THE
GREATEST
SECRET

THE GREATEST SECRET

THE INCREDIBLE POWER OF THOUGHT

Orison Swett Marden

edited by David H. Morgan

MEDIA

MEDIA

Published 2019 by Gildan Media LLC
aka G&D Media
www.GandDmedia.com

Front cover design by David Rheinhardt of Pyrographx

Interior design by Meghan Day Healey of Story Horse, LLC

Library of Congress Cataloging-in-Publication Data is available upon request

ISBN: 978-1-7225-0285-0

10 9 8 7 6 5 4 3 2 1

CONTENTS

INTRODUCTION   9

PART I

THOUGHT, OUR INCREDIBLE LIFE-FORCE

CHAPTER 1 Thinking All Over   15

CHAPTER 2
Steering Thought Prevents Life Wrecks   33

CHAPTER 3 Thoughts Radiate As Influence   38

CHAPTER 4 Preparing The Mind For Sleep   43

CHAPTER 5 Mental Activity During Sleep   50

CHAPTER 6 "As Ye Sow"   60

CHAPTER 7 Be A Mental Chemist   63

CHAPTER 8
Change the Thought, Change the Person 66

CHAPTER 9 The Gift of Imagination 71

CHAPTER 10
The Ability of the Mind To Compel the Body 74

CHAPTER 11 How to Control Thought 79

PART II

THE POWER OF THOUGHT
IN CREATING SELF-CONFIDENCE

CHAPTER 12 The Miracle of Self-Confidence 87

CHAPTER 13 Expect Great Things of Yourself 96

CHAPTER 14 Working For One Thing and
Expecting Something Else 105

CHAPTER 15 Negative Creeds Paralyze 112

CHAPTER 16 Making Dreams Come True 115

CHAPTER 17 How To Get What You Want 125

CHAPTER 18 Being In Tune 136

CHAPTER 19 The Suggestion of Inferiority 142

CHAPTER 20 How Thinking Brings Success 150

CHAPTER 21 How the Mind Rules the Body 156

CHAPTER 22 Self-Motivation by Self-Suggestion 161

CHAPTER 23
Heart-to-Heart Talks and Affirmations 165

PART III

THE POWER OF THOUGHT IN CREATING HEALTH

CHAPTER 24
The Power of the Mind Over the Body 183

CHAPTER 25
Thought Causes Disease and Health 198

CHAPTER 26
Strengthening Deficient Faculties 203

CHAPTER 27 Our Mental Friends and Foes 207

CHAPTER 28 Mental Self-Thought Poisoning 211

CHAPTER 29 Imagination and Health 222

CHAPTER 30
How Suggestions Influence Health 227

CHAPTER 31 Health Through Right Thinking 234

PART IV

THE POWER OF THOUGHT IN CREATING HAPPINESS

CHAPTER 32 Don't Get the Worry Habit! 241

CHAPTER 33 The Source of True Contentment 244

CHAPTER 34 The Aesthetic Mind 248

CHAPTER 35 Holding the Beauty Thought 252

CHAPTER 36 The Divinity of Ideals 255

CHAPTER 37 The Sundial's Motto 260

PART V

THE POWER OF THOUGHT IN CREATING PROSPERITY

CHAPTER 38 How To Attract Prosperity 269

CHAPTER 39 Poverty, A Mental Disability 278

CHAPTER 40
Making Yourself a Prosperity Magnet 289

CHAPTER 41
Success and Happiness Are For You 299

PART VI

THE POWER OF THOUGHT TO PREVENT AGING

CHAPTER 42 How To Stay Young 309

CHAPTER 43 Why Grow Old? 319

INTRODUCTION

a s with all self-help/motivational writers, thought is central in Orison Swett Marden's writings. Control your thoughts, and you control your destiny.

Put differently, we are the product of our thoughts.

That would be a profound but rather straightforward insight were it not for the fact that none of us has truly chosen the thoughts we have grown up with. We have grown up with other people's thoughts: the thoughts of our families, the thoughts of our culture, the thoughts of our religious teachings, the thoughts of our peers, the thoughts of our government, and on and on.

Consequently, none of us has grown up into the full life we desired for ourselves. Maybe we've succeed in business, or in marriage, or in pursuing a well-fitting career, but rarely have any of us done so—if indeed any of us truly has—without having to pass through the crucible of thoughts that were actually keeping us from attaining our happiness, our dreams. To the degree we have attained success in any endeavor, we have attained it through trial-and-error. Not simply the trial-and-error of experience—of the learning curve of experience—but through the trial-and-error of discovering that the ways we were *thinking* about attaining our goals were flawed. We have fallen short here and there, we have missed the mark, as it were, because the thoughts we've held have led us off the path we've sought to be on. Indeed, we have learned that in some instances, the thoughts we've held have been leading us in exactly the opposite direction of our goal.

So the truth is that our thoughts are our destiny, but as some—many? all?—of our thoughts are not truly our own, the destinies we have attained have often not been our destinies, the ones in keeping with our ideals, our dreams, our hopes, our experiences.

All of this makes not only our thoughts the most important aspect of our lives, but a book on *examining* our thoughts, re-thinking our thoughts, sorting out our thoughts, the most important book we can read . . . if we are to achieve the lives of fulfillment we seek. Because remember, our thoughts are our destiny. In the nature—character, quality—or our thoughts, therefore, lies the key to understanding the nature—character, quality—of our lives.

The Greatest Secret: The Incredible Power of Thought, may well, then, be the most important book you will read. For if our thoughts are our destiny, then in reading this book, you will be reading about the very element of life that has led you to the life you're now living. And in so doing, you will have acquired an understanding of how you have come to have the life you have, and how you can change it if you wish.

Because virtually everything in our lives is the product of our thinking, "The Greatest Secret" presents Orison Swett Marden's writings about thought as it pertains to, affects, the central concerns in most of our lives: self-confidence, health, happiness, prosperity, and aging.

Of special interest to many will be Marden's thoughts in Chapter 1: "Thinking All Over." In the latter half of the 20th century, so-called mind/body thinking became quite popular, having a profound affect on attitudes and practices regarding medical treatment that continues to this day. The notion that intelligence was not just located in the brain was considered a new, breakthrough discovery. But as you will read in Chapter 1, it was a fact that was researched and understood in the beginning of the 20th century. What took it so long to make its way into the public consciousness? Why, if it was being researched, studied, and accepted in universities by noted scholars and researchers, was it principally—and so belatedly—introduced to the public by metaphysical writers and speakers? What has taken it so long to still be accepted in the general medical community and practice?

Part V of this book contains a sampling of Marden's writings on thought and prosperity. For a more detailed discussion on the subject of prosperity, readers are recommended to the LifeTime series book entitled *The Key to Prosperity: Conquering Poverty Thinking*, comprising a more extensive discussion by Marden—including practical techniques—of this important subject.

Shakespeare has rightly written, "There is nothing either good or bad, but thinking makes it so." Our thoughts, in other words—or more precisely, how we think—are the basis for how we determine our values. And what we value, determines the quality of our lives.

It is the hope that in the chapters of this book, you will discover the ideas and techniques by which you will be able to live in to the greatest degree in accordance with the ennobling, enriching values of your life.

PART I

THOUGHT, OUR INCREDIBLE LIFE-FORCE

CHAPTER 1
Thinking All Over

modern science has proved that intelligence is not confined to the brain cells, but that we think as a whole, that all the cell life takes part in the thinking process.

Scientists tell us that the individual cells in a piece of flesh taken from any part of the body and placed near a certain drug which is injurious to cell life will draw away as far as they can from this injurious substance. On the other hand, when a substance friendly to cell life is placed near it, the cells will draw as close as possible to this friendly substance and apparently try to absorb it. In other words, these cells manifest a characteristic of intelligent: selection (or, choice).

One reason why our mental attitudes, our hopes, our fears, our joys, our sorrows, have such a tremendous influence upon our bodies, our lives, is because, as Thomas Edison said, every cell in us thinks. And since this is true, we know that every thought, every impression made on the mind, every mental attitude, affects all of the cells of the body—the whole organism.

We have been so accustomed to confining intelligence to the brain alone that it is difficult to think it is a product of the cellular activity of the entire body—brain, muscles, bones, tissues, and all. Yet in fact, we think all over. The mind is the product of activity in all the cells of the body.

The latest scientific investigations seem to show that each one of the tiny microscopical cells of a body, invisible to the naked eye, contains in itself the creative, reproducing, repairing, re-creating qualities, determining the entire future of the body, physically considered, which these cells compose: the plan, the development, the limitation of growth.

Each cell is endowed with intelligence and has a consciousness of its own, and, although each one of these cells has a separate consciousness, the community of cells all works together for the federation of the whole in a most orderly, scientific manner. They build, repair, renew, and maintain the entire organism of the body.

Professor Nels Quevli in his latest book, *Cell Intelligence*, says, "The cell is a conscious intelligent being, and by reason thereof plans and builds all plants and animals in the same manner as man constructs houses, railroads and other structures." He believes that the individual cells of any animal, acting harmoniously with the entire organism, alter the plan of the animal to meet any new demand caused by the changes of habitat of the animal, such as environment, or the changes made in response to the demand for the creature's protection (as in the case of the animals which change their colors to correspond to the coloring of the trees or the rocks upon which they live so as to make them invisible to their enemies).

Quevli believes that the cells in any part of the body contain a property of memory reaching back through the ages to the primordial cells, to the beginning of life itself, and that this, with other characteristics, is passed along by the divisions of the cells. When the cells divide, all the qualities which were in the original cell before the division are passed along to each of the new halves—the new cells, therefore, containing everything which the original cell contained.

We are apt to think of the body as a collection of different organs and that these organs are in a way separate—of different material or construction. But we are in fact one enormous mass of tiny cells closely related to one another.

Because the bones, for example, are harder than the brain, we think there can be little affinity between the two, but, as a matter of fact, all the twelve different tissues of the body are made up of cells of varying consistency, all of which come from one primordial cell—and what affects one cell anywhere in the body affects all. Each cell is an entity or little self, and we are made up of these billions of our little selves or cells.

These tiny selves are like members of a great orchestra which instantly respond to the keynote given them by their leader—in our case, our brains and thoughts. Whatever tune our mentality plays, they play. They become like our thought. Every suggestion, every motive that moves the individual, is reflected in these cells. Every cell in the body vibrates in unison with every thought, every emotion, every passion that sways us—and the result on the cell life corresponds with the character of the thought, the emotion or passion.

The ego is the master spirit, the leader of all the little self or cell communities. All the cells of the body will do its bidding. The ego can think health into the cells or it can think disease. It can think discord or harmony into them. It can think efficiency or inefficiency into them. It can send a success thrill or a failure thrill through all of the cells, a thrill of masterfulness or of weakness. It can send through them a vibration of fear or of courage, of selfishness or of generosity. It can send vibrating through all the cells of the body a thrill of hope or of despair, a thrill of love or of hate—a triumphant vibration or a vibration of defeat, of failure, of disgrace. In short, whatever thought the ego, or I, sends out will stamp itself on every cell in the body, will make it like itself.

Surgeons report that after a great victory, for instance, the wounds of the soldiers heal much more rapidly than the wounds of the soldiers in the defeated army, showing that the mental exhilaration which accompanies the consciousness of victory is a stimulant, a tonic, while conversely the despondency which accompanies defeat, is a physical depressant.

The cells are practically an extension of the brain. Each is a sub-station connected with the central station of the brain. Anger, hatred, jealousy or malice in the brain means anger, hatred, jealousy or malice in every cell in the body. Trouble in the brain means trouble everywhere. Happiness in the brain means happiness everywhere. When the mind is full of hope, bright prospects, the body is full of hope, alert, efficient, eager to work. When there is discouragement in the mind there is discouragement, despondency everywhere in the body.

Ambition is paralyzed, enthusiasm blighted, efficiency strangled.

Every physician knows that certain emotions—worry, fear, grief, depression—will greatly increase the activity and hasten the development of physical diseases. We little realize what we are doing when we are constantly sending messages of discouragement, of fear, of worry through all the billions of cells in the body. We little realize what it means when we talk discouragement, when we give up to the "blues," when we lose courage, faith, hope, confidence in ourselves. It really means panic, disorganization, all through the cell life of the body. Mental depression is felt in every remotest cell. It unnerves every organ, and reduces the entire organism to a state of weakness and inefficiency, if not to utter collapse.

For a long time surgeons have known that certain kinds of cancer are produced by mental influences; that not only cancerous tendencies latent in the system are thus aroused and their development encouraged, but that some kinds of cancers, even when there is no previous hereditary tendency or taint may be absolutely originated in this way. This scientific conclusion has been tremendously emphasized by the great increase in the development of cancer in those who have been hard hit by the war, especially those who have lost relatives or dear friends, or whose loved ones have been frightfully mangled, maimed for life. Their peculiar mental suffering, the mingled worry, grief and anxiety of these people has aggravated cancerous tendencies and originated many new cases of cancer where no previous tendencies to that dread disease existed.

A great Paris specialist, Dr. Theodore Truffler, cites a case where a patient who showed no predisposition whatever to cancer developed it after much mourning for the loss of his two sons in battle. This grief had simulated into a real cancer eruption which before had been apparently unimportant.

Not only do worry, fear, and anxiety and great grief induce cancer, but hatred, grudges, chronic jealousy, also originate several different kinds of cancer, and very materially hasten the development of cancerous tendencies which they do not originate.

Many kinds of skin disease, kidney trouble, dyspepsia, liver trouble, brain and heart trouble, are now known to result from mental causes, such as chronic hatred and jealousy. These keep the blood and other secretions in a state of chronic poisoning, which devitalizes the whole body and encourages the development of latent disease tendencies or of disease germs.

The painful sensation that bad news causes, resulting in people fainting from shock—as when news of a sudden death or frightful accident comes of those dear to them—is not all in the head, it is not all in the brain. The effect of the shock visits every cell in the body. They are depressed all over. The whole cell life feels the shock. Every bit of bad, discouraging news, depression, fear, worry, anxiety, jealousy, hatred—these send their disintegrating messages through all the cell colonies, all the dependencies in the body.

On the other hand, good news, the expectation of better things, the renewal of hope, confidence, the upbuilding of faith in glorious things that are coming in the near future these act like a tonic on those who are "down and out." They refresh and renew the entire being.

The trouble is we have been so in the habit of thinking of the body as outside of the brain itself, as a sort of unintelligent matter, absolutely dependent upon the control of the brain, that it is very difficult for us to grasp the truth, that the intelligence, the planner, the builder, the repairer, is in each cell.

When we are wounded, for instance, we do not deliberately with our brain send a message to the cells to repair and rebuild where the damage has been done, where the tissues have been lacerated or cut away. The cells themselves do that, they are the builders. They built the body originally and they continue to maintain and repair it.

Professor Quevli says that in each division of the cell, or nucleus, a crowd of skilled workers, intelligent builders, exist. He believes in the interesting theory that the planner of the cell, the planner of the individual, is in the microscopical cell itself. How could we imagine a force molding, fashioning, creating, modifying, changing, nourishing, to exist outside of the cell life? The only sound theory is that this force or intelligence is an indestructible part of the cell life itself, that it is the great cosmic intelligence everywhere present. It is life itself—we cannot image it absent from any atom, molecule, or electron in existence, any more than we can image a spot where the mathematical law does not apply, or that two and two do not make four.

Some of our most advanced scientists believe that the cells of the different organs of the body constitute what we may term a community mind or brain, which presides over the life and functions of each particular organ. These community brains, such as the stomach, the liver, the kidneys, the heart, get their instructions from the great central station of intelligence—the brain.

Every cell in the body is an energetic little worker, incessantly laboring for the community to which it belongs. Take, for example, the group of cells which form the liver. The work of this organ is to secrete bile, manufacture sugar, and eliminate poisons which might be fatal to other organs, such as the kidneys. Every cell is occupied in this important work.

Another group of these tiny cell workers, those which form the heart, are continually busy in the service of this great central organ, whose duty is to keep the blood in circulation, never to let it stop an instant, day or night.

A third group of these wonder workers form the stomach. The office of the stomach is to begin the process of digestion, to manufacture from the blood the acid which helps to disintegrate the food. It also does much of the work which the teeth were intended to do, but which we usually neglect.

Another community of cells constitute the kidneys, whose task is to strain out of the blood the poisons which the other organs have not eliminated, and which if allowed to remain would injure the more vital organs.

Here is a group which forms the thyroid gland, whose work is to store up certain salts and other substances for future use, and to assist in regulating the nutrition and the heat of the body.

And here is another group, perhaps the most important, which forms the leader of all the other community centers—the brain. This thinking organ is the seat of distribution of all orders through the marvelous system of nerves, which run from the great central station to every corner of the body, communicating instantly with every one of the billions of the cell citizens in the whole system. Like those in all the other organs, each cell of the brain is constantly at work.

Now, these billions of workers—all specialists in their line, no cell doing the work delegated to another—are dependent on the nourishment which they get from the blood. If the blood is poor, thin, deteriorated by imperfect or insufficient food, or if it is poisoned by dissipation or by wrong thinking, then their work as builders suffers accordingly.

When the blood for any reason is thus impoverished, the cells of the stomach and other digestive organs are too feeble to do their work properly. And when the food is not properly digested, it putrefies and the poisons it generates are absorbed by the body, causing trouble everywhere throughout the system: The heart action is impaired; the circulation of the blood is poor; all the tissues suffer from lack of nutrition; the vigor of the body is depreciated (because the digestive organs can not manufacture force, robustness, out of vitiated blood); and billions of cells suffer from malnutrition, or semi-starvation, and your powers begin to wane. There is a lack of vim and force and fire in your efforts. The cry for food, for nutrition, from the suffering cells goes to the brain. It convinces you that something is the matter, and you say you are sick, you are down and out, you don't feel like anything. Your ambition sags, and off you go to a drug store or a doctor for something which will brace you up, make you feel better.

Perhaps you then begin to fear you are going to be laid up, that you are developing some disease. The terrors of a possible breakdown adds its poisoned burden to the already poor, vitiated blood, and matters grow worse. Instead of radically remedying such an unfortunate condition by satisfying the intelligent cry of the cells, most people begin to add the whip to the tired horse as a stimulant, a tonic, when the horse needs nothing but good wholesome food and rest, harmony in the mental kingdom.

Everywhere in the body Nature tries to save us from our igno-rance, our mistakes, our animal appetites, our dissipations, our wrong thinking. Every cell in the body is constantly on guard, trying to help us, trying to save us from our own ignorance and sins.

Much of what we call intuitive perception about our bodies, for example, is due to the cell intelligence in the various parts of the body. What is it, for instance, that tells us when we have eaten enough to supply the bodily needs? The brain does not know it, because none of the food which we eat at an ordinary meal has had time to affect the brain before the appetite has been satisfied. What is the appetite? It is the demand for nourishment from the different cells of the body. It is not located in any one place. The cells call for food, and it is their intelligence that makes this call. We say we instinctively feel when we have eaten enough. We do not want any more and our appetite declines. But this knowledge does not come from the brain alone. It is a feeling of all the cells of the body—that there is sufficient in the stomach to supply its needs.

The appetite wanes accordingly, but it must be intelligence back of this which makes this decision. The brain cells are simply making a call for their own needs—are calling for sustenance. They are not, in this instance, making calls for the liver, the heart, the kidneys, the muscles to go to work.

The mental healing of disease rests upon the fact that intelligence is not confined to the brain, but that there is intelligence in the cells of the body generally, as has been further proved in the case of the deaf and the blind. In their efforts at self-expression, these people have developed the intelligence of the finger tips to such an extent that actual gray mat-ter cells, similar to those in the brain, have been found there. In other words, gray brain cells are developed in the finger tips of the blind.

It is well known that this gray brain matter found in the finger tips of the blind is also found in other parts of the system, especially in many ramifications of the spinal nerves. It is found everywhere along the tract of the nervous system.

Walking and all of the involuntary movements of the body are controlled by the intelligence of the local cells. We do not stop and pre-meditate, or will, every step. We take each one automatically, without any exercise of the will. An intelligence outside the brain must also keep up the heart beats and the breathing while the brain is uncon-scious during sleep, and even while we are awake, for we make no conscious effort at any time to keep up these functions.

Nor does the expert pianist think of the movements of the fingers when playing. He or she may all the time be thinking of something else, just as we all may well be while performing certain activities—such as driving a car or walking. Our minds may be wandering, and yet we perform intelligently because intelligent cells are distributed throughout our bodies' muscular nervous system.

Admittedly, to say that the brain educates the spinal column and the nervous branches to perform this piano-playing miracle is no sci-entific explanation. The only satisfactory explanation is that all the cells of the body are intelligent, that we think as a whole.

We have inherited the race belief that thinking is confined to the brain. But the fact is the difference between the brain cells and the cells in other parts of the body is not nearly so great as we once thought. Many brain accidents have shown that the destruc-tion of large portions of the brain tissue does not materially affect the power of thought, any more than the destruction of tissue in other parts of the body affects it. Not only this, but large portions of the brain have been removed, and yet the individual has gone on working apparently as before. Here is an interesting experiment performed by a noted scientist which gives a striking proof of cell intelligence outside of the brain. This experiment has been tried again and again.

"If a drop of acid is placed on the lower surface of the thigh of a frog after its head has been cut off, the decapitated frog will rub off the drop of acid with the upper surface of the foot on the same leg. Scientists have cut off this foot after the head was cut off, and the headless animal, after trying time and again to rub off the acid with the same foot as before, will finally use the foot on the other leg and continue until it succeeds in rubbing off the acid."

Here we certainly have proof of intelligence combined with harmonious contractions in order to bring about certain definite results. It is a proof that an intelligent mind acts without a brain.

We know that the brain carries on but a small part of the work of the bodily organism.

All of our involuntary movements, the manufacture of the fluids of the body, of the bodily secretions, the changing of foods into tissues, are not affected by the voluntary brain. The work of the chemical laboratory in the body, which is simply beyond human comprehension, is all carried on by intelligent organ cells outside of the brain. The brain cells, it is true, are more highly sensitized, more responsive, than the cells of some other parts of the body. They form, so to speak, a sort of mouthpiece for the other cells, and this is where they find their outward expression.

There is no doubt that the billions of cells composing the body all belong to one intelligent whole. What affects one cell affects all, so that whatever passes through the brain cells passes through every other cell in the body. We know how instantaneously news, a sudden shock of any sort, received at the central brain station is sent to all the organs. The heart, the kidneys, the liver, all of them are at once affected by it. This shows how intimately they must be tied together. The entire body is evidently a sort of an extended brain.

If someone should scratch one end of a piece of timber a hundred feet long with a nail, and your ear were at the other end of the timber, you could hear the scratch instantly. The distance does not seem to make any difference in the transmission of the sound. In a similar way, every thought, every mood, every emotion goes instantly to every part of the body. For example, you may have just sat down to your Thanksgiving dinner with a ravenous appetite, when the gastric juice is trickling from every gastric follicle in your stomach, and you suddenly receive a phone call announcing a terrible catastrophe, in which some of those dearest to you have been mutilated or killed. Instantly the gastric follicles cease to generate the gastric juice and become dry and parched, as the tongue does as in a fever. The heart and the other organs feel the shock at the same time and are equally distressed, and their action inhibited. In short, the different organs and functions respond instantly to the painful news, showing that whatever enters the mind goes immediately to the entire cell life of the body.

The condition of your cells, of your tissues, of your organs, will depend upon the message which you send to them through your thought, through your convictions regarding them, whether of strength or weakness, of health or disease. You think clear through every cell to the farthest extremities of your body. And as you think regarding your cells, so they are.

Their fate is largely in your hands. They will obey whatever orders you give them. By your mental attitude toward the cells of the various organ communities you can make your physical organs perform their functions normally or abnormally; you can insure health or bring about disease; you can prolong your life or you can shorten it.

We know that by concentrating our thought intensely upon any part of the body the blood vessels in that organ or locality expand, and an extra supply of blood is sent there. In other words, the blood follows the thought. Professor Alexander Graham Bell told me that when on long riding trips in Halifax, in severe weather, he could warm his feet by concentrating his thought upon them, so that in a short time they would be all aglow. This method of quickening the circulation of the blood has been tried so often that scientists no longer question it.

And, in an experiment I refer to again in the chapter entitled "How The Mind Rules The Body," professor Elmer Gates often conducted the following experiment as a proof of the power of mind in this direction: Immersing his hands in two separate vessels of water just even full, he first would concentrate his thought on the right hand until the water in the vessel would overflow; then reversing, he would concentrate on the left until that vessel would overflow.

These experiments give a little idea of what thought can do in stimulating or depressing the blood on which the life of the body depends.

It is well known that the fear thought, the thought for example that you have inherited—*and are developing*—cancer causes congestion in that part of your anatomy on which it is fixed. And if the fear thought becomes chronic, you will have chronic congestion there, which aids in developing the thing you fear.

Take the case of a young girl who is told by her friends that she has probably inherited tuberculosis, because one or both of her parents died of that disease. If every time she is exposed to inclement weather, gets her feet wet, or gets in a draft, she is reminded that she is taking great chances, she develops a fear thought. She concentrates this fear upon her lungs, causing congestion there, irritation, coughing. This increases her fear and causes loss of appetite. Then, of course, she loses nourishment, and there is a general decline in her physical condition.

Naturally a loss in weight follows. This symptom frightens her still more, because victims of tuberculosis are always weighing themselves, imagining they are shrinking. Her fears cause imperfect digestion, imperfect assimilation, and hence imperfect repair and renewal of lost tissue. She begins to lose color and then everybody tells her that she is not looking well. This loss of color is another dread symptom, and so it goes on until the fear, the conviction that she is developing the fateful disease, cuts down the last remnant of her disease-resisting power, and she falls a victim to any latent tubercular germs in her system. She stamps her fear thought on the cell life of her lungs and other organs until they respond to it, become like it, while in fact multitudes of people have tubercular germs in their system which never develop if they hold the health thought and build up a strong disease-resisting power.

Disease germs feed upon the debris or broken-down tissue in the body. They are scavengers and do not feed upon healthy tissue, healthy food. But when the tissues begin to break down through fear, the disease-resisting power deteriorates rapidly until the body gets below what we may call the health line. Then all sorts of scavengers or enemy germs, waiting for their opportunity, begin to feed upon the broken-down tissue; the blood becomes impoverished, and the disease gets a hold on its victim.

There is no doubt that disease in the various organs is often due to utter discouragement which the organ cells have received from the central station—the brain. The cells of the whole body often give up their struggle for life because of the discouragement of the master cells.

Time and again when the heart has ceased to beat, and apparently the last breath has been taken, life has been called back to a seemingly dead body just by strong reassuring words, by arousing and restoring the lost confidence of the cells. When there is supreme confidence of victory in all of the cells of the body, life will not depart. But when the cells in the different organ communities get from the brain the message that the death sentence has been pronounced by the physician, or when the patient gives this fatal prognosis as his own conviction, then there is no hope for the dependent communities to try to save the situation.

Is it strange that the cells of the diseased organs should give up the struggle and cease to fight for life when the brain has given up hope and sent a message of despair through the whole system? These impaired cells were having a hard time of it before. There was probably a panic in the little cell community, and now, when the grand commander of all of, the cells of the body—gives up, the depending organ communities also naturally give up.

On the other hand, when the cells all through the body get the thrill of confidence, of hope, of faith in their strength, from the center of intelligence, then they are comparatively free from danger of death. There is enough vitality, enough latent energy in many a body which has just breathed its last to re-energize and bring it back to life again—if such confidence is restored by the mind that to those seemingly dead cells that their latent forces can once more be utlilized.

Since thought has such a tremendous influence upon the cell life of the body, how important it is that our thoughts and images and emotions should be friendly and not hostile, should be helpful and not injurious! How imperative that we hold only those images, in the mind, visualize only those things which are beneficial, kindly, uplifting to the body, not those things which tend to devitalize, to dwarf and ruin it!

The essential thing is to keep the cells in all of the organs happy, contented, encouraged, harmonious. If we do this, we shall be happy, contented, harmonious ourselves.

And just as your cells—and thus, your body—take on your enthusiasm, your zest, your cheer, your courage, your faith, every time you allow a vicious thought, despondent thought, a thought of failure, of fear, of poverty to enter your mind, every time you allow a foreboding of some threatening event to take hold of you, every time you indulge in jealousy, in envy, in hatred, in revenge, in any evil emotion, every cell in your body is correspondingly affected.

They are encouraged or discouraged, they expand or contract their possibilities at your suggestion.

What you think about the cells of any organ they will return to you in kind. You can no more get the best from the cells of your stomach, and your other digestive organs, for instance, when you are all the time saying uncomplimentary things about them, always discouraging them, abusing them, than you can get the best out of your employees or your children by the same methods. When you treat them in this way, talk against them, antagonize them, they become depressed, and express resentment in non-performance of their functions.

There is everything in expecting your body to perform all its functions normally, healthfully. Think of your human machine as perfect, treat your organs as though they were normal. Expect your body, all the cell communities, to express harmony, not discord. Don't harbor a suspicious attitude toward any of your physical organs. Believe that they are going to do the work which they were intended to do, and to do it properly. Trust them just as you would trust your children, your employees. Believe in them, and treat them kindly. Instead of blaming and abusing, encourage and praise them, and they will perform their functions normally and give you robust health.

If the cells in any organ are diseased, the health suggestion, the health affirmation, the holding of the health ideal in the brain will tend to heal them. To send life currents of healing thought sweeping through any defective or diseased organ tends to stimulate the cell life, to encourage the cell organization—in the stomach, the kidneys, the heart, the liver, the lungs, etc.—to respond to the optimistic suggestion. In other words, thinking health, thinking life and truth into a diseased organ, tends to destroy the disease infection, to arouse latent life force in the cells, and to bring about normal health conditions.

We know that we get out of the various organs about what we expect. The brain is no exception. Expect nothing, get nothing. If you have no confidence in your brain it will return only weakness or mediocrity to you. On the other hand, if you have a firm, vigorous faith in it—if you expect great things from it—it will match your expectation.

Believe in your muscles, trust them, believe they are strong and vigorous, have faith that you can lift an enormous weight or can perform great feats as an athlete, and your five hundred muscles will come to your rescue and redeem your faith.

And all of this is even of animals. When the race horse has lost confidence in its speed it never regains it. As long as the animal believes he can beat the others in the race he wins. But when it has been beaten a few times it gets the habit of being beaten, and cannot regain its confidence. It believes it is going to be beaten, and it is.

The art of radiating health thoughts through and through the whole system until every nerve and fiber, every cell in the body, feels the electric thrill of the health force, is the art of arts. It means the achievement of perfect health, of perfect efficiency and of perfect happiness.

Just as we can antidote disease in the cell life by health thoughts, in a similar way we can send out from the central brain station thoughts of prosperity, of opulence, thoughts of success, affirmations of power, that will antidote the poverty disease.

If we would triumph over all our limitations, we must impress the triumphant thought on every cell. We must radiate through the body not only thoughts of health and strength, but also of courage, hope, confidence, expectation of better conditions. Instead of radiating through our system, as most of us do, the poverty thought, the lack thought, the conviction that we are the slaves of social and economic systems above which we cannot rise, we must radiate the abundance thought, the freedom thought, the expectation of prosperity, of opulence. Instead of stamping the failure thought, the thought of mediocrity, or incompetence upon our cells, we must stamp upon them the conviction of superb ability, of confidence that we can accomplish what we undertake. We must constantly cultivate the habit of radiating the thought triumphant, the habit of radiating masterfulness instead of weakness.

After a little practice in the cultivation of upbuilding thought, the health thought, the success thought, the happy thought, the vibrations of these thoughts will reach every remotest cell in our bodies, and we shall feel the thrill of health, of hopefulness, of expectancy of better things animating and energizing our whole being.

What we think and believe we create.

Always hold the ideal suggestion of everything in life—the ideal suggestion of health; the ideal suggestion of your ability, your efficiency; the ideal suggestion regarding your career, your success, your happiness; the ideal suggestion of your destiny. It will transform your life—lift you from the common to the uncommon.

It will make you an artist in life, instead of a mere artisan.

CHAPTER 2
Steering Thought Prevents Life Wrecks

t hought is everything.

Every human desire—be it the desire for prosperity, happiness, health, a satisfying relationship—begins and is carried out by thought.

All that you seek follows from the attention you give to the thoughts that you have. But how many of us are the captains of our own thoughts?

Here's a parable:

A certain man of no great learning, so runs an old legend, became heir to a ship. He knew nothing of the sea, nothing of navigation or engineering, but he was seized by the notion to take a voyage and command this ship that was now his own. He set sail and told the crew to go ahead with their usual duties, as the multiplicity of tasks required to run a ship bewildered him. Once they were out to sea, however, the work grew simpler, and the captain had time to observe what was going on. As he strolled on the forward deck, he saw a man turning a big wheel, first one way and then another.

"What in the world is that man doing?" he asked a member of the crew.

"That's the helmsman. He's steering the ship."

"Well, I don't see any use in his fiddling away there all the time. There's nothing but water ahead, and the sails can push the ship forward. Put up the sails and let's let her go. When there's land in sight, or a ship coming head on, then we can call on him to do his steering."

The order was obeyed, and soon the ship was being buffeted about by winds—pitching and tossing. Shortly thereafter, it capsized, leaving few survivors.

Are we not all in possession of a great vessel more delicate, more precious, than any sailing craft put to sea—our own minds? But how much attention do we typically give to the steering of our thoughts? Don't most of us let our thoughts go pretty much as they will? Don't we let the winds of anger and passion blow our thinking hither and thither? Don't we let chance friendships, aimless amusements, and workplace gossip sway our lives in directions we would never would deliberately choose? Don't we too often let the control and governance of our thoughts be in the control of others, until we find our own lives capsizing?

The mind governs virtually everything in our world, yet it is a force that we most often neglect and misunderstand. When tribute is paid to some deed of our minds, do we not frequently respond as if the workings of our minds is basically outside of our control—that the inspiration for which we were given praise came not through our own devices, but of its own accord? We agree that the mind is a powerful force, but we think that it's a force that is only possible of being harnessed by those born with the genius to do so. And surely, we think, *we* are not among *those*!

Are we truly the captains of our own ships, guiding them to sure harbors of happiness, peace, and success? To be honest, we're not. Moreover, most of us would say that today, with all the demands the world places on our lives and our time, we *cannot* be. But being so is simpler than we think. We must, though, begin by accepting certain fundamental truths; then we must commit ourselves to putting our own better natures to work.

The ability to control thought in order to modify a character already formed, to change our external surroundings—or at least their effect on us—and to provide ourselves with lives of health, happiness, and success, has more and more been studied and understood. We have discovered that the benefits of thought training are infinite, its consequences eternal—indeed, we hardly yet know the possibilities. Nevertheless, sadly, few of us take the pains to direct our thinking into channels that will do us good. Instead, we continue to leave all to chance, to the myriad circumstances that buffet us about, until finally some dire circumstance—some loss, some fatigue from repeated failure—compels us into action to make some counter-effort.

There can be no more important study, no higher duty owed to ourselves and those about us, than that of thought-control—which is the same thing as of self-control and self-development. Perhaps because most of us believe we have so little control over the flight of our thoughts, we have the impression that directing the activity of our minds is a difficult—if not impossible—affair, something that requires more than we possess in order to accomplish.

Nothing is further from the truth.

All of us, however busy, however educated or uneducated, have within ourselves all that is needed, and all the time needed, to take control of our thoughts in order to remake our characters, if that is what we wish, as well as to affect much of the workings of our bodies and the course of our lives. Granted, each of us will have different problems to solve, different tasks to perform, and different results to aim for, but achieving the goals we wish by watching the thoughts we have is as possible for one person as it is for another.

Before you can do much toward controlling your thoughts, however, you must first truly *sense* the power and importance of your thoughts, not merely accept the truth of this as an intellectual statement. You must *feel*, you must be *convinced*, that a bad thought harms you and a good thought helps you. There must be no playing with fire, here. There must be no careless feeling that it matters little if you are off your guard part of the time. You must know in your inmost consciousness that the thoughts of your every moment have a part in deciding your fate. You must feel that proper control of your own thoughts will cause all good things to come naturally to you, just as all bad things will be your portion if you misuse their powers.

We must not lose sight that we posses in our hands the power to make or mar our natures. A sculptor dares not strike random blows while gazing away from the marble. With eyes steadfast, the sculptor makes every stroke count toward the final result—a result that the sculptor has fixed in his or her mind, corresponding to his or her the plan. We must do likewise in chiseling our characters, forming our environment, making our lives. We must know what we want, know we can get it, and set ourselves directly at the task, never relenting or relaxing in its performance—lest we use this great tool of our minds imprudently and fail to produce for ourselves lives of beauty and harmony, happiness and success.

And we must remember that a sculptor's chisel in the hands of a bungler may mar the loveliest statue, and in the hands of a criminal it may become a burglar's tool or a murderer's bludgeon.

There is a difference between thought and an ordinary tool, how-ever: Thought is always active, so we must, in every moment, commit ourselves to be doing something with it. We cannot lay it down and say we will take it up later. We must keep in mind that every thought—*whether of our own bidding or that we allow come of its own*—forges some aspect of our lives.

We must resolutely determine to take the helm of our own lives, to hold right thoughts and expel wrong ones, to be the captains of the all-important cargo of our minds.

Here's the lesson: Mental control is self-control.

Those who learn this escape the unhappiness and the many hard experiences which depress the lives of those who fail to learn this greatest of all life's lessons.

Controlling our thoughts allows us to bestow upon ourselves all the great blessings that are waiting to flow into us from our own life forces.

CHAPTER 3
Thoughts Radiate As Influence

Our thoughts, while most powerfully acting on our own lives, by no means exhaust their force there. They are not held prisoners within our minds or bodies. Potent with influence, they fly from us every instant, working for weal or for woe.

"Every thought which genius and piety throw into the world alters the world," said Emerson. This must not be taken merely to mean printed thoughts, or thoughts spoken from pulpit or rostrum, or even thoughts spoken at all. Our most secret, unuttered thoughts go forth and affect the world, the people all about us.

We each have an atmosphere peculiar to ourselves—pervaded by all of our characteristics, our ambitions and aspirations; absolutely determined by the thoughts that govern all our actions. The quality of our thoughts enter into our every voluntary act. And we give everybody with whom we come in contact the impression of our ideals.

It is not what you say so much as the bearing of your thought toward others that forms their estimate of you. Do not flatter yourself that you are known only by what you say; that you are measured by what you consciously *choose* to give people about yourself. You create in others the impression which you hold in your own mind. What you think about modifies and reaffirms others' opinions of you. They feel the quality of your thought, they *know* whether it has power or weakness, whether it is clean, lofty, and noble, or base and low. They can tell by your silent radiations the character of your ideals, and they estimate you accordingly. In fact, this conviction which has come from their silent impression of you may be held firmly, even against your verbal protest to the contrary. As Emerson put it, "What you are speaks so loud, I cannot hear what you say."

It does not mater what we *pretend* to be. We cannot radiate anything unlike ourselves. Those who know us will take our *real* measure, not the pretended one.

We can best estimate the effect we produce on others by analyzing the effect other persons have upon us. We know our real friends by the bearing of their thought toward us. They are constantly radiating themselves into our consciousness. We know that they feel generous and magnanimous toward us—even when we let ourselves and them down.

It does not matter how pleasant, agreeable, or considerate a person may be toward us. If that person holds antagonistic thoughts, mean thoughts, carries a grudge, is not what he or she pretends to be, our instincts will penetrate beneath their pretense and unmask their real self—and while the person thinks he or she is deceiving us, we feel instinctively what (who) he or really is.

In the home and in the office, in every relation of life, radiation of one's own thoughts plays an important part. No care and effort can be too great to ensure that our radiating influence is always helpful, uplifting, beneficent.

How much harm can be done in a single day by casting a dark shadow across some bright life, depressing buoyancy, crushing hopes, strangling aspirations—more harm than we can often be undone in years. We would be appalled if we could see pass before us, in vivid panorama, the wrecks of a lifetime caused by cruel thought. A stab here, a thrust there, a cruel, malicious sarcasm, bitter irony, ungenerous criticisms, jealous thought, envious thought, hatred, anger, revengeful thought are all going out constantly from many a mind on their deadly missions.

Some people make us feel mean and contemptible in their presence. They call out of us meanness which we never knew we possessed and make us almost despise ourselves. Marriage sometimes reveals undesirable qualities which neither husband nor wife suspected in themselves before.

Some people emit a sort of miasmatic atmosphere, which poisons everything that comes within its reach. No matter how generous and magnanimous we felt before, when these characters come near us we shrivel and shrink within ourselves and there is no responsiveness, no spontaneity possible until they go out of our presence. Like disturbed clams, we shut ourselves up as tightly as possible until we feel that we are out of danger. We cannot be ourselves when near such people. We try to be agreeable with them, but somehow everything is forced; we cannot be sociable with them. We seem ill at ease until they have departed; then we feel that a heavy weight is lifted from us, and we are ourselves again.

Other people act like a tonic or an invigorating and refreshing breeze. They make us feel like new beings. By their presence they stimulate our thoughts, quicken our faculties, sharpen our intellect, open the flood-gates of language and sentiment, and awaken the poetic within us. These diverse effects come from the radiation or expression of personality, and we ourselves are producing like effects on others all the time. We radiate what we feel and believe, our fleeting moods and our deep-seated convictions. What we think most about and strive to become, we radiate to others in our every letter, in every conversation, in our manner, in our life. Spirit is contagious, and will be quickly perceived or even taken on by those with whom we come in contact. If the mind is in harmony and peace, if it is strong and healthy, we radiate health, peace, and harmony wherever we go.

As we can only communicate the quality of our thought at the moment, how important that we control these thoughts, and make them clean, pure, true thoughts, instead of foul, demoralizing, doubtful ones.

It is simply cruel to hold a suspicious thought of another until you have positively proved its authenticity. That other person's mind is sacred; you have no right to invade it with your doubting thoughts and pictures of suspicion.

We should keep our wicked thoughts at home. But as this is in fact seldom possible, then we should at the least not harbor them—any more than we would allow ourselves to hold thoughts of sin or crime.

When you find yourself holding an evil thought toward another, an unhealthy thought, you should call, "Halt! About face!" Look toward the sunlight; determine that, if you cannot do any good in the world, you will not scatter seeds of poison, the venom of malice and hatred.

Be one of those who is always radiating success thoughts, health thoughts, joy thoughts, uplifting, helpful thoughts, scattering sunshine wherever they go. These are the helpers of the world, the lighteners of burdens, the people who ease the jolts of life and soothe the wounded and give solace to the discouraged.

Learn to radiate joy, not stingily, not meanly, but generously. Fling out your gladness without reserve. Shed it in the home, on the street, on the car, in the store, everywhere, as the rose sheds its beauty and flings out its fragrance.

When we learn that love thoughts heal; that they carry balm to wounds; that thoughts of harmony, of beauty, and of truth always uplift, beautify, and ennoble; that the opposite carry death, destruction, and blight everywhere—we will then learn the true secret of right living.

CHAPTER 4
Preparing the Mind for Sleep

he period of sleep is a wonderful period of growth, for the mind as well as for the body. It is a time when you can attract your desires; it is a propitious time to nurse your vision.

Few people, however, ever think of preparing the mind for sleep, although doing so is even more necessary than preparing the body for sleep. Most of us take great pains to put the latter in order: we and undress, take a warm bath, massage the face with some sort of refreshening salve, cold cream, or oil; we make sure that our sleeping room is properly ventilated and that our bed is clean and comfortable, but we don't give a thought to the matter of preparing our minds for rest.

Yet, if we retire holding a grudge against a neighbor, a resolve to "get even" with somebody who has injured us; hatred or jealousy in our hearts, or envy of another's success, and we go to sleep nursing these feelings, we more often than not will awaken in a depressed, exhausted state, feeling bitter, pessimistic, irritable, unhappy. The destroyer of our physical and emotional health was at work all night, running amuck among the delicate brain and nerve cells, furiously tearing down what beneficent Nature had taken such pains to build up.

Instead of making our subconscious mental processes build us up during the night, many of us we allow them to tear us down. We grow weary and age in the night, when just the reverse ought to be the case, for Nature herself has ordained that night should be the building, the renewing, time of life.

I know people whose lives have been revolutionized by adopting the practice of putting themselves in a harmonious condition, getting in tune with the Infinite before going to sleep. Formerly they were in the habit of retiring in a bad mood—tired, discouraged over anticipated evils, worrying about all sorts of things. They would discuss their misfortunes at night with friends or spouses—thinking over the unfortunate conditions of their affairs, their mistakes, and the possible unfavorable consequences that might result from them. Naturally, their minds were in an upset condition when they fell asleep, and, as might be expected, the melancholy, disturbing pictures of the misfortunes they feared—vividly exaggerated in the stillness of the night—became etched deeper and deeper on their brains and did their baleful work, making real rest and reinvigoration absolutely impossible.

When these people changed their pre-bedtime habits and retired in a peaceful frame of mind, they awoke stronger, fresher, more vigorous, more resourceful, better able to cope with difficulties, to make plans and to carry them out than when they depleted their physical and mental resources by robbing themselves of their best friend: Nature's restorative, sleep.

Many people who hear me speak or read my books and magazine writings about this practice of preparing the mind for sleep, tell me that despite what they hear and read, they cannot stop thinking after they go bed. Their brains are so active, doing their next day's work, that they cannot stop the mental processes for hours

Of course you cannot stop all thinking the first night you start trying to form the new habit, when you have practiced the old night-thinking habit for years; when perhaps as far back as you can remember you have gone to bed every night worrying, thinking, planning—planning ahead for the coming days, weeks, months . . . perhaps planning ahead for the coming year. But if you persist, and make it a cast iron rule to allow no anxieties or fears, no business troubles or discords of any kind to enter your bedroom, you will succeed in accomplishing your object.

Think of your bedroom as the your sacred place for rest, where the things that trouble and harass and vex during the daytime shall find no entrance. Put this legend over the door, or in some conspicuous place where you can see it: "This is my holy of holies, the place of supreme peace and power in my life from which all discord must be shut out." When you undress and lie down, say to yourself, "I have done my best during the day. Now I am going to drop thinking, drop worrying and planning, and get a good, refreshing sleep."

Clear your mind not only of all anxious, worrying business thoughts, but also of all ill will or hatred toward another. Resolve that you will not harbor an unpleasant, bitter or unkind thought toward any human being, that you will wipe off the slate of your memory everything you have ever had against any one; that you will forget whatever is unpleasant in the past and start with a clean slate. Imagine that the words "Harmony," "Peace," "Love," "Goodwill to every living creature" are emblazoned in letters of light all over the walls of your room. Repeat them over and over until that other self just below the threshold of your consciousness becomes saturated with the ideas they convey, and after a while you will drop into slumber with a serene, poised mind, a mind filled with happy, joyous, creative thoughts.

Of course, until the new habit is fixed, thoughts will intrude themselves in spite of you, but you needn't harbor them. You needn't allow yourself, under any circumstances, to go on thinking about business or any discordant thing after you retire any more than you would allow a madman to slash you with a knife without making any attempt to defend yourself. You can, if you only persist in the new and better way, fall asleep every night like a tired child, and awake in the morning just as refreshed and happy. Your subconscious self will, after a while, carry out your behests without any conscious effort on your part. This sleepless subconscious self is, in fact, one of the most effective agents you have to help you accomplish whatever you desire. Insomnia, for instance, which is the curse of so many Americans, may be entirely overcome by its aid.

If you are a victim of insomnia, and if your insomnia is a result of bad or irregular habits, then needless to say, you, the victim must first of all change your pre-bedtime habits before you can expect any relief. You have gotten used to going to bed every night with the thought firmly fixed in your consciousness that you are once more not going to sleep, and you have become, to a great extent, the victim of your belief: The conviction in your subconscious mind that there is something the matter with your sleeping ability is largely responsible for the continuance of your trouble.

We know by experience that we can convince ourselves of almost anything by affirming it long enough and often enough. The constant repetition, after a while, establishes the belief in our minds that the thing is true. Consequently, we can establish the sleep habit just as easily as any other habit.

It is perfectly possible by means of affirmation, the constant repetition in heart-to-heart talks with ourselves to regain our power to sleep normally. Your subconscious self, that side of your nature which presides over the involuntary or automatic functions during sleep, as well as while you are awake, can be made to obey your suggestions—even your desire to overcome insomnia. Say to this inner self: "You know there is no reason why you should not sleep. There is no defect in your physical or mental make-up which keeps you awake. You ought to sleep soundly so many hours every night. There is no reason why you should not, and you are going to do so tonight."

Repeat similar affirmations during the day. Say to yourself, "This sleeplessness is only a bad habit. If I were ill physically or mentally, if I had any serious defect in my nervous system which would give any excuse for insomnia, it would be a different thing, but I haven't anything of the sort. I am simply the slave of a senseless obsession and I am going to break it. I am going to begin right away. I am going to sleep better tonight, tomorrow night, and the next night. I am going to get through with this habit that I have created. Nothing keeps me awake but my conviction, my fears and worries that I am not going to sleep."

Prepare your mind for sleep in the way already suggested by emptying it of all worry and fear, all envy and uncharitableness, everything that disturbs, irritates, or excites. Crowd these out with thoughts of joy, of good cheer, of things which will help and inspire. Compose yourself with the belief that you will go to sleep easily and naturally; relax every muscle and say to yourself in a quiet drowsy voice, "I am so sleepy, so sleepy, so sleepy." The subconscious self will listen and in a short time will automatically put your suggestion into practice.

We are a bundle of habits. We perform most of our life functions with greater or less regularity, so that they become practically automatic, and in many ways, regularity, system, and order are imperative for our health, our success and our happiness. This is especially true in regard to sleep. We must keep regular hours, be systematic in our habits, or our sleep is likely to suffer.

If you play as hard as you work, refresh and rejuvenate your-self by pleasant recreation when your work is done, and then at a regular hour every night prepare your mind for sleep—just as you prepare your body—giving it a mental bath and clothing it in beau-tiful thoughts, you will in a short time establish the habit of sound, peaceful, refreshing sleep.

Form the habit of making a call on the Great Within of yourself before retiring. Leave there the message of self-betterment and self-enlargement—that which you yearn for and long to realize but do not know just how to attain. Registering this call, this demand for some-thing higher and nobler in your subconsciousness before you drift off to sleep—putting it right up to yourself—will work like a leaven during the night. After a while, all the building forces within you will unite in furthering your aim—in helping you to realize your vision, whatever it may be.

There are marvelous possibilities for health and character, success and happiness building, during sleep. Instead of making an enemy of your subconscious self by giving it destructive thoughts to work with at night, worrisome thoughts that will destroy much of what you have accomplished during the day, make it your friend by giving it strong, creative, helpful thoughts with which to go on creating, building for you during the night.

Every thought dropped into the subconscious mind before we go to sleep is a seed that will germinate in the night while we are uncon-scious and will ultimately bring forth a harvest of its kind. By nightly impressing upon your subconscious your desires, picturing as vividly as possible your ideals, what you wish to become and what you long to accomplish, you will be surprised to see how quickly that wonder-ful force in the subjective self will begin to shape the pattern, to copy the model which it is given—to overcome unwanted tendencies which the willpower may not be strong enough to correct in the daytime.

You will find that you will be able to correct the habits which are wounding your self-respect, humiliating you, marring your usefulness and efficiency—perhaps sapping your life. If, as now seems clear, the subconscious mind can build or destroy, can make us happy or miserable according to the pattern we give it before going to sleep, if it can solve the problems of the inventor, of the discoverer, of the troubled business person, why do we not use it more? Why do we not avail ourselves of this tremendous mysterious force for life-building, character-building, success-building, happiness-building, instead of for life-destroying?

One reason is that we are only just beginning to discover that we can control this secondary self or intelligence, which regulates all the functions of the body without the immediate orders of the objective self. We are getting a glimpse of what it is capable of doing by experiments upon hypnotized subjects, when the objective mind, the mind which gets most of its material through the five senses, is shut off and the other, the subjective mind, is in control.

We are finding that it is comparatively easy while a person is in a hypnotic state to make wonderful changes in disposition, and to correct vicious habits, mental and moral defects, through suggestion.

There is no doubt that so far as the subjective mind is concerned, we are in a similar condition when asleep as we are when in a hypnotic trance, and experiments have shown that marvelous results are possible by talking to ourselves, using auto-suggestion—pre-hypnotic suggestions, if you will—prior to sleep.

If you want to make yourself beautiful in character, in disposition, in person, think beautiful thoughts into your mind as you fall asleep. Speak to it of beautiful things as you are drifting off to sleep

In the marvelous interior creative force lies the great secret of life. Blessed is they who find it.

CHAPTER 5
Mental Activity During Sleep

physiologists tell us that the mental processes which are active on retiring, continue far into the night. Those mental impressions we have upon retiring, just before going to sleep—the thoughts that dominate the mind—continue to exercise influence long after we become unconscious.

We are told, too, that wrinkles and other evidences of age are formed as readily during sleep as when awake, indicating that the way the mind is set when falling asleep has a powerful influence on the body.

Many people cut off the best years of their lives by the continuation in their sleep of the wearing, tearing, rasping influences that have been operating upon them during the day.

Thousands of business and professional men and women are so active during the day, live such strenuous, unnatural lives, that they cannot stop thinking after they retire, and sleep is driven away, or only induced after complete mental exhaustion. These people are so absorbed in the problems of their business or vocations that they do not know how to relax, to rest; so they lie down to sleep with all their cares—just as a tired camel lies down in the desert with its great burden still on its back. The result is that, instead of being benefitted by refreshing, rejuvenating sleep, they get up in the morning weary, much older than when they retired, when they ought to get up full of vigor, with a great surplus of energy and bounding vitality—strong and ambitious for the day's work before them. The corroding, exhausting, discord-producing operations which are going on when they fall asleep and which continue into the night, counteract the good they would otherwise get from their limited amount of sleep.

It is more important to prepare the mind for sleep than the body. The mental bath is even more necessary than the physical one.

The first thing to do is to get rid of the worrying, racking influences which have been operating upon us during the day—to clean the mental house—to tear down all the dingy, discouraging, discordant pictures that have disfigured it and hang up bright, cheerful, encouraging ones for the night.

Never allow yourself, under any circumstances, to retire in a discouraged, despondent, gloomy mood, or in a fit of temper. Never lie down with a frown on your brow; with a perplexed, troubled expression on your face. Smooth out the wrinkles—drive away grudges, jealousies, all the enemies of your peace of mind. Let nothing tempt you to go to sleep with an unkind, critical, jealous thought toward another in your mind.

It is bad enough to feel unkindly toward others when under severe provocation, or when in a hot temper, but you cannot afford to deliberately continue this state of mind after the provocation has ceased and spoil your sleep. You cannot afford the wear and tear. It takes too much out of you. Life is too short, time too precious to spend any part of it in unprofitable, health-wrecking, soul-racking thought.

Be at peace with all the world at least once in every twenty-four hours. You cannot afford to allow the enemies of your happiness to etch their miserable images deeper and deeper into your character as you sleep. Erase them all. Start every night with a clean slate.

If you have been impulsive, foolish, unkind during the day in your treatment of others; if you have been holding a revengeful, ugly, or jealous attitude toward others, wipe off your mental slate now and start anew. Obey the injunction of St. Paul, "Let not the sun go down upon your wrath."

If you have difficulty in banishing unpleasant or torturing thoughts, read an inspiring book—something that will take out your wrinkles and put you in a happy mood, and will reveal to you the real grandeur and beauty of life; that will make you feel ashamed of your petty meannesses and narrow, uncharitable thoughts.

Saturate your mind with pleasant memories and with dreams of great expectations. Just imagine yourself the man or woman you long to become, filled with happiness, prosperity, and power. Hold tenaciously the ideal of the character you most admire, the personality to which you aspire—the broad, magnanimous, large-hearted, deep-minded, lovable soul which you wish it were possible for you to become. The habit of such beautiful life-picturing and the power of reverie on retiring will very quickly begin to reproduce itself, outpicture itself in your life.

After a little practice, you will be surprised to see how quickly and completely you can change your whole mental attitude, so that you will face life the right way before you fall, asleep.

A prominent business man told me recently that his great weakness was his inability to stop thinking after retiring. This man, who is very active during the day and works at a high tension, has a sensitive nervous makeup, and his brain keeps on working after he falls asleep as intensely as it did during the day. In this way he is robbed of much sleep—and what he gets is so troubled and unrefreshing, that he feels all used up the next day.

I advised him to cultivate the habit of closing the, door of his business brain at the same time that he closed the door of his business office.

"You should," I said, "insist on changing the current of your, thoughts when you leave your business for the day, just as you change your environment, or as you change your clothes for dinner when you go home in the evening. Turn your thoughts to your wife and children, to their joys and interests; talk to them, play games with them, read some humorous or entertaining story, or some strong, interesting book that will lift you out of your business rut. Go out for a long walk or a ride; fill your lungs with strong, sweet, fresh air; look about you and observe the beauties of nature. Or have a hobby of some kind to which you can turn for recreation and refreshment when you quit your regular business. Be master of your mind. Learn to control it, instead of allowing it to control you and tyrannize you.

"Hang up in your bedroom, in a conspicuous place where you can always see it, a card bearing in bold, illuminated letters, this motto: 'No Thinking Here.'

"Shut off all thinking processes of every kind when you retire for the night, relax every muscle; let there be no tension of mind or body, and in a short time you will find that sleep will come to you as easily and naturally as to a little child—as untroubled, as sweet, and as refreshing as that of a child."

To all who are troubled as this man was, I offer the same advice, for its adoption proved very successful in his case.

It is a great art to be able to shut the gates of the mental powerhouse on retiring, to control oneself, to put oneself in harmony with the world, to expel from he mind everything which jars or irritates—all malice, envy, and jealousy, the enemies of our peace and happiness—before we go to sleep. It is an art that all can acquire.

Indeed, have you ever thought of the possibilities of spiritual and mental development during sleep? Has it ever occurred to you that while the processes of repair and upbuilding are proceeding normally in the body, the mind also may be expanding, the soul as well as the body may be growing?

As a matter of fact, few people realize what an immense amount of work is carried on automatically in the body under the direction of the subconscious mind. If the entire brain and nervous system were to go to sleep at night all of the bodily functions would stop. The heart would cease to beat; the stomach, the liver, the kidneys and the other glands would no longer act, the various digestive processes would cease to operate, all the physical organs would cease working, and we would stop breathing.

One of the deepest mysteries of Nature's processes is that of putting a part of the brain and nervous system, and most of the mental faculties which were in use during the day, under the sweet ether of sleep, while she repairs and rejuvenates every cell and every tissue— but at the same time keeping in the most active condition a great many of the bodily processes and even certain of the mental and creative faculties. These latter are awake and alert all the time while the sleeper is in a state of unconsciousness.

Most of us probably have had the experience of dropping to sleep at night discouraged because we could not solve same vexing problem to our satisfaction—and behold, in the morning, without any conscious effort on our part, the problem was solved; all its intricacies were unraveled, and what had so puzzled us the night before was perfectly clear when we woke up in the morning. Our conscious, objective self did not enter the mysterious laboratory where the miracle was wrought. We do not know how it was wrought. We only know that it was done somehow, without our knowledge, while we slept.

Some of our greatest inventions and discoveries have been worked out by the subconscious mind during sleep. Many an inventor who went to sleep with a puzzled brain, discouraged and disheartened, unable to make the connecting link between theory and practical application, awoke in the morning with his or her problem solved.

Mathematicians and astronomers have had marvelous results worked out while they slept, answers to questions which had puzzled them beyond measure during their waking hours.

Writers, poets, painters, musicians, all have received inspiration for their work, while the body slumbered.

Many people attempt to explain these things on a purely physical basis. They attribute the apparent phenomenon to the mere fact that the brain has been refreshed and renewed during the night, and that, consequently, we can think better and more clearly in the morning. That is true, so far as it goes, but there is something more—something beyond this. We know that during sleep ideas are suggested and problems actually worked out along lines which did not occur to the waking mind.

Most of us have had experiences, of some kind or another which show that there is some great principle, some intelligent power back of the flesh, but not of it, which is continually active in our lives, helping us to solve our problems. One of the most interesting instances of this is given in the biography of the great scientist, Professor Louis Agassiz, by his widow:

"He [Professor Agassiz]," she wrote, "had been for two weeks striving to decipher the somewhat obscure impression of a fossil fish on the stone slab in which it was preserved. Weary and perplexed, he put his work aside at last, and tried to dismiss it from his mind. Shortly after, he waked one night persuaded that while asleep he had seen his fish with all the missing features perfectly restored. But when he tried to hold and make fast the image, it escaped him.

"Nevertheless, he went early to the Jardin des Plantes, thinking that on looking anew at the impression, he should see something which would put him on the track of his vision. In vain—the blurred record was as blank as ever. The next night he saw the fish again, but with no more satisfactory result. When he awoke it disappeared from his memory as before. Hoping that the same experience might be repeated, on the third night he placed a pencil and paper beside his bed before going to sleep.

"Accordingly, towards morning the fish reappeared in his dream, confusedly at first, but at last with such distinctness that he had no longer any doubt as to its zoological characters. Still half dreaming, in perfect darkness, he traced these characters on the sheet of paper at the bedside. In the morning he was surprised to see in his nocturnal sketch features which he thought it impossible the fossil itself should reveal. He hastened to the Jardin des Plantes, and, with his drawing as a guide, succeeded in chiseling away the surface of the stone under which portions of the fish proved to be hidden. When wholly exposed it corresponded with his dream and his drawing, and he succeeded in classifying it with ease."

We are all familiar with examples of the sometimes incredible feats performed by somnambulists. While fast asleep, they will get up and dress, lock and unlock doors, go out and walk and ride in the most dangerous places, where they would not attempt to go when awake. Many have been known to walk along the edges of roofs of houses, the banks of rivers, or close to the edge of precipices, where one false step would precipitate them to death. They will speak, write, act, and move as if entirely conscious of what they are doing. They will answer questions put to them while asleep and carry on a conversation rationally.

In this respect the state of the sleep walker is similar to that of a person in a hypnotic trance, who can be acted on from without and remain wholly unconscious. Surgical operations have been performed upon a hypnotized person without the use of anesthetics; and there is no doubt that this also would be possible during profound sleep. The subjective mind is much more susceptible to suggestion when the objective mind is unconscious. There is no resistance on account of prejudice or external influences.

That we are on the eve of marvelous possibilities of treating disease during sleep there is not the slightest doubt. The same is true of habit forming, mind changing, of mind improving, of strengthening deficient faculties, of eradicating peculiarities and idiosyncracies, of neutralizing injurious hereditary tendencies, of increasing ability. The possibilities of changing the disposition and of mind building during sleep are only beginning to be realized.

We are beginning to realize that all of our experiences during the day, all of our thoughts, emotions and mental attitudes, the multitude of little things which seem to make but a fleeting impression, are not in reality lost. Every day leaves its record on the brain, and this record is never erased or destroyed. Each is dropped into the subconscious mind where it is ever on call.

I heard recently, for example, of a prominent banker who lost a very important key, the only one to the bank treasures. He claimed that it had not been lost in the ordinary way, but was stolen. Suspicion was at once attached to the employees. A prominent detective was placed in the bank, and after watching and questioning every one on the staff, he became convinced that none but the banker himself knew anything about the key.

Every detective is necessarily something of a mind reader, and this one, believing firmly in his own theory, suggested a simple plan for recovering the key. He told the banker to quit suspecting the employees and worrying about burglars getting the bank's treasures, and instead to relax his overwrought mind and go to sleep with the belief that he himself had put the key away, somewhere, and that it would be found in the morning. "If you do this," he said, "I believe the mystery will be solved."

The banker did as the detective suggested, and on getting up the following morning he was instinctively led to a certain secret place, and, behold, there was the key. He was not conscious that he had put it there, but after finding it he had a faint recollection of previously going to this place.

The banker's objective or conscious mind was probably busy with something else when he put the key away. Only his subconscious self had any knowledge of what he was doing. Then when he missed the key his fears, his worry, his anxiety, his suspicions and generally wrought-up mentality made it impossible for his subjective mind to reveal the secret to him. But after his mind had become poised and he was again in tune with his subjective intelligence, the information was passed along.

Now if, as we have seen, the subconscious mind can perform real work, real service for us, why should we not use it especially during sleep? Why should we not avail ourselves of this enormous creative force to strengthen all our powers and possibilities, to piece out, virtually to lengthen our time, our lives? Think what it would mean to us in a lifetime if we could keep these sleepless creative functions always in superb condition so that they would go on during the night working out our problems, unraveling our difficulties, carrying forward our plans, while we are asleep!

It is now established beyond a doubt that certain parts of the brain continue active during the night when the rest of it is under the anesthetic of sleep. But we have hardly begun to realize what a tremendous ally this sleepless creative part of the brain can be made in our mental development. It is well known that most of the growth of the child, of its skeleton, muscles, nerves and all the twelve different kinds of tissues in its body takes place during sleep, that there is comparatively little during the activities of the day. It is not so well understood that our minds also grow during the night; that they develop along the lines of the ideals, thoughts and emotions with which we feed them before retiring.

We never awake just the same being as when we went to sleep. We are either better or worse. We changed while we slept. While our senses are wrapped in slumber, the subjective mind is busily at work. It is either building up or tearing down. It is my firm belief that by an intelligent, systematic direction of this sleepless faculty of the brain we can actually make it create for us along the line of our desires. I know persons who have performed wonders in reforming themselves by self-suggestion on retiring at night, holding the happy, inspiring, helpful suggestion in the mind up to the point of unconsciousness. Persons have overcome ugly tempers and dispositions in this way as well as other undesirable traits.

Most people, by not putting the mind in proper condition before going to sleep, not only do not intelligently use this marvelous creative agency but they destroy all possibility of beneficial results from its action.

Be sure that when you fall asleep there is only that in your consciousness which will help you to be more of a man, more of woman. Determine that your mind, when you lose conscious thought, shall have in it no worrisome images, but only beautiful images and thoughts of hope and goodwill toward every living creature; that there shall be no failure thought, no poverty thought, no ugly discordant thought, but that everything shall be bright, cheerful, hopeful, helpful and optimistic.

CHAPTER 6
"As Ye Sow"

s it not a strange fact that while we know with absolute certainty
that what we sow or plant in the soil will come back to us in exact
kind, that it is absolutely impossible to sow corn and get a crop
of wheat, we entirely disregard this law when it comes to mental
sowing?

On what principle can we expect a crop of happiness and contentment when for years we have been sowing seed thoughts of exactly
the opposite character? How can we expect a crop of health when we
are all the time sowing disease thought seeds?

We would think a farmer insane who should sow thistle seeds all
over the farm and expect to reap wheat. But we sow fear thoughts,
worry thoughts, anxious thoughts, doubt thoughts, and wonder that
we are not in perpetual harmony.

The harvest from our thoughts is just as much the result of law as
that of the farmer's sowing. How simple our great life problems would
become if we could only realize that the mental laws are just as sci-

entific as the physical laws! Every thought generated in the brain is a seed which must produce its harvest—thistle or rose, weed or wheat.

If there is any one law of the universe emphasized over and above all others, it is that like produces like everywhere and always.

Everybody who sees your present character, your moral harvest, knows what you put into the soil of your youth. They do not need to go back and inquire about your childhood; the crop tells the story; you are simply reaping what you have sown. You do not expect to get the fragrant breath of the rose from sowing thistle seeds. How can you expect to sow the thistles of revenge and brutality and reap a harvest of kindness and happiness?

On the other hand, if we sow the charitable, magnanimous, encouraging, uplifting thought, we shall reap the golden harvest of harmony and beauty and joy. If we sow the thoughts of abundance, of plenty, we shall tend to reap prosperity; while if we sow the mean, pinched, stingy failure thoughts, we shall reap a poverty harvest.

When we see a sour, repulsive face, we know that it is a harvest of selfish, vicious sowing. And when we see a serene, confident face, we know that it has come from the sowing of harmonious, helpful, unselfish thought seeds.

A person who should take a knife and begin to slash his or her flesh until the blood flowed would be shut up in an insane asylum. Be do we not all the time slash our mental selves with edged thought-tools—hatred, revenge, anger, jealousy—and yet we think ourselves sane, normal?

Every thought is a seed which produces a mental plant exactly like itself. *If there is venom in the seed thought-plant there will be venom in the fruit*—which will poison the life, destroy happiness and efficiency.

If you sell yourself to your desires, you must expect the harvest to correspond. Life is just to us. It gives us what we pay for, and we receive only as we pay. *Nature keeps a cash store.* She gives us everything we pay for: we take away nothing for which we did not leave the price.

If you want to produce a crop of prosperity, you must not sow failure or poverty seeds, seeds of discouragement or doubt.

If you want to produce a character-crop of beauty, sweetness, and loveliness, you must sow seeds of kindness, love, and helpfulness.

There is no guess-work about this processes. There is, instead, an absolutely inexorable law: Like *must* produce like.

Many complain because their harvest is so full of thorns, thistles, and weeds. But if they analyzed their lives, they would find that they had been sowing seeds of limitation, fear, envy, blame, lack of self faith and hope, and the like. If they had sown seeds of optimism, prosperity, belief, self-confidence, tenacity, they would have had a very different kind of harvest.

We may complain of our condition today, but in time we will have to face the truth that we are simply reaping what we sowed yesterday.

There is no dodging this reaping. Everything we do, every thought that passes through our minds, is a seed which we throw out into the soil of the world, and which must give a harvest like itself.

If you are not content with your current circumstances, your current harvest, if it is not providing you with the sustenance you seek, begin sowing differently today—different actions, different behaviors, and most importantly, different thoughts—and tomorrow you will have the harvest that nourishes you.

CHAPTER 7
Be A Mental Chemist

Many of us keep our minds more or less poisoned much of the time because of our ignorance of mental chemistry. We suffer from mental self-poison and do not know how to prevent it, but the time will come when every intelligent person will know how to apply the proper antidotes for special forms of mental poisoning.

We shall find that it is just as easy to counteract an unfriendly, disagreeable, malicious thought by turning on the counter thought, as it is to rob the hot water of its burning power by turning on the cold-water faucet. We shall be able to regulate the temperature of our thought just as we now are able to regulate as the temperature of our water. If the water is too hot we simply turn on the cold faucet. In a like manner, when we feel our brain heating up with hot temper, we shall simply turn on the love thought, the peace thought, and the anger heat will be instantly counteracted.

I know of a many, for example, who has lost all his property, all his family, and has been left alone in the world—a poor and homeless old man. Yet no one can ever detect a tremor of complaint or a weakness anywhere in his nature, simply because he has so completely learned the science of right thinking that he can shut out of his mind or neutralize with its mental antidote anything which would cause him pain or injury. He neutralizes discord with harmony, error with truth.

He has become such an adept at mental chemistry that the very moment he is touched with the poison of hatred and jealousy, he antidotes it with love, the spirit of goodwill. The shafts of malice and envy can not get near him. He looks upon these things as no part of the truth of his being.

Hatred cannot live an instant in the presence of love. The Golden Rule will kill all jealousy and revenge. They cannot live together.

The trouble with most people is that they try to drive out the bad in themselves instead of antidoting it with the good. They try to force hatred out of their minds without the assistance of its antidote.

What you allow to live in your heart, harbor in your mind, dwell upon in your thoughts, are seeds which will develop in your life and produce things like themselves. Hate seed in the heart can not produce a love flower in your life. A sinister thought will produce a sinister harvest. The revenge seed will produce a bloody harvest.

We cannot drive darkness out of a room, but we can let in the light—and the darkness flees.

Remember that every morbid mood, every discordant, weak thought is a symptom of a poisoned mind. You have the antidote: the opposite thought. Your mind remedy is always present. The antidote for all error is truth, for all discord, is harmony. You do not have to pay a physician. You have your own chemist always with you. When you have learned the secrets of mental chemistry you can instantly stop every symptom and check every approach of mind disease.

Primitive people have great faith in the fact that their Creator put into certain barks, plants, and minerals remedies for every physical ill. But we are beginning to learn that we carry the great panacea for all our ills *within ourselves*; that the antidotes for the worst poisons—the poisons of hatred, jealousy, anger, and selfishness—exist in the form of love, charity, and goodwill in our minds.

Every true, beautiful, and helpful thought is a suggestion which, if held in the mind, tends to reproduce itself there—clarifying your ideals and uplifting your life. While these inspiring and helpful suggestions fill your mind, their opposites cannot put in their deadly work, because the two cannot live together. They are mutually antagonistic—natural enemies. One excludes the other.

Learn the secret of scientific mental chemistry. Acquire the inestimable art of holding the right suggestion in your mind, so that you can triumph over any dominant note in your environment when it is unfriendly to your highest good.

CHAPTER 8
Change the Thought, Change the Person

many people have an idea that the brain is not susceptible of any very great change—that its limits are fixed by the destiny of heredity, and that about all we can do is to give it a little polish and culture.

There are plenty of examples, however, of individuals who have completely revolutionized portions of their brains, and have made strong faculties of those which were weak at birth or deficient from lack of exercise. There are many instances where certain mental faculties have been almost entirely wanting, and yet have been built up so that they have powerfully buttressed their whole character.

Take courage, for instance. Many very successful people were once so completely devoid of this quality that the lack threatened to wreck their whole future. But they developed it until it became strong.

This was done by the cultivation of self-confidence—by holding the constant suggestion of courage in their minds; by the contemplation of brave and heroic deeds; by the reading of the life stories and works of great heroes; by the suggestion that fear is a negative quality, the absence of the natural quality of courage which is everyone's birthright—and by the constant effort to do courageous deeds.

When the world was young, our brain was very primitive, because the demand upon it was largely for self-protection and the acquisition of food, which called only for the development of its lower, its animal part. Gradually, however, there was a higher call upon it and a more varied development, until today, in the highest civilization, it has become exceedingly complex.

Every new demand of civilization makes a new call upon the brain, and, just as the physique of animals and humans has been modified to meet varying conditions of climate and maintenance, the brain has developed faculties and powers to meet the fresh calls of a more complicated life—developing new cells and strengthening weak ones whenever the latter were called upon for helpful activity.

The late professor William James of Harvard said that the slightest thought changes the brain structure, leaving its telltale work. The character of our thoughts, then, is constantly changing the structure of our brains.

The nature of our thoughts also affects the nature of our characters. Hold any particular thought in the mind persistently until it has formed grooves in the brain-tissue and become dominant in the brain structure, and you have permanently changed your character in that direction. You are, in that particular, a new person. The habit of holding revengeful, hateful thoughts, for example, in time turns a sweet character into a sour one.

If you are deficient, if you have any weak faculties, traits, which you wish to strengthen, concentrate your thought upon the quality you desire. The cells presiding over that portion of the brain will be strengthened by holding your thought there.

Holding a creative, affirmative, confident thought will strengthen the faculty, just as doubt and lack of confidence will weaken it.

If you wish to cultivate or to improve a weak or deficient faculty, just hold the picture of it in its perfect form. Do not hold the defective, faulty image. Think of the desired quality and live it in your thoughts as you would like to have it. In every way to exercise it so that new and better brain cells will be formed and the weak ones strengthened. If you are vacillating, for instance, if you lack decision, just assume a decisive mental attitude. Constantly affirm that you are able to decide wisely, firmly, finally. Do not allow yourself to think that you are weak.

Instead of trying to root out a defect or a vicious quality directly, cultivate the opposite quality. Persist in this, and the undesired quality will gradually die. *"Kill the negative by cultivating the positive."*

The craving for something higher and better is the best possible antidote or remedy for the lower tendencies which one wishes to get rid of. When the general habit of always aspiring, moving upwards and climbing to something higher and better is formed, the undesirable qualities and the vicious habits will fade away; they will die from lack of nourishment. Only those things grow in our nature which are fed. The quickest way to kill them is to cut off their nourishment.

But not only can we strengthen mental weaknesses and deficiencies, but it is perfectly possible to increase our general ability through the power of suggestion. Indeed, the susceptibility of all the mental faculties to improvement, to enlargement, is something remarkable.

The science of brain-building is teaching us how to prevent and how to eliminate idiosyncrasies and peculiarities and how to strengthen weaknesses which now handicap so many of us. Many of us, for example, have the impression that our abilities are something that is inherited, and that while we may polish them a little, they cannot add to it or enlarge it. But we are beginning to see that *all* the mental faculties are capable of very great enlargement. In fact, there is not a single faculty which can not be very materially improved in a comparatively short time.

In time, we shall learn that symmetrical brain development is what gives power, and that to develop some particular faculty or faculties and allow others, which are perhaps equally as important, to atrophy and shrivel from disuse, is not scientific education, and that this one-sided development is hindrance to our development.

All reforms must result from changing the mind; from a complete reversal of the mental attitude; a turning about and facing the other way.

Learn to assert stoutly the possession of whatever you lack. If it is courage or staying power that you seek, assert these qualities as yours by divine right. Stoutly refuse to give them up. Be thoroughly convinced that they belong to you, that you actually possess them, and you will win.

We tend to become like our aspirations. If we constantly aspire and strive for something better and higher and nobler, we can not help improving. The ambition that is dominant in the mind tends to work itself out in the life. If our ambition is sordid and low, we shall develop these qualities, for our lives follow our ideals.

Parents, teachers, and reformers are beginning to see that they call out of those whom they wish to help just what they see in them, because their suggestive thought arouses its affinities. The subject *feels* their thought. If it is a helpful, inspiring one, it tends to uplift him. If, on the other hand, it is concentrated upon his defects, these very qualities which they try to erase are only etched deeper and made more indelible.

The same principle applies to our own imperfections; our own unfolding. If we over-emphasize the bad in ourselves, if we are always criticizing our shortcomings and weaknesses and castigating ourselves for not doing better, we only deepen the unfortunate pictures in our consciousness and make them more influential in our lives.

On the other hand, if we visualize the larger possible man or woman and see only what is sublime in ourselves, we shall be able to make infinitely more of ourselves and open up the glorious possibilities of what may properly be called our divine development.

CHAPTER 9
The Gift of Imagination

I know of an elderly, Italian lady who has, for many years, been an invalid and has rarely been out of her house, and yet she says she has the most delightful times imaginable on her mental vacations. She travels abroad every day, revisits the scenes familiar in her childhood, climbs the Alps, and walks through the streets of the cities of Italy, once so dear to her. She rides the wind as she sits for hours on the veranda of her old Sorrento home, watching sailboats skimming across the bay of Naples. She watches the oranges and lemons ripening on the trees. She takes mental trips to the leading theaters, and reviews again the plays and operas which she saw in her younger days. She reads Shakespeare, and sees all the great Shakespearean actors and actresses in her mind's eye, who never tire of repeating their roles for her. Oftentimes when in pain she takes off on her mental trips, and when she comes back she is refreshed with new hope and new courage for fighting her physical battles. For hours, this sweet lady not only forgets all aches and pains which make her an invalid, she forgets the physical chains which enslave her in doors—and she wanders over the earth at will. These mental trips, she says, are often more enjoyable than the physical ones, because she has none of the annoyances and discomforts of travel and none of the expense. She says that if people only knew the possibilities of enjoyment through the picturing power of the imagination, the whole human race would be happy.

Regrettably, our training and education do not half emphasize the possibilities of enjoyment through the imagination, which is ever available to each of us, to transport us in the twinkling of an eye into whatever we can dream.

One of the great secrets of those who surprise everybody by the enormous amount of work they accomplish and pleasure they experience in the midst of what for others would be stress, is their ability to take frequent mental recesses. Little vacations. I know, for example, several people so hemmed in and confined by perpetual hard work that it is almost impossible for them to be long away from their places of business or their professions—yet although they are subject to conditions that would worry others into an early grave, they always seem to be serene, fresh, and buoyant, because they have acquired the happy art of taking mental vacations. I have interviewed some of these people, and they tell me that no matter how trying, or how exasperating their work, or how annoying the conditions may be about them, they seek opportunities to lift themselves out of their troubles and into a harmonious and blissful mental condition which nothing material can touch or mar. They have so educated their imaginations that they can create new worlds and live in them. They go back to the old home or farm and relive happy moments from their childhood days and friendships. They wade and fish in brooks, climb mountains, tramp in the forest, and meander through the meadows.

It does not take long to freshen a jaded mind if one knows the secret art. And that is the art of imagination. The imaginative faculties are wings which enable us to soar away quickly into joys ineffable—to fly away at will from our harassing, embarrassing, unwanted, surroundings; from things that discourage, disgust, and annoy; from lives of grasping and deadlines and drudgery; from the "blues."

Imagination helps the prisoner to fly out of the cell. John Bunyan was in prison when he wrote his masterpiece *The Pilgrim's Progress*. He used his imaginative faculty to create such characters as Christian, Evangelist, Faithful, Hopeful, and Giant Despair—fictitious characters who representative of moods, feelings, beliefs, attitudes, and capacities of human nature, live forever in our hearts.

No matter how badly things may be about you or what blunders or mistakes harass you, no matter what misfortunes overtake you, imagination is to your opportunity for fulfillment in times of duress like the captured bird which young boys harass, tease, and torment, yet which wrenches away from them and in an instant soars into the air and is free again.

The great truth of your self-fulfillment is that the sacred longings of your imagination were given to you as a constant reminder that you can make your life sublime; that no matter how disagreeable or unfriendly your surroundings may be, you can—*because* of your imagination and *by* your imagination—lift yourself into something better for yourself, something that you see in your imaginative vision.

CHAPTER 10
The Ability of the Mind
to Compel the Body

I t is a common experience for actors who are ill to be cured for a time and to be entirely forgetful of their aches and pains under the stimulus of ambition and the brain-quickening influence of their audiences.

I know of an actor who suffered such tortures with inflammatory rheumatism that even with the aid of a cane he could not walk two blocks, from his hotel to the theater. Yet, when his cue was called, he not only walked upon the stage with the utmost ease and grace, but was also entirely oblivious of the pain which a few moments before had made him wretched. A stronger motive drove out the lesser, made him utterly unconscious of his trouble, and the pain for the time was gone. It was not merely covered up by some other thought, passion, or emotion, but it was temporarily annihilated; and as soon as the play was over, and his part finished, he was crippled again.

It is an unusual thing for singers or actors and actresses to be obliged to give up their parts even for a night, but when they are off duty or on their vacations, they are much more likely to be ill or indisposed. There is a common saying among actors and singers that they cannot afford to be sick.

That "imperious must" which compels actors to do their level best, whether they feel like it or not, is a force which no ordinary pain or physical disability can silence or over-come. And it is a compelling quality that we all experience. Somehow, even though we may feel that it is impossible for us to make any further effort, if a crisis comes, when an emergency is upon us—in whatever moments when we feel the prodding of this imperative, imperious necessity—there comes a latent power from within us which answers the call—and we do what we thought was the impossible.

General Grant was suffering greatly from rheumatism at Appomattox, but when a flag of truce informed him that Lee was ready to surrender, his great joy not only made him forget his rheumatism but also drove it completely away—at least for some time.

The shock occasioned by the great San Francisco earthquake cured a paralytic who had been crippled for fifteen years. Men and women who had been practically invalids for a long time, and who were scarcely able to wait upon themselves, worked like Trojans when this crisis came, carrying their children and household goods long distances to places of safety.

We do not know what we can bear until we are put to the test. Many a delicate mother, who thought that she could not survive the death of her children, has lived to bury her husband and the last one of a large family, and in addition to all this has seen her home and last dollar swept away—yet she had the courage to bear it all and to go on.

When the need comes, there is a power deep within us that answers the call.

A person who shrinks from the prick of a pin, and who, under ordinary circumstances, can not endure without an anesthetic the extraction of a tooth or the cutting of flesh even in a trivial operation, can, when mangled in an accident, far from civilization, stand the amputation of a limb without as much fear and terror as he might suffer at home from the lancing of a whitlow.

I have seen a dozen firemen go to their deaths in a fire without showing the slightest sign of fear. These men did not shrink even when they realized that every means of escape had been cut off. The last rope thrown to them had been consumed; the last ladder had crumbled to ashes, and they were still in a burning tower one hundred feet above a blazing roof. Yet they showed no sign of fear when the tower sank into the seething caldron of flame.

When I was in Deadwood, in the Black Hills of South Dakota, I was told that in the early days there—before telephone, railroad, or telegraph communication had been established—the people were obliged to send a hundred miles for a physician. For this reason the services of a doctor were beyond the reach of persons of moderate means. The result was that people learned to depend upon themselves to such an extent that it was only on extremely rare occasions, usually in a case of severe accident or some great emergency, that a physician was sent for. Some of the largest families of children in the place had been reared without a physician ever coming into the house. When I asked some of these people if they were ever sick they replied, "No, we are never sick, simply because we are obliged to keep well. We cannot afford to have a physician, and even if we could it would take so long to get him here that the sick one might be dead before he arrived."

One of the most unfortunate things that has come to us through what we call "higher civilization" is the killing of our faith in our power of disease resistance. We make great preparations for sickness. We expect it, anticipate it, and consequently have it. It is only a block or two to a physician, a drug-store is on every other corner, and the temptation to make an appointment with a physician or to get drugs at the slightest symptom of illness tends to make most of us more and more dependent on outside help and less confident in controlling our physical discords.

On the other hand, during the frontier days there were little villages and hamlets which physicians rarely entered, and the people often developed great powers of disease resistance.

There is no doubt that the doctor habit in many of us has a great deal to do with our parents calling the doctor whenever there was the least sign of disturbance in us. The result is that we have grown up a doctor picture, a medicine picture, in our minds—and these pictures influence our subsequent lives.

Is it not more rational to believe that the Creator would put the remedies for our ills within ourselves—in our own minds where they are always available—than that He would store them in herbs and minerals in remote parts of the earth, where but only a small portion of the human race would ever discover them, and countless millions would die in total ignorance of their existence?

There is a latent power, a force of indestructible life, an immortal principle of health, in every individual, which if developed would heal all our wounds and furnish a balm for the hurts of the world.

How rare a thing it is for people to be ill upon any great occasion in which they are to be active participants. How unusual for those even in very delicate health to be sick—or *too sick*—upon a particular day on which they have been invited to am occasion in their honor, royal reception, or a visit to the White House!

Multitudes of men and women would be sick in bed if they could afford it; but the hungry mouths to feed, the children to clothe, these and all the other obligations of life so press upon them that they cannot stop working; they must keep going whether they feel like it or not.

Many of the greatest things in the world have been accomplished under the stress of the "imperious must"—merciless in its lashings and proddings to accomplishment—that strenuous effort which we feel we must make when driven to desperation, when all outside help has been cut off, and we are forced to call upon all that is within us to extricate ourselves from some unfortunate situation.

This little insistent "must" dogs our steps; drives and bestirs us; makes us willing to suffer privations and endure hardships, inconveniences, and discomforts; and work slavishly, when in fact inclination otherwise tempts us to take life easy.

And it is this little insistent "must" that teaches us that there is a power in the mind that indeed can move mountains.

Would that we learn how to tap this power in times other than crises!

CHAPTER 11
How to Control Thought

there is no reason why we should allow the mind to wander into all sorts of fields and to dwell upon all sorts of subjects at random. With a little practice, in other words, we can control and concentrate the mind in any reasonable way we please. Attention, in other words, controlled by the will and directed by reason and higher judgment, can so discipline the mind that it will dwell on higher ideals—until high thinking has become a habit. Then the lower ideals and lower thinking will drop out of consciousness, and the mind will be left upon a higher plane. It is only a question of discipline.

Many and varied are the methods prescribed by writers for gaining thought control. But if we compare the techniques, we will find that there are certain concepts in common among the various writers and methods, as the following brief survey of writings will reveal.

"It is not possible to give explicit directions for an American substitute for Hindu Yoga practice," writes W. J. Colville, "as the general needs of the Anglo-Saxon race are not the same outwardly as those of their

Oriental brethren; but the great words *concentration* and *meditation* are just as forceful and full of meaning in the West as in the East. To concentrate on one's beloved goal, to see before the mental eye the prize as though it were already won, while we are all the while intensely conscious of moving nearer to its externalization, is so to place ourselves in relation with all that helps us on our way, that one by one obstacles vanish, and what seemed once too hard for human strength to accomplish appears now plain and even simple. The greatest need of all is to keep the goal in sight and not let interest flag or inward vision waver.

"A good lesson for all to practice is to take some special aspiration into the silence, and there realize its fulfillment with all the intensity of your visualistic ability. See yourself in the very place in which you most desire to be engaged, in the very work you would love best to accomplish. A little persistent industry in this exercise will soon relieve the intellect of worry, and gradually open up the understanding to perceive how to accomplish the otherwise unaccomplishable.

"But there is no substitute for work in all the universe, therefore let no one imagine that a state of inoperative, dreamy contemplation is one to be recommended. Outward work must follow inward contemplation. True meditation does not absolve us from the need of making effort, but it is a means for revealing to us what efforts we need to make and how to make them."

A similar process for controlling thought is recommended by a writer who says, "Go into the silence, concentrate your mind, polarize thought, breathe in the power and strength that is ever within the reach of all, and in unlimited supply, from which nothing but our own action or rejection can cut us off."

"The atmosphere about us is a product of thought. Thought makes it what it is, and thought alone can change it when it will," says Floyd B. Wilson, in *Paths to Power*. "The atmosphere that marks strong individuality is universally conceded to be the product of the invisible emanation of thought centered on an idea. Your atmosphere, being a product of thought, must receive all its power and force through the creative energy that gives it existence.

"Our proposition as to control, therefore, now reduces itself to this: If we know ourselves masters of our mental apparatus, we know we can control our thoughts and thus dictate our atmosphere. If, in silence, we daily hold ourselves passive—receptive for the particular good we most desire—we open the way for the creation of the atmosphere that is sought. One must come to these sittings as nearly passive as possible; but above all free from doubt. To many it will be found serious work to learn to hold themselves passive. The moments spent in this way will do more to advance you to the end than any other thing you can do."

Speaking more especially of the means of controlling the thought for the benefit of the body, Charles Brodie Patterson writes, "Let us keep the mind clear and bright, fill it with wholesome thoughts of life, and be kindly in our feelings toward others. Let us have no fear of anything, but realize that we are one with universal power—that power which can supply our every need; that health, strength, and happiness are our legitimate birthright, that they are ever potential in our inner lives, and that our bodies may express them now. If we take this mental attitude and adhere steadfastly to it, the body will very soon manifest health and strength."

In the light of these various directions from those who have drawn them from their own experience and that of others, it does not seem so difficult to raise our standard of living substantially by instilling into our thoughts the higher practice of awareness and forcing out the lower habit of lack of focus.

But how do we attain this level of awareness? How do we prevent the many distracting passions from interfering with our focused awareness?

"It is not necessary to engage in battle the small army of lesser passions," says Horace Fletcher, "if you concentrate your efforts against anger and worry, for the former are all children of these parents. Oppose anger and worry with a bold front, make one heroic stand against them, and they and all their children will fly. Disown them once and the ability to re-adopt them will have disappeared with them."

In a later book, Mr. Fletcher further reduces to one the enemy of harmonious, focused thought, calling anger and worry only forms of fear. And W. W. Atkinson concurs, writing, "Worry is the child of Fear, and bears a strong family resemblance to its parent. Treat the Fear family as you would any other kind of vermin—get rid of the old ones before they have a chance to have progeny."

So once we gain the power of concentration, we must cultivate perfect fearlessness and confidence—with which come cheerfulness and efficiency, and which result in happiness and prosperity.

If, then, we surround ourselves with a positive atmosphere, if we keep all negatives, all destroyers—all thoughts that suggest discord, disease, disaster, and failure—out of our minds and hold there only those words and thoughts which create and upbuild, we will very soon change the character of our entire mind—eventually thrusting out of our minds the enemies of success and happiness the moment they attempt to enter. We will harbor only noble words and thoughts—those which encourage, which bring light and beauty, which inspire and ennoble—welcoming these as eagerly as we will shun the others.

In pursuit of this desired level of consciousness and harmonious thought, the following rules in *Power of Will*, by Frank C. Haddock, seem practical and suggestive:

"Resolutely, persistently, and intelligently maintain a true and psychic field by constant exercise of strong will power toward all high realities: beautiful objects, right ideas, health, peace, truth, success, altruism, right-minded persons, the best literature, art, science, the noblest movements and institutions of the times, and a true religion.

"In contact with other people, maintain in your personal atmosphere a perfect and constant calm. Let this be so complete that it may not betray the effort to secure it, either in disturbed ether waves, or in movements which the other person's subconsciousness will recognize as coolness or suppressed hostility.

"Avoid all excitement.

"Send out no antagonisms.

"Reveal to the inner consciousness of other people nothing in your mind calculated to injure their feelings.

"Banish from your field all feelings of contempt and ridicule.

"Permit no vibrations of anger or irritation to escape into your field.

"Banish absolutely all thought waves of fear for persons with whore you are dealing.

"Banish all thought waves of distrust as to success with such persons.

"Maintain a personal atmosphere that is surcharged with the dynamic force of confident expectancy."

PART II

THE POWER
OF THOUGHT
IN CREATING
SELF-CONFIDENCE

CHAPTER 12
The Miracle of Self-Confidence

nothing else will so nerve you to accomplish great things as to believe in your own greatness, in your own marvelous possibilities. Count those as enemies who shake your faith in yourself, in your ability to do the thing you have set your heart upon doing—for when your, confidence is gone, your power is gone. Your achievement will never rise higher than your self-faith.

The miracles of civilization have been performed by men and women of great self-confidence, who had unwavering faith in their power to accomplish the tasks they undertook. The race would have been centuries behind what it is today had it not been for their grit, their determination, their persistence in finding and making real the thing they believed in and which the world often denounced as chimerical or impossible.

There is no law by which you can achieve success in anything without expecting it, demanding it, assuming it. There must be a strong, firm self-faith first, or the thing will never come. There is little room for chance in this world. Everything must have not only a cause, but a sufficient cause—a cause as large as the result.

A stream cannot rise higher than its source. No matter how great the ability, how large the genius, or how splendid the education, the achievement will never rise higher than the confidence. Great success must have a great source in expectation, in self-confidence, and in persistent endeavor to attain it.

Those can who think they can, and those can't who think they can't. That is an inexorable, indisputable law:

It does not matter what other people think of you, of your plans, or of your aims. No matter if they call you a visionary, a crank, or a dreamer—you must believe in yourself. You forsake yourself when you lose your confidence. Never allow anybody or any misfortune to shake your belief in yourself. You may lose your property, your health, your reputation, other peoples' confidence even, but there is always hope for you so long as you keep a firm faith in yourself. If you never lose that, but keep pushing on, the world will, sooner or later, make way for you.

A soldier once took a message to Napoleon in such great haste that the horse he rode dropped dead before he had delivered the paper. Nevertheless, he carried on and got the message to the general. Napoleon dictated his answer and, handing it to the messenger, ordered him to mount his own horse and deliver, it with all possible speed.

The messenger looked at the magnificent animal, with its superb trappings, and said, "Nay, General, but this is too gorgeous, too magnificent for a common soldier."

Napoleon said, "Nothing is too good or too magnificent for a French soldier."

The world is full of people like this poor French soldier, who think that what others have is too good for *them*; that it does not fit their humble condition; that they are not expected to have as good things as those who are "more favored." They do not realize how they weaken themselves by this mental attitude of self-depreciation or self-effacement. They do not claim enough, expect enough, or demand enough of themselves.

You will never become a giant if you only make a pygmy's claim for yourself; if you only expect a pygmy's part. There is no law which can cause a pygmy's thinking to produce a giant. The statue follows the model. The model is the inward vision.

Most people have been educated to think that it was not intended they should have the best there is in the world; that the good and the beautiful things of life were not designed for them, but were reserved for those especially favored by fortune. They have grown up under this conviction of their inferiority, and they will be inferior until they claim superiority as their birthright. A vast number of men and women who are really capable of doing great things, do small things, live mediocre lives, because they do not expect or demand enough of themselves. They do not know how to call out their best.

One reason why the human race as a whole has not measured up to its possibilities, to its promise; one reason why we see everywhere splendid ability doing the work of mediocrity; is because people do not think half enough of themselves.

We do not fully realize to what extent we can really be masters of ourselves. We fail to see that we can control our own destiny, make ourselves do whatever is possible; make ourselves become whatever we long to be.

"If we choose to be no more than clods of clay," says Marie Corelli, "then we shall be used as clods of clay for braver feet to tread on."

The persistent thought that you are not as good as others, that you are a weak, ineffective being, will lower your whole standard of life and paralyze your ability.

There is everything in assuming the part we wish to play, and playing it royally. If you are ambitious to do big things, you must make a large program for yourself, and assume the part it demands.

There is something in the atmosphere of those who have a large and true estimate of themselves, who believe they are going to win out. Something in their very appearance wins half the battle before a blow is struck. Things get out of the way of the vigorous, affirmative person—things which are always tripping the self-depreciating, negative person.

Those who are self-reliant, positive, optimistic, and undertake their work with the assurance of success, magnetize their conditions. They draw to themselves the literal fulfillment of the biblical promise in Matthew 25:29: "For unto every one that hath shall be given, and he shall have abundance."

Set your so resolutely, so definitely, and with such vigorous determination toward the thing you would accomplish, and put so much grit into your resolution, that nothing on earth can turn you from your purpose until you attain it.

This very assertion of superiority—the assumption of power, the, affirmation of belief in yourself, the mental attitude that claims success as an inalienable birthright—will strengthen your whole being and give power to a combination of faculties which doubt, fear, and a lack of confidence would undermine.

The reason why so many fail is that they do not commit themselves with a determination to win at any cost. They do not have that superb confidence in themselves which never looks back—which burns all bridges behind it. There is just uncertainty enough as to whether they will succeed to take the edge off their effort, and it is just this little difference between doing pretty well and flinging all oneself, all one's power, into one's effort, that makes the difference between mediocrity and a grand achievement.

If you doubt your ability to do what you set out to do; if you think that others are better fitted to do it than you; if you fear to let yourself out and take chances; if you lack boldness; if you have a timid, shrinking nature; if the negatives preponderate in your vocabulary; if you think that you lack positiveness, initiative, aggressiveness, ability; you can never win anything very great until you change your whole mental attitude and learn to have great faith in yourself. Fear, doubt, and timidity must be turned out of your mind.

All the greatest achievements in the world began in longing—in dreamings and hopings, which for a time were nursed in despair, with no light in sight. But this longing kept the courage up and made self-sacrifice easier until the thing dreamed of—the mental vision—was realized.

"According to your faith be it unto you."

Our faith is a very good measure of what we get out of life. The person of weak faith gets little; the one of mighty faith gets much.

The intensity of your confidence in your ability to do the thing you attempt is related to the degree of your achievement.

We are very apt to think of those who have been unusually successful in any line as greatly favored by fortune. And, relatedly, we try to account for their success in all sorts of ways but the right one. The fact is that we find that when they first started out in active life, they held the confident, vigorous, persistent thought of and belief in their ability to accomplish what they were undertaking. Their mental attitude was set so stubbornly toward their goal that the doubts and fears which dog and hinder and frighten the less confident—those who hold a low estimate of themselves, who ask, demand, and expect but little—got out of their path, and the world made way for them.

We must not only believe we can succeed, but *we must believe it with all our hearts.*

We must have a positive conviction that we can attain success.

Those man whose minds are set firmly toward achievement do not appropriate success, *they are success.*

No lukewarm energy or indifferent ambition ever accomplished anything. *There must be vigor in our expectation* in our faith, in our determination, in our endeavor. *We must resolve with the energy that does things.*

Not only must the desire for the thing we long for be kept uppermost, but there must be strongly concentrated intensity of effort to attain our object.

As it is the fierceness of the heat that melts the iron ore and makes it possible to weld it or mold it into shape, as it is the intensity of the electrical force that dissolves the diamond—the hardest known substance—so, too, *it is the concentrated aim, the invincible purpose,* that wins success. Nothing was ever accomplished by a half-hearted desire.

We think ourselves into smallness, into inferiority by thinking downward. We ought to think upward, then we would reach the heights where superiority dwells.

There is a great difference between those who think that "perhaps" they can do, or who "will try" to do a thing, and those who "know" they can do it—who are "bound" to do it; who feel within themselves a pulsating power, an irresistible force equal to any obstacle that may stand or come in their way.

This difference between uncertainty and certainty, between vacillation and decision, between the one who wavers and the one who decides things, between "I hope to" and "I can," between "I'll try" and "I will"—this little difference marks the distance between a thing half-done and a thing accomplished; between mediocrity and excellence.

Self-faith walks on the mountain tops, hence its superior vision. It sees what is invisible to those who follow.

It is not egotism. It is knowledge, and it comes from the consciousness of possessing the ability requisite for what one undertakes.

What miracles self-faith has wrought! What impossible deeds it has helped to perform!

It was the sustaining power of a mighty self-faith that enabled Columbus to bear the jeers and imputations of the Spanish cabinet; that sustained him when his sailors were in mutiny and he was at their mercy in a little vessel on an unknown sea; that enabled him to hold steadily to his purpose, entering in his diary day after day— "This day we sailed west, which was our course."

It was this self-faith which gave courage and determination to Fulton to attempt his first trip up the Hudson in the *Clermont*, before thousands of his fellow citizens, who had gathered to howl and jeer at his expected failure. He believed he could do the—thing he attempted though the whole world was against him.

Self-faith took Dewey past cannons, torpedoes, and mines to victory at Manila Bay; it carried Farragut, lashed to the rigging, past the defenses of the enemy in Mobile Bay; it led Nelson and Grant to victory.

Self-faith has been the great reserve in the world of invention, discovery, and art. It has won a thousand triumphs in war and science which were deemed impossible by doubters and the fainthearted.

Perhaps there is no other one thing which keeps so many people back as their low estimate of themselves. They are more handicapped by their limiting thought, by their foolish convictions of inefficiency, than by almost anything else, for *there is no power in the universe that can help a man do, a thing when he thinks he cannot do it.* Self-faith must lead the way. You cannot go beyond the limits you set for yourself.

It is one of the most difficult things for we mortals to really believe in our own bigness, in our own grandeur; to believe that our yearnings and hungerings and aspirations for higher, nobler things have any basis in reality or any real, ultimate end. But our yearnings are, in fact, the signs of our ability to match them, of our power to make them real: *The thing you long for and work for comes to you because your thought has created it; because there is something inside you that attracts it. It comes because there is an affinity within you for it. Your own comes to you, because it is always seeking you.*

Whenever you see those who have been unusually successful in any field, remember that they have usually *thought* themselves into that position—their mental attitude and energy have created it. It is the outcome of their self-faith, of their inward vision of themselves.

Faith opens the door that enables us to look into the soul's limitless possibilities and reveals such powers there, such unconquerable forces, that we are not only encouraged to go on, but feel a great consciousness of added power because we have touched omnipotence, have a glimpse of the great source of things.

Faith is that something within us which does not guess, but knows. It knows because it sees what without it we would not be able to see. It is the prophet within us, the divine messenger appointed to accompany us through life to guide and direct and encourage us. It gives us a glimpse of our possibilities, and thereby keeps us from losing heart, from quitting our upward life struggle.

Our faith knows because it sees what we cannot see. It sees resources, powers, potencies which our doubts and fears veil from us. Faith is assured, is never afraid, because it sees the way out; sees the solution of to a problem.

Faith never fails; it is a miracle worker. It looks beyond all boundaries, transcends all limitations, penetrates all obstacles and sees the goal.

It is doubt and fear, timidity and cowardice, that hold us down and keep us in mediocrity—doing petty things when we are capable of sublime deeds.

"Believe in yourself with all your might." That is, believe that your destiny is inside of you, that there is a power within you which, if awakened, aroused, developed, and matched with honest effort, will not only make a noble man or woman of you, but will also make you successful and happy.

CHAPTER 13
Expect Great Things of Yourself

What would be the probable success of an animal tamer who went into a cage with ferocious wild beasts for the first time full of fear, doubt, uncertainty? What that tamer said, "I will try to conquer these wild animals, but I really do not believe I can do it. It is a pretty tough proposition for a human being to try to conquer a wild tiger from the jungles of Africa. There may be those who can do it, but I doubt very much whether I can."

If lion tamers should face wild beasts with such an attitude of weakness, doubt, and fear, they would very soon be torn to pieces. Bold courage is all that would save them. The tamer must conquer with the eye first, and there must be a lot of winning, gritty stuff back of the eye—for the slightest show of fear would probably be fatal; the least indication of cowardice might cost him the tamer his or her life.

What is true of lion tamers is true for us all: We cannot achieve unless we actually believe we are going to get what we are working for. Or at least approximate to it.

The mind must lead. The pattern precedes the weaving of the web; the ideal must go ahead. *We always face in the direction of our faith.* It is what we believe we can do that we accomplish or tend to.

If we analyze great achievements and those who accomplish them, the most prominent quality in evidence is self-confidence. Those with absolute faith in their ability to do what they undertake are the most likely to succeed, even when such confidence seems to outsiders audacious, if not foolhardy.

To acknowledge lack of ability, to give way to a temporary doubt, is to give failure so much advantage. We should never allow self-faith to waver for a moment, no matter how dark the way may seem. Nothing will destroy our confidence nor the confidence of others so quickly as a doubt in our own minds. Many people, fail because they radiate their discouraged moods and project them into the minds of those about them. If you are always putting a low rating on yourself, marking yourself down, you may be sure that others will not take the trouble to mark you up. They will not take pains to see if you have not rated yourself too low.

I never knew anyone who had a small, belittling estimate of himself or herself to do a great thing. We can never get more out of ourselves than we expect. If you expect large things from yourself, and demand them, if you hold the large mental attitude toward your life and work, you will get much bigger results than if you depreciate yourself and look only for little results.

If you think you are peculiar, that you are not like other people, that you are different and can not achieve what they do—if you harbor these impressions—you are not in a position to overcome what you regard as a handicap. The consciousness of possessing such qualities keeps you from being yourself.

People who are constantly depreciating themselves, effacing themselves, who believe that they never will amount to anything of consequence make a corresponding impression upon others, for they look as they feel.

Your own estimate of yourself, of your ability, your standing, the weight you carry, and of the figure you cut in the world, will be out-pictured in your appearance, in your manner.

If you feel very ordinary you will appear very ordinary. If you do not respect yourself you will show it in your face. If you feel poor, you may be sure that nothing very rich will manifest itself in you.

On the other hand, if you always contemplate the very qualities which you long to possess, they will gradually become yours, and you will express them in your face and manner. You must feel grand to look grand. There must be superiority in your thought before it can be expressed in your face and your bearing.

Whatever qualities you attribute to yourself, in other words, you will manifest in the impression you make upon others.

Confidence is the very basis of all achievement. There is a tremendous power in the conviction that we can do a thing.

Those who have great faith in themselves are relived from doubts as to their ability, from the great many uncertainties as to whether they are in their right place, and from fears regarding their future.

Freedom is essential to achievement. We cannot do our greatest work when our minds are cramped with worry, anxiety, fear, or uncertainty, any more than we can do our best physical work with our bodies' in a cramped position. Absolute freedom is imperative for the best brain work. Uncertainty and doubt are great enemies of that concentration which is the secret of all effectiveness.

Confidence has ever been the great foundation stone. It has performed miracles in every line of endeavor.

Self-faith is the great connecting link between the objective and the subjective states. It is our faith that enters the Great Within of us, the holy of holy of our lives, and touches the divine. Faith opens the door of the true source of life, and it is through faith that we touch Infinite Power.

Our life is grand or ordinary, large or small, in proportion to the insight and strength of our self-faith.

Many people do not trust their faith; because they do not know what it is. They confuse it with fancy or imagination, but it is the voice of a Power Within in touch with Omnipotence. It is a spiritual faculty which does not guess or think or doubt, but which knows, for it sees the way out which the other faculties can not see. It is knowledge just as real as the knowledge which we gain through the senses. Faith is a great elevator of character and has a wonderful influence on the ideals. It lifts us to the heights and gives us glimpses of the promised land. It is "the light of truth and wisdom." On the other hand, the suggestion of inferiority has caused more individual wretchedness, tragedies, and failures in life than anything else.

Even the best race horse could not win a prize if its confidence were destroyed. This is one of the things the trainers are always careful to retain, for the animal's confidence that it can win is a very great factor in victory.

It is faith that unlocks our power and enables us to use our ability. It has been the great miracle-worker of the ages. Whatever will increase your confidence in yourself increases your power.

Self-faith is the best substitute for genius; in fact, it is closely allied to genius.

Faith is the great leader in every achievement. It shows the path which leads the way to our possibilities. Faith is the faculty or instinct which knows, because it sees the possibilities within; it does not hesitate to urge us to undertake great things, because it sees reserves in us capable of accomplishing them.

No one has ever yet been able to make a satisfactory explanation of the philosophy of faith. What is that will hold many to their tasks, keep up their courage and hope under the most trying, heartrending conditions? What is it that will enable them to endure—and with fortitude, even cheerfulness—all sorts of suffering, the pangs of poverty, and which will sustain and reassure them after their last dollar has gone? When friends and family—those they love best—misunderstand them or do not believe in them? What is it that sustains and enheartens these people so that they endure what would kill them a hundred times if they were without it?

We stand in wonder before the heroes who often lose everything in the world but their faith in what they had set their hearts upon:

Faith always takes the first step forward. It is a soul sense, a spiritual foresight, which peers far beyond the physical eye's vision—a courier which leads the way, opens the closed door, sees beyond the obstacles, and points to the path which the less spiritual faculties could not see.

There is little fear for the future in those who have a deep-seated faith in themselves. Their self-faith is more than a match for difficulties. Self-faith has always been the poor person's friend and best capital. Those with no assets but colossal faith in themselves have accomplished wonders, where capital without self-faith has failed.

If you believe in yourself, you will be much more likely to do the larger things you are capable of than if you were to hold the self depreciatory, lack-of-confidence attitude.

If, however, you go about with an apologetic air as though you would *pick up anything that anybody else dropped and be glad to get it*, that you do not expect much of yourself; that you do not believe that the grand things, the good things of the world are intended for you, you will pass for a very small person. Moreover, it is a fact that others' estimate of us has a great deal to do with our place in life and what we achieve. It is not alone the subjective effect of *our belief in ourselves* that enables us to get results; it is also largely the effect of that self-faith on others. When we feel a sense of mastery, of having risen to our dominion, we talk confidence, radiate victory, and overcome doubts in others. Everybody believes we can do the thing we undertake. The world believes in the conqueror, the one who carries victory in his or her very appearance.

I know a man who creeps into aboard meeting where he is a director as though he were a nobody, entirely unworthy of his position, and he wonders why he is a mere cipher on the board, why he carries so little weight with other members, why he is hardly ever deferred to.

He does not realize that he has lived with himself a good while and by this time ought to know himself better than others who see him only occasionally and naturally take him at his own rating. If he labels himself all over with the tags of inferiority, if he walks and talks and acts like a nobody and gives the impression that he does not think much of himself anyway, how can he expect others to do for him what he will not do for himself?

The only inferiority in us is what we put into ourselves. We think ourselves into smallness, into inferiority by thinking downward. We ought to think upward, if we would reach the heights where superiority dwells.

One of the most unfortunate phases of theology is in the idea of the debasement of humanity—that we have fallen from our grand, original estate. The truth is that we have always been advancing as race, always improving, but our progress has been greatly hampered by this belittling idea.

The human being God made never fell. It is only our inferior way of looking at ourselves, our criminal self-depreciation, that has crippled and deteriorated us.

The trouble with us is that we do not keep our good qualities sufficiently in sight; we do not think half well enough of ourselves. If we did, we would have a much better expression, would present a divine appearance.

It makes all the difference in the world to us whether we go through life as conquerors, whether we go about as though we believed we amounted to something, with strong, vigorous, self-confident, victorious air, or whether we go about with an apologetic, self-effacing, get-out-of-other-people's-way attitude.

It does not matter how great or grand our general abilities may be, our self-estimate will determine the results of our efforts. We are never stronger than our faith, we never undertake anything greater than our self-confidence dictates.

More than any other, *our greatest deficiency is that of self-faith.*

The majority of us are many times weaker in confidence than any other faculty.

It does not matter how strong your mental or physical skills are if they are not backed by a vigorous faith. Faith puts all the other faculties to work. It powerfully encourages all the other faculties—and courage is a tremendous force in one's life. A purpose backed up by the superb courage of faith so that you find neither comfort, rest, nor satisfaction until you are successful, will perform miracles, no matter what circumstances may conspire to hinder you.

Our faculties work under orders, and they tend to do or produce what is expected of them. If we expect a great deal, make a great demand of them, and insist on their helping us to carry out our ambition, they fall into line and proceed to help us. If, on the other hand, we do not have confidence enough to make a vigorous demand, a strenuous effort, if we waver or are in doubt, our faculties will lose their courage, and their effort will be perfunctory, will lack efficiency.

One reason so many fail or at best plod along in mediocrity is because they see so many obstacles and difficulties looming up so threateningly that they lose heart and are in a discouraged condition much of the time. This mental attitude is fatal to achievement, for it makes the mind negative, noncreative. It is confidence and hope that call out the faculties and multiply their creative, producing power.

The habit of dwelling on difficulties and magnifying them weakens the character and paralyzes the initiative in such a way as to hinder one from ever daring to undertake great things. The person who sees the obstacles more clearly than anything else is not the person to attempt or do any great thing. The one who does things is the one who sees the end and defies the obstacles: If the Alps had looked so formidable to Napoleon as they did to his advisers and other people, he would never have crossed them in midwinter.

Great things are done under the stress of an over-powering conviction of one's ability to do what one undertakes. There is irresistible force in a powerful affirmative expressed with unflinching determination.

Faith was given to support us, to reassure us when we cannot see light ahead, or solve our problems. It is to us what the compass is to the mariner in a storm. We feel the same assurance when as that mariner when we cannot see anything ahead—because our self-faith compass points onward true to our destination.

It is infinitely easier to force a huge shell through the steel plates of a ship when projected with lightning speed from the cannon than to push it through slowly. So the world makes way for those who know which way they are going and who project themselves with vigor.

The things which are always tripping the hesitating, the doubtful, the weak, get out of the way of the vigorous, positive, decisive. Difficulties are great or small in proportion as you are great or small. They loom up like mountains to one person and dwindle to mole hills to another. It is only those of little faith who are afraid of hard things, who shrink before obstacles—because they lack the momentum to force them out of their way.

Do not be afraid of taking responsibilities. Make up your mind that you will assume any responsibility which comes to you along the line of your legitimate career and that you will bear it a little better than anybody else ever before has. There is no greater mistake in the world than that of postponing present responsibility thinking that you will be better prepared to assume it later. It is accepting these positions as they come to you that gives you the preparation—for we can do nothing of importance easily, effectively, until we have done it so many times that it becomes a habit. On the very resolution to do the thing which is best for you—no matter how disagreeable, no matter how humiliating, no matter how much you may suffer from sensitiveness or a feeling of unpreparedness—depends the development of your character and quality of your life.

Do not be afraid to demand great things of yourself. Powers which you never dreamed you possessed will leap to your assistance. The habit of expecting great things of ourselves calls out the best in us. It tends to awaken forces which but for the greater demand, the higher call, would remain latent.

You will find a stimulating effect in always considering yourself as lucky or fortunate. It is a great thing to form a habit of expecting good from every experience in life. Just think what it means to have everybody think you are lucky and expect that what you undertake will turn out well!

Is there any reason why you should go through the world whining, tagging at somebody else's heels trailing, imitating, copying somebody else, afraid to call your soul your own? Hold an up-building, ennobling, sublime picture of yourself and your divine possibilities. Hold up your head and learn to think well of yourself. Have a good opinion of yourself and your ability to do what you undertake.

For if you do not, nobody else will.

CHAPTER 14

Working For One Thing and Expecting Something Else

ost people do not face life in the right way. They neutralize a large part of their effort because their mental attitude does not correspond with their endeavor—so while working for one thing, they are really expecting something else. They discourage, drive away, the very thing they are pursuing—by holding the wrong mental attitude towards it.

To be ambitious for wealth and yet always expecting to be poor, to be always doubting your ability to get what you long for, is like trying to reach East by traveling West. There is no philosophy which will help someone to succeed who is always doubting his or her ability to do so, and thus attracting failure.

The person who would succeed must think success, must think upward. He or she must think progressively, creatively, constructively, inventively, and, above all, optimistically.

You will go in the direction in which you face. If you look towards poverty, towards lack, you will go that way. If, on the other hand, you turn squarely around and refuse to have anything to do with poverty—to think it, live it, or recognize it—you will then begin to make progress towards the goal of plenty.

Many of us work at cross purposes, because, while we would like to be rich, we believe in our hearts that we shall not become so—and so our mental attitude, the pattern which our life processes follow makes impossible the very thing we are working for. As long as we carry about a poorhouse atmosphere with ourselves, we will make a poorhouse impression—and that will never attract money.

Thoughts are magnets which attract things like themselves. So you must ever be careful. Never allow yourself to complain of your lot, to say, "I am poor," "I can never do what others do," "I have not the ability that others have," "I am a failure," "Luck is against me," as you are making it all the more difficult to get rid of these enemies of your peace and happiness—for every time you think of them they will go a little deeper and deeper into your consciousness.

There is no possibility of your producing just the opposite of what you are holding in your mind, because your mental attitude is the pattern which is built into the life. Your accomplishments are achieved mentally first.

A fatal penalty awaits you, therefore, if you are always looking on the dark side of everything—always predicting evil and failure; always seeing only the seamy, disagreeable side of life. You are drawing to yourself what you see, what your thoughts are looking for.

The habit of looking at everything *constructively*, from the bright, hopeful side, the side of faith and assurance, instead of from the side of doubt and uncertainty; and the habit of believing that *the best* is going to happen, that the right must triumph; the faith that truth is bound finally to conquer error, that harmony and health are the reality and discord and disease the temporary absence of it—*this is the attitude of the optimist, which will ultimately reform the world.*

Optimism is a builder. It is to the individual what the sun is to vegetation. It infuses life, beauty, and growth into everything within its reach. Our mental faculties grow and thrive in it just as the plants and trees grow and thrive in the physical sunshine.

Nothing has the power to attract things unlike itself. Everything radiates its own quality and attracts things which are akin.

Stop thinking trouble if you want to attract its opposite. Stop thinking poverty if you want to attract wealth. Do not have anything to do with the things you have been fearing. They are fatal enemies to your advancement. Cut them off. Expel them from your mind. Forget them. Think the opposite thoughts just as persistently as you can, and you will be surprised to see how soon you will begin to attract the very things for which you long.

The mental attitude which we hold toward our work or our aim has everything to do with what we accomplish. If you go to your work with the attitude of a slave lashed to your task and see in it only drudgery; if you work without hope, see no future in what you are doing beyond getting a bare living; if you see no light ahead, nothing but poverty, deprivation, and hard work all your life; if you think that you were destined to such a hard life, you cannot expect to get—anything else than that for which you look.

If, on the other hand, no matter how poor you may be today, you can see a better future; if you believe that some day you are going to rise out of humdrum work, that you are going to get up out of the basement of life into the drawing-room, where beauty, comfort, and joy await you; if you keep your eye steadily upon the goal which you hope to reach and feel confident that you have the ability to attain, you will accomplish your aspiration.

Keeping the faith that, we shall sometime do the thing which we can not now see any possible way of accomplishing, just holding steadily the mental attitude, the belief that we will accomplish it, that somehow, some way, it will come to us, the clinging to our vision, gets the mind into such a *creative* condition that it becomes a magnet to draw the thing desired.

I have never known any who believed in themselves and constantly affirmed their ability to do what they undertook, who always kept their eye constantly on theirs goal and struggled purposefully toward it, who did not make a success of life. Aspiration becomes inspiration and then realization. What we vigorously resolve to do, believe in with all our heart, confidently expect, the mental forces tend to realize. The very intensity of expectation enlists the vigor of all the mental processes in trying to accomplish things. In other words, all the forces of the mind fall into line with our expectation and resolution. Our expectancy, our determination to achieve the thing on which we have set our heart, forms a pattern, a working model, which the mind endeavors to reproduce in reality. It is the mental picture which is used as the model for the creative forces.

Keep your mind in an uplifting, upbuilding attitude. Never allow yourself for an instant to harbor a doubt that you are finally going to accomplish what you undertake.

Doubts are treacherous, they destroy your creative ability, neutralize ambition. Constantly say to yourself, "I *must* have what I need; it is my right and I am going to have it."

There is a great cumulative, magnetic effect in continually holding in your mind continually the thought that you were made for success, for health, for happiness, for usefulness, and that nothing in the world but yourself can keep you from it.

Form a habit of repeating this affirmation, this faith in your ultimate triumph; hold it *tenaciously*, *vigorously*, and after a while you will be surprised to find how the things come to you which you have so longed for, yearned for, and struggled towards.

I have seen a man, when all the results of half a lifetime of struggle and sacrifice had been swept away by financial disaster, when he had nothing left but his grit, determination, and a great family of hungry mouths to feed, who would not even for an instant admit that he would not get on his feet again. There was no use talking discouragement to that man! You might as well have tried to discourage Napoleon. With clenched fists and a determination which did not recognize defeat, he kept his eye resolutely on his goal and pushed on. In a few years he was on his feet again.

We were not intended to be puppets of circumstances, slaves to our environments. We were intended to *make* our environment, to *create* our conditions.

Nothing comes to us without cause, and that cause is mental. Our mental attitude creates our condition of success or failure. The result of our work will correspond with the nature of our thoughts, our habitual mental attitude. To produce, the mind must be kept in a positive, creative condition. A discordant, worrying, despondent, poverty-facing mental attitude will quickly render the mind negative, and will produce a troop of mental enemies that will effectually bar your way to success and happiness.

Our mental faculties are like servants. They give us exactly what we expect of them. If we trust them, if we depend upon them, they will give us their best. If we are afraid, they will be afraid.

Negative people *wait* for things to happen. They have a feeling that somehow things are going to happen, and that in the meantime, they can not do much to change them.

It is the positive constructive mental attitude that has accomplished all of the great things in the world. It is the creative, aggressive, pushing power of faith—self-faith—that is back of all achievement. A strong, vigorous character creates a condition that will force things to happen. Knowing that nothing will move of itself, he is always putting into operation forces that do things.

People such as this, endowed with great expectancy and determined to reach their goals, let what will stand in their way—but by their very resolution get rid of a lot of success enemies which trip up the weak and the irresolute.

There is a mysterious power in the Great Within of us which we can not explain, but which we all feel to be there, which tends to carry out our commands, our resolves, whatever they may be.

For example, if I persist in thinking and affirming that I am a nobody, that I am not as good as other people, I shall after a while begin to really believe this, and then a fatal acceptance will be registered in my subconsciousness, and the mental machinery will begin to reproduce the "nobody" pattern.

Unfortunately, many positive minds *do* become negative by influences which destroy their self-confidence. They gradually lose faith in themselves. Perhaps this begins through the suggestion of incompetence from others, the suggestion that they do not know their business or are not equal to the position they hold. After a while, through this subtle suggestion, initiative is weakened; the victims do not undertake things with quite the same vigor as formerly; they gradually lose the power of quick decision, and soon fear—to decide anything of importance. Their minds become vacillating. Thus, instead of the leaders they once were, they become followers.

On the other hand, if I stoutly affirm that I am heir to all the good things in the universe and that they belong to me as my birthright, if I firmly declare my faith in myself and constantly assert that I am able to carry out superbly the great life purpose which is indicated in my bent, assert that power is mine, that I will have nothing to do with sickness, with doubt or discouragement, I then make my mind so positive, so creative in its assertive attitude that instead of destroying, it produces, instead of tearing down—builds up for me the very thing for which I long.

The mind acts under law. The mental faculties will not give up their best unless they are marshaled by order. They are like soldiers. They must have a leader, a general, who enforces order, method. They rebel, mutiny, under weak leadership.

You will find a tremendous help in constantly affirming that you are the person you wish to be; not that you hope to be, but that you actually *are* now: You will be surprised to see how quickly the part which you assume will be realized in your life, will be outpictured in your character.

The art of all arts is to make one's life a perpetual victory. To do this, we must keep our minds up to their maximum power—radiating a confident, courageous, fearless impression; carrying the confident air which accompanies the conquering habit.

Most of us, however, go through life neither successes nor failures, neither rich nor poor. We live most of our lives balanced between lack and a little, because part of the time our minds are productive, creative, and part of the time negative, hence unproductive. So we oscillate like a pendulum: When we get a little courage, hope, enthusiasm, we produce a little, because our minds are creative; when we lose heart, become discouraged, are filled with doubts and fears, our minds become negative, uncreative, non-producing, and we slide back again to want.

Over and over affirm your self-confidence, your birthright of deservingness. The time will come when you will be able to keep your mind in a productive, creative attitude all the time.

Then your life will be filled with an abundance of all that is good.

CHAPTER 15
Negative Creeds Paralyze

the power to do is largely a question of self-faith, self-confidence. No matter what you undertake, you will never do it until you think you can. You will never master it until you first feel the mastery and do the deed in your mind. It must be thought out or it can never be wrought out. It must be mind accomplishment before it can be a material one.

There is no science in the world, however, which will bring a thing to you while your thought repels it, while doubt and suspicion linger in the mind. None of us can surpass our self-imposed bounds or limitations. If we would get up in the world, we must learn to deny our belief in limitation. We must throw all negative suggestions to the wind. We must think success before he can achieve it. We must affirm continually with decision and vigor that which we wish to accomplish or be.

How can we expect to rise in the world if we are all the time saying to ourselves, "I can't do this thing. It is useless to try; I know I can't do it. Other may do it, but I know *I* can't." Speaking this way, we have become victims of the chronic "can't." Negation has mastered us. "I can't" has become the habit of our lives. All self-respect and self-confidence, all consciousness of ability, have been undermined and destroyed. Our achievements cannot rise higher than our thoughts.

Contrast this with those who always say, "I will." No matter what obstacles confront them, they say, "I will do the thing I have undertaken." It is the constant affirmation of their determination to do the thing that increases their confidence in themselves—as well as in their power to do the thing—until they actually do it.

Our achievements cannot rise higher than our thoughts.

As long as you contemplate any personal defect—mental, moral, or physical—you will fall below your possible attainment; you cannot approach your ideal, your standard.

As long as you allow negative, destructive, tearing-down processes to exist in your mind, you cannot create anything, and you will be a weakling.

If you could only once realize the demoralizing influence of holding the sickly ideal, the failure ideal, in the mind until the standards of excellence are all dragged down to the level of mediocrity or commonness, you would never again be content to dwell in the valley of failure, to live in the basement of your life.

How, for instance, can you be free, prosperous, and happy while you are imprisoned and enslaved by the poverty thought, the conviction that you are poor and unlucky, and that you can never accumulate money as others do?

In what condition are you to fight for prosperity when you have lost confidence in your ability and are convinced that opportunity is for others and not for you? You will not be able to make a strenuous, energetic effort to release yourself from your condition while you hold the failure thought. You will not believe that you can push away the limitations which hedge you in. You will see no way to regain your confidence and self-trust, to get a foothold. Instead, you will think poverty, talk poverty, act poverty, dream poverty, and then wonder why you are unlucky—all the while not realizing that you are making your condition a self-fulfilling prophecy. You are making yourself a negative magnet, repelling all the success qualities and attracting only those of failure. You have lost your magnetic power to attract the forces which can extricate you from the environment you disdain.

Negatives never accomplish anything. There is no life in a negative, nothing but deterioration, destruction, death. Negatives are great enemies of the success candidate. Those who are always talking down everything, who are always complaining of hard times and bad business, poor health and poverty, attract to themselves all the destructive, negative influences about them, neutralizing all of their endeavors.

Constructive thought abandons those who are always thinking destructively, and using destructive language, for such people have nothing kindred with the positive, nothing to attract it. Create principles cannot live in a negative, destructive atmosphere, and no self-esteeming achievement can take place there.

Negatives will paralyze your ambition; they will poison your life. They will rob you of power. They will kill your self-confidence until you are a victim of your situation instead of a master of it.

Banish these ghosts, these unrealities, these enemies of your success and happiness, forever from your mind. Rise up out of the valley of despair and despondency, out of the miasma which has poisoned the air around you, out of the foulness which has suffocated you all these years, into the atmosphere of excellence, of power, of beauty; then you will begin to accomplish something in life, to be somebody.

No matter what the conditions you face, you have the power to overcome them. And that power is the power of your thinking.

The power of your mind is the power of your self-confidence.

CHAPTER 16
Making Dreams Come True

Whatever an individual or a people concentrates upon it tends to get, because concentration is just as much of a force as is electricity The person who concentrates upon law, thinks law, dreams law, reads everything he or she can get hold of relating to law, steals into courts and listens to trials at every chance is sure to become a lawyer.

It is the same with any other vocation or art—medicine, engineering, literature, music; any of the arts or sciences. Those who concentrate upon an idea, who continue to visualize their dreams, to nurse them, who never lose sight of their goal, no matter how dark or forbidding the way, get what they concentrate on. They make their minds powerful magnets to attract the thing on which they have concentrated. Sooner or later they realize their dreams.

Washington, in a letter written when he was but twelve years old, said: "I shall marry a beautiful woman; I shall be one of the wealthiest men in the land; I shall lead the army of my colony; I shall rule the nation which I help to create."

General Grant, in his "Memoirs," says that as a boy at West Point, he saw General Scott seated on his horse, reviewing the cadets, and something within him said, "Ulysses, some day you will ride in his place and be general of the army."

What could have kept Ole Bull from becoming a master musician? Who or what could keep back a boy who would brave his father's displeasure, steal out of his bed at night, and go into the attic to play his "little red violin," which haunted his dreams and would not let him sleep? What could keep a Faraday or an Edison, whom no hardships frightened, from realizing the wonderful visions of boyhood?

If you can concentrate your thought and hold it persistently, work with it along the line of your greatest ambition, nothing can keep you from its realization. But spasmodic concentration, spasmodic enthusiasm, however intense, will peter out. Dreaming without effort will only waste your power. It is holding your vision, together with persistent, concentrated endeavor on the material plane, that wins.

There are thousands of devices in the patent office in Washington which have never, been of any use to the world, simply because the inventors did not cling to their vision long enough to materialize it in perfection. They became discouraged. They ceased their efforts. They let their visions fade, and so became demagnetized and lost the power to realize them. Other inventors have taken up many such "near" successes, added the missing links in their completion and have made them real successes,

If we were to send out our desires intensely; to visualize them until our very mentalities vibrated with the things we long for, and to work persistently in their direction, we would attract them.

Everywhere there are disappointed men and women who have soured on life because they could not get what they longed for—a musical or art education, the necessary training for authorship, for law or medicine, for engineering, or for some other vocation to which they felt they had been called. They are struggling along in an uncongenial environment, railing at the fate which has robbed them of their own. They feel that life has cheated them, when the truth is they have cheated themselves. They did not insistently and persistently send out their desires and longings; they did not nurse them and positively refuse to give them up; above all, they did not put forth their best efforts for their realization.

There are three things we must do to make our dreams come true:

Visualize our desire.

Concentrate on our vision.

Work to bring it into the actual.

The implements necessary for this are inside of us, not outside. No matter what the accidents of birth or fortune, there is only one force by which we can fashion our life material: mind.

The power that makes our desire, our vision, a reality is not in our environment or in any condition outside of us; it is within us.

There is some unseen, unknown, magnetic force developed by a long-continued concentration of the mind upon a cherished desire that draws to itself the reality which matches the desire. We cannot tell just what this force is that brings the thing we long for out of the cosmic ether and objectifies it, shapes it to correspond with our longing. We only know that it exists. The cosmic ether everywhere surrounding us is full of undreamed of possibilities, and the strong, concentrated mind reaches out into this ether, this sea of intelligence, attracts to it its own, and objectifies the desire.

All human achievements have been pulled out of the unseen by the mind reaching out and fashioning the vast material everywhere available for its disposal into the shapes which matched the wishes, the desires, of the achievers.

All the great discoveries, great inventions, great deeds have been wrought out of the actual by the perpetual thinking of and visualizing these things by their authors. These grand characters clung to their vision, their visions became mighty magnets that attracted out of the universal intelligence the realization of their dreams.

The idea of the telephone was flashed into the mind of Professor Alexander Bell by the drawing of a string through a hole in the bottom of a tin can, by means of which he found that the voice could be transmitted. The idea took such complete possession of the inventor that it robbed him of sleep and, for a time made him poor. But nothing could rob him of his vision or prevent him from struggling to work it out of the visionary stage into the actual

I lived near Professor Bell, in the next room, indeed, while he worked on his invention. I saw much of his struggle with poverty, heard the criticisms and denunciations of his friends, as he persisted in his visionary work until the telephone became a reality—a reality without which modern life could not be conducted.

The brain cells grow in response to desire. Where there is no desire there is no growth. The brain develops most in the direction of the leading ambition, where the mental activities are the most pronounced. The desire for a musical career, for instance, develops he musical brain cells. Business ambition develops that part of the brain which has to do with business, the cells which are brought into action in executive management, in administering affairs, in money making. Wherever we make our demand upon the brain by desire that part responds in growth.

A poor girl, the daughter of humble people in Maine who thought that to become a public singer was an unforgivable sin, could not in the beginning see any possible way to realize the dreams she held in secret, but she kept visualizing her dream, nursing her desire and doing the only thing for its realization her parents would allow—singing in a little church choir. Gradually the way opened, and one step led to another until the little Maine girl became the famous Madame Nordica, one of the world's greatest singers. Her brain had been continually developing along the line of hers vision, drawing to her the material to make it real.

No matter if you are a poor girl away back in the country and see no possible way of leaving your poor old father and mother in order to prepare for your career, don't let go of your desire. Whether it be music, art, literature, business or a profession, hold to it. No matter how dark the outlook, keep on visualizing your desire and light and opportunity will come to enable you to make it a reality. Whatever the Creator has fitted you to do, He will give you a chance to do—if you cling to your vision and struggle as best you can for its attainment.

Think of the Lillian Nordicas, the Lucy Stones, the Louisa Alcotts, the Mary Lyons, the Dr. Anna Howard Shaws, the thousands of women who were hedged in just as you are, by poverty or forbidding circumstances of some sort, yet succeeded in spite of everything in doing what they desired to do, in being what they longed to be. Take heart and believe that God has given you also "all implements divine to shape the way" to your soul's desire

The trouble with many of us is that we are afraid to believe this. We fear that fate will mock us, cast back to us our mental visions empty of fruition. We do not understand the laws governing our thought forces any more than we understand the laws governing the universe. If we had faith in their power, our earnest thoughts and efforts would germinate and bud and flower just as does the tiny seed we put into the earth.

Most of us instead of treating our desires seriously, trifle with them as though they were only to be played with, as though they never could be realities. We do not believe in their divinity. We regard our heart longings, our soul yearnings as fanciful vagaries, romances of the imagination. Yet we know that every invention, every discovery or achievement that has blessed the world began in a desire, in a longing to produce or to do a certain thing, and that the persistent longing was accompanied by a struggle to make the mental picture a reality.

It is difficult for us to grasp the fact that ambition, accompanied by effort, is actually a creative power which tends to realize itself. Our minds are like that of the doubting disciple, who would not believe that his Lord had risen until he had actually thrust his finger into the side which had been pierced by a cruel spear. Only the things that we see seem real to us when, as a matter of fact, the most real things in the world are the unseen.

We never doubt the existence of the force that brings the bud out of the seed, the foliage and the flower out of the bud, the fruits, the vegetables from the flower. It is invisible. We cannot sense it, but we know that it is there. No one can see or hear or feel gravitation, or the forces which balance the earth and whirl it with lightning speed through space, bringing it round its orbit without a variation of the tenth of a second in a century, yet who can doubt their reality? Does any one question the mighty power of electricity because it cannot be seen or heard or smelled?

The potency of our desires of our soul longings, when backed by the effort to make them realities, is just as real as is that of any of the unseen forces in Nature's great laboratory. The great cosmic ether is packed with invisible potentialities, and whatever comes out of it to you comes in response to your call. Everything you have accomplished in life has been a result of a psychic law which, consciously or unconsciously, you have obeyed.

Do not make the mistake of thinking that the way will not open because you cannot now see any possible means of achieving that for which you long. The very intensity of your longing for a certain career, to do a certain thing, is the best evidence that you have the ability to match it, and that this ability was given you for a purpose— even to play a divine, a magnificent part in the great universal plan.

The longing is the forerunner of achievement. It is the seed that will germinate if nurtured by effort.

Just imagine you are carrying a lantern which will advance with you and give light enough for the next step. It is not necessary to see to the end of the road. All the light you need is for the next step. Faith in your vision and persistent endeavor will do the rest.

Send out your wishes, cherish your desires, force out your yearnings, your heart longings with all the intensity and persistency you can muster, and you will be surprised to see how soon they will begin to attract their affinities, how they will grow and take tangible shape, and ultimately become actual things. Fling out your desires into the cosmic ether boldly with the utmost confidence. Therein you will gather the material which shall build into reality the castle of your dreams.

The great disadvantage in our time is not lack of chance or opportunity but of losing our vision, of letting our ambition die.

Think how the seed must be tended and nurtured before it will give forth the new life. See how the delicate bud has to be coaxed by the sun and air for many weeks—sometimes even months, even—before it pushes its head up through the tough sod to the light. Suppose the seed were to say, "It is impossible for me to get out of this dark earth. There is no light here. I am so tender the slightest pressure will break me and stop my growth forever. The only way out of my prison is to push up through this tough sod, and it would take a tremendous force to do that. I would be crushed, strangled, before I got half way through."

But no. Something in the bud moves it into attempting the "impossible," and behold, ultimately it rears its tender head above what it considered the great enemy of its progress. Moreover, the dark sod, the very thing which it thought was going to make its future impossible, becomes its support and strength. The very struggle to get up through the soil has strengthened its fiber and fitted it to cope with the elements above, with the storms it must meet.

So even in you live in some remote place—far away from a thriving metropolis and libraries and culture—yet you feel that you are a born engineer, but see no possible way to get a technical education, don't lose heart or hope. Get what books you can on your specialty.

Cling to your vision. Push out in every direction that is possible to you. It may take years, but if you are true to yourself your concentration on your desire, your pushing toward it, will open a door into the light and before you know it you will be on the road to your goal.

Just like the tender plant, you may be hemmed in by seemingly insurmountable obstacles; you may not see a ray of light through the sod of hard, forbidding circumstances, but hold your vision and keep pushing. In your struggle you will develop strength, you will find sunshine and air, growth and life. If you are shut in by an uncongenial occupation and feel tempted to lose heart and give up your dreams because you can see no way to better yourself. This is just the time to cling to them, and to insist that they shall come true. Without knowing it you may be just in the middle of the sod, and if you keep pushing where you are, in season and out of season, you will come to the sunlight and the air, to freedom.

The master key which will unlock that door that seemingly is keeping you back is not in the hand of fate. You are fashioning it by your thoughts.

Very few of us, however realize the close relationship that exists between vision, mind, and accomplishment. If I were asked to name the principal cause of the majority of failures in life I should say it was the failure to understand this, to grasp the relation of thought to accomplishment. The gradual fading out of one's dreams, the losing of one's vision, may be traced to this cause.

When we first start out in life we are enthusiasts. Our vision is bright and alluring and we feel confident we are going to win out, that we shall do something distinctive, something individual, unusual. But after a few setbacks and failures we lose heart, and faith in our vision dies. Then we gradually awaken to the fact that our ambition is beginning to deteriorate. It is not quite as sharply defined as formerly. Our ideals are a trifle dimmed, our longings a trifle less insistent.

We try to find reasons and excuses for our lagging efforts and waning enthusiasm.

We think it may be from overwork—that we are tired and need a rest. Or that our health is not quite up to standard, and that, by and by our former intense desire to realize our dreams will return. And then, before we realize it, this atrophying of will process, which is so insidious, has burned out our fires.

The trouble was that our grip on our vision was not strong enough. We did not half understand the power of the mind, when firmly and persistently clinging to our vision, to help us to our goal.

What we get out of life depends very largely on our fidelity to our vision.

How much of a grip has your vision on you? Does it clutch you with a force that nothing but death can relax, or does it hold you so lightly that you are easily separated from it, discouraged from trying to make it real?

Two sailors force the same breeze to send their boats in opposite directions. It is not the wind, but the set of the sail that determines the port.

Those who are made of the stuff that wins hang on to their vision even to the point of starvation, for they know that there is only one way of bringing it down to earth—and that is by clinging to it through storm and stress, in spite of every obstacle and discouragement.

Never mind what discouragements, misfortunes or failures come to you, let nobody, no combination of unfortunate circumstances, destroy your faith in your dream of what you believe you were made to do. Never mind how the actual facts seem to contradict the results you are after. No matter who may oppose you or how much others may abuse and condemn you, cling to your vision, because it is sacred. It is the God-urge in you. You have no right to allow it to fade or to become dim.

Your final success will be measured by your ability to cling to your vision through discouragement. It will depend largely upon your stick-to-it-ive-ness, your bulldog tenacity. If you shrink before criticism and opposition you will demagnetize your mind and lose all the momentum which you have gained in your previous endeavor. No matter how dark or threatening the outlook, keep working, keep visualizing your life dream, and some unexpected way will surely open for its fulfillment.

Put out of your mind forever any thought that you can possibly fail in reaching the goal of your longing. Set your face toward it. Keep looking steadfastly in the direction of your ambition, whatever it may be. Resolve never to recognize defeat, and you will, by your mental attitude, your resolution, create a tremendous force for the drawing of your own to you. If you have the grit and stamina to stick, to persevere to the end, if you persistently maintain the victorious attitude toward your vision victory will crown your efforts.

Desire is at the bottom of every achievement. We are the product of our desires. What we long for, strive for, the vision we nurse, is our great life shaper, our character molder.

CHAPTER 17
How to Get What You Want

We are human magnets. Or, more precisely, our minds are magnets.

A piece of magnetized steel will attract only the products of iron ore. It has no affinity for wood, copper, rubber, or any other substance that has not iron in it. Similarly, we are constantly drawing to us, establishing relations with, the things and the people that respond to our thoughts and ideals.

Our environment, our associates, our general condition are the result of our mental attraction. These things have come to us on the physical plane because we have concentrated upon them, have related ourselves to them mentally; they are our affinities, and will remain with us as long as the affinity for them continues to exist in our minds.

Your thoughts, your viewpoints, your conception of what your status and position in life will be, your ideal of your future, will draw you exactly to that their realization like a lodestone. Focus your mind, your predictions, your expectations on poverty, failure and wretchedness; banish ambition, hope, expectation of good things; give full sway in your mentality to fear, worry, doubt, anticipation of evil, and your mental magnet will draw you unerringly to squalid surroundings, to an inferior position, to association with persons of a lower order of mind on a meaner social plane.

The great trouble with all of us who are struggling with unhappy or unfortunate conditions is we are not thinking right, and so we are not attracting the right things.

"Think the things you want." The profoundest philosophy is locked up in these few words. Think of them clearly, persistently, concentrating upon them with all the force and might of your mind, and struggle toward them with all your energy. This is the way to make yourself a magnet for the things you want. But the moment you begin to doubt, to worry, to fear, you demagnetize yourself from your true aspirations, and the things you desire flee from you. You drive them away by your mental attitude. They cannot come near you because you are separating yourself from them. Indeed, just as tow magnets with reversed polarities move away from each other, you are repelling them. You are going in one direction, and the things you want are going in the opposite direction.

No matter how discouraging your present outlook, how apparently unpromising your future, cling to your desire and you will realize it. Picture the ideal conditions, visualize the success, which you long to attain—imagine yourself already in the position you are ambitious to reach. Do not acknowledge limitations, do not allow any other suggestion to lodge in your mind than the success you long for, the conditions you aspire to. Picture your desires as actually realized and hold fast to your vision with all the tenacity you can muster. This is the way out of your difficulties; this is the way to open the door ahead of you to the place higher up, to better and brighter conditions.

That something within you which longs to be brought out, to be expressed, is the voice of God calling to you. Don't disregard it. Don't be afraid of your longings; there is divinity in them. Don't try to strangle them because you think they are much too extravagant, too Utopian. The Creator has not given you a longing to do that which you have no ability to do.

One reason why the lives of many of us are so narrow and pinched, small and commonplace, is because we are afraid to fling out our desires, our longings, afraid to visualize them. We become so accustomed to putting our confidence only in things that we see on the physical plane, in that which is evident to the senses, that it is very difficult for us to realize that our true power, the force that truly does things, resides in the mind. Instead of believing in our possessing of the things we desire, we believe in our limitations, in our restrictions. We demagnetize ourselves from our desires by wrong thinking and lack of faith. We see only the obstacles in our path, and forget that a determined, steadfast mind is greater than any obstacle that can oppose.

Benjamin Disraeli knew this when he said, "Man is not the creature of circumstances. Circumstances are the creatures of man." He demonstrated its truth in his own life. With many circumstances apparently dead against him at the start, the resolute young Jew overcame all obstacles, and reached the goal of his ideal. He became Prime Minister of England, and was made Earl of Beaconsfield by his sovereign, Queen Victoria.

Those who have climbed up in the world have seen themselves climbing, have pictured themselves actually in the position they longed to be in. They have climbed up mentally first. They have kept a vision of themselves as ever climbing to higher and higher things. They have continually affirmed their ability to climb, to grow up to their ideal. If we ever hope to make our dreams come true, we must do as they did; we must actually live in the conscious realization of our ideal. This is means by which we will split the difficulties ahead of us, which will open the doors which shut us from what we seek as our own.

If you are discouraged by repeated failures and disappointments, suffering the pangs of thwarted ambition; if you are not doing the thing you long to do; if life is not yielding the satisfaction, the success and joy of happy service; if your plans do not prosper; if you are hampered by poverty and a narrow, crude, uncongenial environment, there is something wrong—not with the world, but with yourself. You are not thinking right. You are not visualizing yourself as you long to be.

We are pictures of what we have thought, believed, and done in the past. Every moment of our lives we are experiencing the result of thought. The outward things that have been acting on us, shaping the conditions in which we live, are chiefly the fruits of our own motives, thoughts and acts. What we believe, what we think, what we expect, shapes our lives. Through the control and direction of our thoughts, backed up with corresponding efforts on the physical plane, we can attract to us all our heart's desires.

How often do we hear it said of someone, "Everything that person does succeeds," or "Everything he or she touches turns to gold." Why? Because these people are man is constantly picturing the success of every undertaking and are backing up their vision by their effort. By clinging to their vision, by vigorous resolution and persistent, determined endeavor, they are continually making themselves a powerful magnet to draw their own to themselves. Consciously or unconsciously, they are using the force by the use of each of us may mold ourselves and our circumstances.

By persistent right thinking, backed by the steady exercise of our wills, we can remake ourselves and our circumstances. It is purely a matter of right thinking. Every time we visualize the thing we long for, every time we see ourselves in imagination in the position we long to fill, we are forming a habit which will tend to make our highest moments permanent, to bring our vision out of the ideal into the actual.

If each of us only knew the possibilities lying in our visualizing powers, it would revolutionize our lives.

At one time, most of the country between Omaha and the Rocky Mountains was a vast barren desert, and it looked as though it was thought that it would be absolutely worthless. Many wondered why the Creator ever made such a dreary waste as these millions of acres presented, and when it was suggested in Congress that the Government assist in building a railroad across this desert from the Missouri River to the Pacific Slope, even men like Webster laughed at the idea. Webster said that such an undertaking would be a wicked waste of public money, and he suggested the importation of camels for the purpose of carrying the United States mail across the Western desert. He believed this was the only use that could be made of those waste lands.

But the vision seen by the men who conceived the Union Pacific Railroad was no idle dream; it was a foreshadowing of the reality. Before a rail had been laid, these men saw great thriving cities, vast populations and millions of fertile farms springing up like magic where others without a vision of its possibilities saw nothing but alkali plains, sage brush and coyotes. It was these men, men who were not limited by appearances, by what the senses told them, who transformed the desert into a thing of beauty and untold wealth.

Human beings are like this arid desert, packed with marvelous possibilities which are just waiting for that which will arouse their latent forces and make the germs of those wonderful possibilities blossom into beauty and power. What we need is a firm belief in the vision of ourselves which we see in the moment of our highest inspiration.

As soon as we feel the touch of the awakening, arousing, energizing power of an unalterable faith in our ability to be "the thing we long for," our lives will blossom into beauty and grandeur.

The realization of our power to create ideals and to make these live in reality is destined to revolutionize the world, because we build life through our ideals. This power to build mentally is the pathway of achievement, the way which will lead to the millennium. We cannot accomplish anything, do anything, create anything except through an ideal, a vision.

"The vision that you glorify in your mind," says James Allen, "the ideal that you enthrone in your heart—this you will build your life by, this you will become.

"The thoughtless, the ignorant, and the indolent, seeing only the apparent effects of things and not the things themselves, talk of luck, of fortune and chance. Seeing a man grow rich, they say 'How lucky he is!' Observing another become intellectual, they exclaim 'How highly favored he is!' And noting the saintly character and wide influence of another, they remark, 'How chance aids him at every turn!' They do not see the trials and failures and struggles which these men have voluntarily encountered in order to gain their experience; have no knowledge of the sacrifice they have made, of the undaunted efforts they have put forth, of the faith they have exercised, that they might overcome the apparently insurmountable, and realize the vision of their heart."

The reason why so many people fail to realize their ideals is that they are not willing to do their part to make it real. Remember that the longing, the desire to do a certain thing, is merely sowing the seed of your ambition. If you stop at this you will get about as much harvest as the farmer would get who puts seeds in the ground without preparing the soil, without fertilizing it and keeping the weeds down.

You must back up that which your heart longs to realize with an honest purpose to do your best, a dead-in-earnest effort to make your vision real. The mere holding of the desire to do so, no matter how persistently or strongly you hold it, will not help you to realize your dreams. You must not only sow the seed of desire and longing, you must do all the nourishing, cultivating, caring for—or you will only reap a thistle harvest. We see men and women everywhere reaping a very thistly, a very weedy harvest from the sowing of mere longings. These people can scarcely get enough out of their harvest to keep them alive, simply because they have taken no care of their seed after the planting.

The constant nursing, cultivating the desire, the ambition, keeping our heart's longings and soul yearnings alive, wholesome and healthy by active endeavor, is the only way in which we can match our dreams with their realities.

What we think most about is constantly weaving itself into the fabric of our career, becoming a part of ourselves, increasing the power of our mental magnet to attract those things we most ardently desire.

However, the law is neither moral nor unmoral, the nature of the object concentrated on does not affect its action. It may be the noble vision of a Jeanne d'Arc, of a Savonarola, or of a Lincoln, or it may be a wholly selfish, or an unworthy object: whatever our vision, the attractive, constructive forces will lead toward the realization of it. Dreaming and thinking and pushing along any line, whatever it may be, will produce like results. The idea is that the everlasting dreaming and pushing, the alertness to take advantage of opportunity, the constant visualizing of the thing one yearns for most, will inevitably bring the desired results—based on the mental vision, which bring us the things we desire.

The framework of your life structure is invisible. It is on the, mental plane. You are laying the foundation for your future, fixing its limits by the expectations you are visualizing. You cannot do anything bigger than you plan to do. The mental plans always come first. Your future building will merely be carrying out in detail what you are visualizing today. The future is simply an extension of the present. You are right now by your thought habit, by your prevailing mental attitude, making your place in life. You are locating yourself, settling what you are to be. In other words, you are right now making your future, deciding what your position in the world shall be. And it will be broad, ever growing, ever expanding, or it will become narrower, more pinched and rutty, according to your mental plan, according to the vision you hold.

The only world you will ever know anything about, the only world that is true for you at this moment, is the one you create mentally. The environment you fashion out of your thoughts, your beliefs, your ideals, your philosophy is the only one you will ever live in.

A mental magnet cannot attract opposite qualities. It can only attract things like itself, and it is our privilege to give the magnet its quality. We can inject hate into it. Or jealousy. Or envy. Or revenge. We can in a very short time demagnetize the magnet which was pulling good things so that it will attract bad things. It is for us to decide the quality of the magnetic current that shall flow out from us, but the mind is always a magnet sending out and attracting something, and this *something* which flows back to us always corresponds to the mental outflow.

Whatever is in the mind at the moment is the thing you are inviting to come and live with you. Your suspicion attracts suspicion. Jealousy brings more jealousy, hate more hate, just as love brings love to meet it, as friendliness brings more friendliness, as sympathy and good will toward all draw the same to you from others and increase your popularity and magnetic power.

We build as we think. Our lives follow our thoughts. As we think so we are. Many so limit themselves by their gloomy doubts and fears that they utterly dwarf their divine powers and possibilities. They do not realize that they are their own jailers, that they are holding themselves in the very conditions they despise. They have not learned how to make themselves magnets for the things they desire. They do not know that our own is seeking us and will come to us, whether it is property, friends, love, happiness, or any other legitimate desire— unless we drive it away by our antagonistic thought.

The limit of your thought will be the limit of your possibilities. Your limited ideal of yourself will limit your execution. You will never get any higher than your vision and your faith in that vision.

No matter how unfortunate your environment, or how unpromising your present condition, if you cling to your vision and keep struggling toward its realization, you are mentally building, enlarging your ideal, increasing the power of your mental magnet to attract your own.

Never mind opposition, never mind criticism, never mind if others call you a fool or a crank—they called the greatest inventors, artists, scientists, composers the same. Be true to the mysterious message within, the divine voice which bids you up and on. No matter what other things you have to give up, no matter what sacrifices you have to make, let everything else go if necessary, but cling to the ideal which haunts your dreams, for it points to the star of your destiny, and if you follow it you will come out of the darkness into beauty and brightness. Your highest ideal, the vision of your life work which you long to make real, is your best friend. Keep as close to it as you can, stick to it, and it will lead you to your goal. You may not understand why the star has been put so high above you and why so many mountains of obstacles and difficulties intervene, but if you keep your eye on the star and listen to the voice of your soul which bids you climb on, you will reach it.

Just because you are struggling in some work which your whole nature rebels, because there is no one to help you support your aged parents or an invalid brother or sister, do not conclude that your vision must perish. Keep pushing on as best you can, and affirming your power to attain your desire. Hundreds and thousands of poor men and women with poorer opportunities than yours have done immortal deeds because they had faith in their ideal and in their power to attain it.

It is by the perpetual focusing of his thought upon the solving of scientific problems, added to his faith in his ability to solve these problems, that Edison attracted to himself the forces which made him the greatest living inventor. His mind always ran ahead of him, visualizing the invention he was trying to bring out into objective reality. He was always picturing himself a little higher up, a little further on, and his success has followed his vision and his faith.

Suppose Edison had lost faith in his vision. Suppose he had allowed obstacles to discourage him and had said to himself, "Thousands of men have been thinking along these lines, trying to solve these problems for a long time, and have failed, and how can I expect to succeed? Why should I waste my time and energies in trying to do what they found impossible?" Do you think he would have become the power he became? Of course not. He couldn't. Doors always open, opportunities always come, to the man or woman who trusts and works, but nothing comes to the weak, doubting heart, the faint endeavor, nothing comes to those who do not believe in their divinity, their power to overcome.

No matter bow dark and forbidding the way, just imagine that you are carrying a lantern which always advances with you and gives you light enough for the next step, and although it looks very dark and discouraging a little distance ahead, when you arrive there the light will arrive also. All the light you need is for the next step, to know that you are going in the right direction.

Science tells us the eagle's wings developed in response to the eagle's desire to fly, to soar into the ether. Your longings, your yearnings for something higher and grander, your aspirations, backed by an invincible purpose, will call out your wings, will develop your latent power, so that you will rise above your mediocre environment to the full measure of your possibilities.

If we each were taught to keep our soul vision inviolable, never to tamper with that sacred something within which always points heavenward, that something which no matter how poor or iron our environment bids us look up and not down, aspire and not grovel, we—and civilization—would advance with marvelous strides.

We rise with our vision. All elevation, all progress, therefore, is first mental. It is based on faith in a visualized ideal. Everything starts with a vision, and the result always corresponds to the nature of the vision and our faithfulness to it.

Visualization will some day be found to be one of the great secrets of character building and achievement. Effort follows visualization as achievement follows effort. We are always gravitating toward the vision we hold our minds, and we will never make headway in any other direction than toward that which is our dominant thought, our dominant desire, our dominant motive. To be the best you can be, therefore, is to truly follow your inspiration; follow what your soul longs to do.

"A desire in the heart for anything," says H. Emile Lady, "is God's sure promise sent beforehand to indicate that it is yours already in the limitless realm of supply."

CHAPTER 18
Being In Tune

nothing could induce Ole Bull to play in public until his violin was in perfect tune. It did not make any difference how long it took him or how uneasy his audience became, if a string stretched the least bit during a performance, even though the discord was not noticed by anyone but himself, the instrument had to be put into harmony before he went on. A poorer musician would not be so particular. He would say to himself, "I will run through this piece no matter if one string is down a bit. No one may detect it but; myself."

Great music teachers say that nothing will ruin the sensitiveness of the ear and lower the musical perception and standard so quickly as using an instrument out of tune or singing with others who can not appreciate fine tone distinctions. The mind after a while ceases to distinguish delicate shadings of tone. The voice quickly imitates and follows the musical instrument accompanying it. The ear is deceived, and very soon, the singer forms the habit of singing off key.

It does not matter what particular instrument you may be using in the great life orchestra, whether it be the violin, the piano, the voice, or your mind expressing itself in literature, law, medicine, or any other vocation—you can not afford to start your concert with the great human race for your audience without getting it in tune.

Whatever else you may do, do not play out of tune, sing out of tune, or work out of tune. Do not let your discordant instrument spoil your ear or your mental appreciation. Familiarity with discord will wreck your success perceptions. Not even a Paderewski could win exquisite harmonies from a piano out of tune.

Mental discord is fatal to quality in work. The destructive emotions—worry, anxiety, hatred, jealousy, anger, greed, selfishness—are all deadly enemies of efficiency. One can no more do one's best work when possessed by any of these emotions than a watch can keep good time when there is friction in the bearings of its delicate mechanism. In order to keep perfect time, the watch must be exquisitely adjusted. Every wheel, every cog, every bearing, every jewel must be mechanically perfect, for any defect, any trouble, any friction anywhere will make absolutely correct time impossible. The human machinery is infinitely more delicate than the mechanism of the finest chronometer, and it needs regulating, needs to be put in perfect tune, adjusted to a nicety every morning before it starts on the day's run, just as a violin needs tuning before the concert begins.

Have you ever watched a centrifugal wringer in a laundry? It wobbles so badly when it first begins to revolve that it seems as though it would tear itself to pieces. But gradually, as the velocity increases, the motion becomes steadier and steadier, and the machine speeds with lightning rapidity on its center. When it once gains its perfect balance nothing seems to disturb it, although when it first began to revolve the least thing made it wobble.

Correspondingly, a thousand and one trifles which disturb those who have not found their mental center do not affect the poised, self-centered souls at all. Even great things—panics, crises, failures, fires, the loss of property or friends, disasters of any kind—do not throw them off their balance. They have found their center, their equilibrium, and no longer vacillate between hope and despair.

A poised, balanced mind unifies all the mental energies of the system, while the mind that flies all to pieces at the least provocation is constantly, demoralized: the mental forces are scattered; there is a lack of mental coordination, cohesion, and consequent power.

Harmony is the secret of all effectiveness, and harmony is simply keeping ourselves in tune.

This means maintaining poise, serenity, amiability, and sweetness of temper—the combination of enable us to cooperate with the perpetual renewal processes constantly going on within us, which are otherwise destroyed by friction.

The poised soul is so entrenched in the calm of eternal harmony that it is beyond the reach of disaster or the fear of it. Such a serene soul is like a huge iceberg, balanced by the calm in the depths of the sea. It laughs at the giant waves which beat against its sides and the storms which lash it. They do not even cause it a tremor, because its huge bulk—which enables it to ride calmly and serenely without perturbation when lashed by the ocean of fury—is in perpetual calm in the depths below.

It is strange that those who are very shrewd in other matters should be so shortsighted, so ignorant, so utterly foolish in regard to the importance of keeping their marvelous, intricate, and delicate mental machinery in tune every day. Many business people who could have accomplished a great deal more during the day with infinitely less effort, and could go home in a much fresher condition, instead drag themselves wearily through a discordant day and find themselves completely exhausted at night, because they failed to take a little time to put themselves in tune before going to work in the morning.

A New York business man told me that he never allowed himself to go to his office in the morning until he had put his mind into perfect harmony with the world. If he had the slightest feeling of envy or jealousy, if he felt selfish or unfair, if he did not have the right attitude toward his partners or any of his employees, he would clear his mind of any of these forms of discord either before leaving his home or while traveling to work. He said that he discovered that if he started out in the morning with a right attitude of mind toward everybody, he got infinitely more out of the day than he otherwise would; that whenever he has allowed himself to go to work in the past in a discordant condition he had not obtained nearly as good results, and he made those about him unhappy, to say nothing of causing increased wear and tear upon himself.

One reason the lives of so many of us are so ineffective is that we do not rise above the things that untune our minds—the things that irritate, annoy and worry us, and produce discord. Many of those who do only mediocre things really have a great deal of ability, but are so sensitive to friction that they can not do effective work. If, they say, they only had someone to steer them, to plan for them, to keep discord away from them and to help them keep in harmony, they could do remarkable things. But the truth is that those who do great things are obliged to acquire this "art of arts" for themselves. No one can exercise it for them. Indeed, they have discovered that no one can accomplish anything very great in this world unless he or she is able to be superior to the thousand and one things which would otherwise irritate and distract his or her attention.

How little we appreciate the marvelousness of the exquisite mechanism of the mind. We force it to do work when it is jaded and out of tune; when its spontaneity is gone and its standards are low. We force it into work by all sorts of stimulants and will-power.

The mind was intended as an instrument of a happiness—for an existence grand and sublime. Yet, we strain its exquisite gossamer mechanism until it is often prematurely injured, overstrained, ruined for its finest work.

We ought to so school ourselves that no matter what happens we should not lose our presence of mind, our balance. We should always keep our equilibrium so as to be able, no matter what happens, to do the level-headed thing, the wise thing, the right, square thing.

Somewhere in my travels I have seen what appeared to be a great stone face carved out of the side of a huge cliff, a face scarred and scratched by the sharp edge of gravel and sand hurled against it during the tremendous sand storms of the desert. Everywhere we see human faces similarly scratched and scarred by tempests of passion—by chafing, fretting and worrying—until the divine image is almost erased, and all power of accomplishing effective work has been destroyed.

How little we realize the power there is in harmony! It makes all the difference in the world in our life and work as to whether we are balanced and serene or are continually wrought up—full of discords and errors, harassed with all sorts of perplexing, vicious things.

If we could only learn the art of keeping ourselves in harmony, we could multiply our effectiveness many times and add years to our lives.

I have seen a great speakers shorn of their power and made perfectly miserable by gnats and mosquitoes. They could not think. They could not use half of their great mental powers. It took all of their time to fight these little pests. In like manner, the efficiency of the great majority of us is seriously marred by little irritating annoyances.

If you wish to attain exquisite mental poise, you must dive into the depths of your being, where there is eternal calm which no mental tempest can disturb. You must put yourself into harmony with the great creative, beneficent power within that heals all your hurts and diseases—where you are not only able to unfold all your faculties harmoniously, but are also conscious of a marvelous happiness . . . a peace of mind.

CHAPTER 19
The Suggestion of Inferiority

In olden times criminals, fugitives from justice, and slaves were branded. The words, "I am a fugitive," "I am a thief," or others indicating their crime or their inferior status were seared on some part of the body with a red hot iron.

In Rome robbers were branded on the forehead with a degrading letter. Laborers in mines, convicts, and gladiators were also branded. In Greece slaves were sometimes branded with a favorite poetical passage of their master. In France the branding iron used on slaves and criminals often took the form of the fleur-de-lis. In England deserters from the army were marked with the letter "D," and vagabonds, robbers and brawlers were branded in some way to advertise their disgrace.

The barbarous custom of branding human beings with the badge of crime or inferiority persisted in America even after it had been discontinued in the mother country. Hawthorne's *The Scarlet Letter* gives us a vivid picture of the suffering inflicted on the moral delinquent by

Puritan moralists in Colonial days. The tragic heroine, Hester Prynn, is never allowed to forget her misdeed. The sinister scarlet letter with which she is branded proclaims her shame to every one she meets.

The mere idea of this stamping human beings with an indelible badge of disgrace, of inferiority, shocks us moderns. Yet in truth, we do not hesitate to mark people today with the scarlet letter of outlawry, the brand of ostracism. Even now, in some of our penal institutions, we continue to put the criminal badge on our prisoners by clothing them in stripes, thus perpetually keeping before them the suggestion that they are criminals, outlaws, apart from their kind.

There are certain inalienable rights which human beings inherit from their Maker, rights which no fellow being, no human law or authority is justified in taking away. No matter what offense a person may commit against society we have no right to degrade him or her below the level of a human being; we have no right so to bombard that person with the suggestion of degradation, of inferiority, that we are almost certain to make that person less a man or woman; to lower that individual's estimate of himself or herself to such a degree that we rob him or her of the power even to attempt to regain his or her self-respect and any position in society. We have no right to insist that those who work for us shall wear a badge of inferiority. We have no right to thrust the suggestion of inferiority perpetually into the mind of any human being.

One of the greatest injuries we can inflict on any one is to convince that person that he or she is a nobody, that he or she has no possibilities and will never amount to anything. The suggestion of inferiority is responsible for more blighted ambitions, more stunted lives, more failures, more misery and unhappiness than almost any other single cause. Just as the, constant dripping of water will wear away stone, so the constant iteration of a statement will cause its acceptance by the average person. Even though the facts may be opposed to it, a constant suggestion presented to the mind impresses us in spite of ourselves and tends to a conviction of its truth.

When the weight of the Civil War was nearly crushing Lincoln, when it was the fashion to denounce and criticize and condemn him, when he was being caricatured as a hideous monster in the jingo press all over the world, one day, walking the floor in the White House, he was overheard saying to himself, "Abe Lincoln, are you a dog or are you a man?" During these dark days it would appear that Lincoln sometimes had a doubt as to whether he was really the man his closest friends knew him to be, or the caricature an antagonistic press pictured him.

The curse of the inferiority suggestion not only tends to destroy our faith in ourselves, but it often makes even the innocent take on the appearance of guilt. When Capt. Alfred Dreyfus, a French military officer, was convicted, through a foul conspiracy based on anti-Semitism, of the crime of treason against France, he showed outwardly all the manifestations of guilt. When stripped, in the presence of a vast multitude, in a public square in Paris, of all his insignia of rank as an officer in the army of France, the epaulettes and buttons being cut from his uniform and his sword broken, although conscious of his innocence of the crime imputed to him, he actually looked like the guilty thing he was accused of being. All but a very few close friends in the vast concourse that witnessed his public disgrace believed that even his appearance corroborated his guilt. The brain of the unfortunate Dreyfus was a wireless receiving station for the hatred, the contempt of millions of people who believed they were looking at a vile traitor who had sold valuable military secrets to Germany.

Many young employees, especially if they are at all sensitive, are irreparably injured by nagging, fault-finding, employers, who are constantly reminding them of their shortcomings, scolding them for every trivial mistake, and never giving them a word of praise or encouragement, no matter how creditable their work, or how well they deserve it.

Enthusiasm is the very soul of success and one cannot be enthusiastic about one's work, one cannot take continued pride in it, if he or she is constantly being told that it is no good, that it is in fact disgracefully bad, that he or she should be ashamed of himself or herself, and that he or she ought to quit if he or she can't, do better. This fault-finding and continual suggestion of inferiority has ruined many a life.

Young writers, for instance, often gets a serious setback in their early efforts because of a severe criticism, an unqualified condemnation of their first book by a reviewer, or the return of their manuscript with an editor's sneering suggestion that the aspiring writer made a mistake in his or her calling. Harsh critics, editors and book reviewers have deterred many young writers from developing their talent. The fear of further criticism or humiliation, of being called foolish, dull or stupid, has blighted in the bud the career of many talented people who under encouragement might have done splendid work. If an individual is of a sensitive nature even though he or she really has great ability, such rebuffs often so dishearten the individual that he or she never has the confidence to try again.

The perpetual suggestion of inferiority holds more people back from doing what they are capable of than almost anything else. In the Old World—China, Japan, India, in England and other European countries, for example—who can measure the harm it has done in the form of "caste." Think what superb men and women have been held down all their lives, kept in menial positions, because they were reared in the belief that once a servant always a servant; that because their parents were menials they must also be menials

What splendid brains and fine personalities we see serving in hotels, restaurants and private households in Europe—often much superior to the proprietors themselves. Saturated with the idea that the child must follow in the parent's footsteps, though they may be infinitely superior in natural ability to those they serve, these individuals remain waiters or waitresses, butlers, coachmen, maids, gardeners or humble employees of some sort. No matter what talents they possess they are held in leash by the ingrained conviction of generations that the accident of birth has decided their position in life. They are convinced that the barriers established by heredity and by caste, an outworn feudal system, are insurmountable.

How delightfully the gentle humorist Barrie satirizes this Old World condition in his play, *The Admirable Crichton*. How skillfully he portrays the clever and resourceful butler, Crichton, who in the crucible of a great emergency proves himself a born leader, a man head and shoulders above the noble lord, his master.

When the yacht carrying the master and his family, Crichton and some other servants, is wrecked, they escape with their lives to a desert island. In their desperate plight the barriers of caste are broken down, and master and man change places. Removed from an artificial environment, where hereditary rank and wealth determine the status of the man, Nature unmistakably asserts herself, and Crichton, by the tacit consent of all, becomes leader. By the force of his inborn ability he controls the situation. He commands, the others obey. Yet when they are rescued by a passing ship and brought back to England, old conditions at once resume their sway. Crichton, without a murmur, or thought of change, falls back to his former menial position, and all goes on as before.

While we Americans laugh at, or severely criticize and denounce, the snobbishness of class distinctions in other countries, we are guilty of similar snobbishness, especially in regard to one section of our fellow-Americans—the black people. No matter how highly educated, how able, how refined or charming a man or a woman, if he or she has but a drop of Negro blood, we brand him or her with the stigma of race inferiority.

I always feel sympathy for the black people who must suffer keenly from the discrimination against their race. They have seen white people avoiding them everywhere; refusing to sit down beside them in public places, in churches, on trains and cars, everywhere they can possibly avoid it. In the South they were once not permitted to ride in the same trains with whites, and in other parts of the country, while they were allowed travel on the ordinary day coaches, they were not allowed on the Pullman cars, except as waiters and porters. Our hotels, private schools, public places, and even many of our churches, have practiced similar discrimination The churches pretend to draw no color lines, but by their attitude most of them have practically done so.

Everywhere they turn in this land of ours where we boast that every man is "born free and equal," black people are embarrassed, placed at a disadvantage. In all sorts of ways white people are constantly humiliating them, reminding them that they belong to an inferior race, and they take their places according to the valuation of those born to more favorable conditions. This constant suggestion of inferiority has done much to keep black people back, because it has added tremendously to their sense of real or fancied inferiority and has been a discouragement to their efforts to make themselves the equals of those who look down upon them.

We cannot help being influenced by other people's opinion of us. It makes us, according to its nature, think more or less of ourselves; of our ability. We are similarly, affected by our environment. We unconsciously take on the superiority or inferiority of our surroundings. Employees who work in cheap, shoddy stores or factories soon become tagged all over with the marks of inferiority, the cheap John methods employed in the establishments in which they work and, spend their days.

If the employees in a store like Tiffany's or Altman's, for example, were to be mixed up with those of some of the cheap, shoddy New York stores, it would not take much discernment to pick out the worker in the superior environment from the one in the inferior. To spend one's best years selling cheap, shoddy merchandise will inevitably leave its mark on those who do so. Even though we may struggle against it, we are unconsciously dyed by the quality of our occupation, the character of the concerns for which we work.

In making your life choice, avoid as you would poison shoddy, fakery concerns which have no standing in their community. Keep away from occupations that have, a demoralizing tendency. Every suggestion of inferiority is contagious, and helps to swerve life from its possibilities. Every influence in our environment is a suggestion which becomes a part of us. If we live with people who lack ambition, who are slovenly, slipshod, or with people of loose morals, of low flying ideals, we tend to reflect their qualities. If we mingle much with those who use slangy, vulgar, incorrect English, people who are not careful about their manners or their expression, these things will reappear in our own conversation and manners. If we read inferior books, or associate with perpetual failures, with people who botch their work and botch their lives our own standards will suffer from the contagion.

It does not matter whether inferiority relates to manner, to work, to conversation, to companions, to thought habits—wherever it occurs, its tendency is to pull down all standards and to cut down the average of achievement. We are all living sensitive plates on which the example, the thoughts and suggestions of others, our own thoughts and habits, our associations and surroundings indelibly etch themselves.

I wish I could burn it into the consciousness of each of you who wants to make a success of life, that you cannot do so while you associate yourself with inferiority and harbor a low estimate of yourself.

Get away from both. Have nothing to do with them. If you are a victim of the inferiority suggestion, deny the suggestion, drive it from your mind as the greatest enemy of your welfare.

You can only do what you think you can. If you hold in mind a cheap, discreditable picture of yourself; if you doubt your efficiency you are shackled, you are not free to express yourself: You erect a barrier between yourself and the power that achieves.

The mere mental acknowledgment or feeling that you are weak and inefficient, is contagious. It is sensed by other people and their thought is added to yours in undermining your self-confidence, which is the bulwark of achievement. No matter what others say or think of you, always hold in mind a lofty ideal of yourself, a picture of your own efficiency. Never allow yourself to doubt your ability to do what you undertake. You can not be inferior, because you are made in God's image. You can, if you will, make a masterpiece of your life, because it is part of His plan that you should.

CHAPTER 20
How Thinking Brings Success

a strong man hypnotized into a belief that he cannot rise from his chair becomes powerless to do so till the spell is removed.

A frail woman, nerved out of necessity to save a life, can carry a person heavier than herself from danger. Both instances could in some sense rightly be referred to as strictly physical, yet in both cases the mental attitude, not the physical ability, is what determined the result. When, therefore, a task to be done consists *wholly* of mental activity, as do most kinds of success winning, how much greater must be the power of the thought and mental attitude in bringing about results!

I wish it were possible to impress everyone with the tremendous power which the mind has on bringing about success: All the conquerors of the world, whether on battlefields, in trade, or in moral struggles, have won by the attitude of mind in which they went at the work they had to do.

The belief in environmental limitations, the conviction that we cannot rise out of our circumstances, that indeed we are *victims of circumstances*, is responsible for a weakening of our achievement faculties and an undermining of our executive ability which cause untold tragic failures—as well as a large part of the poverty and wretchedness of humanity. Such belief is, unfortunately, the norm, yet it produces abnormal conditions.

Dominion in our own circumstances is our birthright, but we have adopted weakness and limitation. We have claimed poverty, wretchedness, and slavery in place of riches, happiness, and freedom.

But how can we rise out of our wretchedness unless we *think and believe* we can?

Is there any science whereby a one *can*, when one thinks one *can't*?

Is there any philosophy whereby one can rise, unless one looks up?

Is there any way by which one can succeed while one thinks, talks, and lives failure?

We cannot go in opposite directions at the same time. Until we erase "fate" and "can't" and "doubt" from our vocabulary, we cannot rise. We cannot get strong while we harbor convictions of our weakness. We cannot have certainty in the presence of doubt; we cannot be happy while we dwell on our miseries or misfortunes.

We might as well expect to become healthy and strong by always thinking and talking about our poor health, saying that we never expect to be robust, as to expect our executive faculties to be strong and vigorous while we are perpetually doubting our ability to do what we undertake.

Nothing more weakens the mind and renders it totally unfit for effective thinking as our constant acknowledgment of our doubt in our ability to accomplish.

The majority of persons who fail begin by doubting their ability to do the things they attempt—because by admitting doubt into their minds, they are letting an enemy into their camp, a spy who will betray them.

Doubt belongs to the failure family, and once admitted and not expelled will introduce "Mr. and Mrs. Take-it-Easy," "Mr. and Mrs. Let-up-a-Little," "Mr. and Mrs. Let-Go-When-It-Gets Hard," "Mr. and Mrs. Wait"—as well as other members of the failure family. And once these families get into the mind, they attract other qualities like themselves, and therein lies the end of ambition: Your longing for prosperity and yearning for achievement will all be vain while you are entertaining these thought. They will exhaust your energy, destroy your power for attracting success. Failure will soon be in the ascendancy in your mind and in your actions.

The moment you admit weakness, the moment you confess defeat, you are gone. There is no hope for the person who has lost stamina, who has given up the struggle. You can't do anything with him or her.

If we hold perpetually the thought that we are down and cannot rise, that success is for others but not for us, we, in so doing, adjust ourselves to our thoughts and to make any other conditions than those we think, impossible.

How can you expect to be lucky when you are always talking about your ill luck? As long as you think you are a poor miserable worm of the dust, you will be that. You cannot rise above your thought; you cannot be different from your conception of yourself. If you really believe you are unlucky, you will be so. There are no drugs, or patent medicines, or influences in the world that can get you out of this condition until you change your thought; and a reversal of thought will bring about a reversal of conditions in the body, as surely as the sun and the rain unfold the petals of a rosebud. There is no mystery about it; it is purely scientific.

People who do great things are powerful in their affirmations. They have tremendous positive ability; they do not know the meaning of negatives. Their power of assertion and their conviction of ability to do are so strong that the opposite does not occur to them. When they make up their minds to do a thing, they take it for granted that they can do it. They are not filled with doubts and fears, no matter how people may scoff, and cry "Crank." Indeed, nearly all the great men and women who have pushed progress along have been called cranks. The world said they had "wheels in their heads." Yet we owe the blessings of modern civilization to the sublime confidence of such men and women in themselves, that indomitable faith in their mission which nothing could shake. The history of all great forward movements is contained in their biographies.

What if Copernicus and Galileo had given up when they were denounced as cranks and insane? Science of today is built on their unshaken confidence that the world is round and that the earth moves around the sun instead of the sun around it!

Suppose Columbus had given up and lost confidence in himself when Europe was laughing at him as a crank!

Suppose Cyrus W. Field had lain down after a dozen years of fruitless endeavor to span the sea, when cable after cable had parted in mid-ocean! Suppose he had listened to his relatives, who said he was wasting his fortune, and would die in poverty!

Suppose Fulton had given up under ridicule when a book was written to prove that a ship could not carry coal enough to force its way across the ocean! (He lived to see that very book brought across the sea in a steamship.)

What if Alexander Graham Bell had lost faith in himself when he had expended his last dollar in experimenting on the principle of the telephone, and when the world called him a crank?

Colossal faith in oneself often excites antagonism and even ridicule, but this quality is essential to all great achievement. Without this sublime faith, this confidence in her mission, how could the fragile village maiden, Joan of Arc, have led and controlled a French army? Without this power how could she have led those thousands of stalwart men as if they were children? This divine confidence multiplied her power a thousandfold, until even the king obeyed her.

It was this grand self-confidence and faith in a just cause that led Andrews Jackson, with a handful of men, to administer a most crushing defeat to an army of trained English soldiers at New Orleans.

It was such faith that enabled General Zachary Taylor at Buena Vista, with 5,000 American soldiers, to defeat Santa Anna, who had 20,000 men.

Confidence, absolute trust, is a creative force which generates, produces, and achieves—while distrust tears down, annihilates, and destroys.

A strong self-faith, by eliminating doubt and uncertainty, wonderfully increases the power of concentration, because it withdraws distracting motives. It makes possible a steady pushing forward, with no scattering of energy.

Successes in all endeavors all have this spirit of invincible affirmation, while if we analyze failures, we shall find that most of them are weak in their self-faith, that they lack the abounding confidence in themselves that marks successful persons.

The mind cannot act with vigor in the presence of doubt. Wavering in the mind makes wavering execution. There must be certainty, or there is no efficiency. The unschooled who believe in themselves, who have the faith that they can do the thing they undertake, often put to shame the college-bred whose over-culture and wider outlook often bring an increased sensitiveness, a lessening of self-confidence, and decision weakened by constant weighing of conflicting theories.

Never allow yourself or any one else to shake your confidence in yourself, to destroy your self-reliance, for this is the very foundation of all great achievement. When it is gone, your whole structure falls. As long as you have it, there is hope for you.

Confidence, unbounded, unshaken faith in yourself, which even amounts to boldness at times, is absolutely necessary in all great undertakings.

CHAPTER 21
How the Mind Rules the Body

ore and more, and by people of varying views, the power of thought is being considered to be omnipotent in how we function. And scientific experiments, instead of destroying this notion, have been substantiating it, through demonstrations of seemingly incredible results.

As early as the 18th Century, for example, the famous American physician William Beaumont, was presented with a youth who had a gunshot wound in the abdomen—a wound that would not close. This unique situation led Beaumont to conduct an extensive study of the digestive system—more than 200 studies over several years with numerous patients. Of importance to us here, is that one of the conclusions he arrived at was the great effect depressing or elevating emotions had on digestion and other bodily functions. In one instance, a telegram announcing disaster caused the collapse of the follicles that were actively secreting gastric juice in a patient's stomach, leaving the patient's food undigested for hours!

Toward the end of the 18th Century, professor Elmer Gates at Washington proved that by thinking intently of his hand when it was placed in a basin full of water and willing that blood should flow to that hand, he was able to make the water spill over the basin. He could measure the amount of extra blood that had been sent to his hand, since it corresponded to the amount of overflowed water. Admittedly, not everyone can do this same experiment on first trial—perhaps not in a hundred trials—but the evidence was now in that the mind could be trained in ways to control the body!

In another study by this same professor, which he published in a paper in 1879, he demonstrated that the very makeup of our breath can be affected by our thoughts! In this fascinating study, he showed that within five minutes after a patient became angry, there appeared in his breath a chemical compound produced by the emotion. Moreover, this compound, when extracted and administered to other humans and animals, caused stimulation and excitement! In his paper, he indicated that "experiments show that irascible, malevolent, and depressing emotions generate in the system injurious compounds, some of which are extremely poisonous; also, that agreeable, happy emotions generate chemical compounds of nutritious value which stimulate the cells to manufacture energy."

Shortly after these experiments, professor W. G. Anderson at Yale University succeeded in practically weighing a thought—or perhaps to put that more accurately, the result of a thought's action. A student was poised on a balance so that his center gravity was at the midpoint of the balance When he was asked to solve mathematical problems, the increased blood flowing to his head changed his center of gravity, causing an immediate dip of the balance. The more complicated the problems the student was asked to perform, the greater the student's intensity of thought, the greater became the shift in his center of gravity. Repeating the nine multiplication table, for instance, caused a greater displacement of the student's center of gravity than repeating the table of fives.

Carrying the experiment further, the professor had the student imagine himself doing leg gymnastics. As the student performed the feats mentally, blood flowed into his limbs in quantities sufficient to tip the balance, according to the movement he was visualizing. Over the course of performing these purely mental activities, the student's center of gravity shifted four inches, or as much would have occurred if he'd raised both arms above his shoulders! These experiments were repeated on a large number of students—and with the same results.

To further test the influence of mind on the body, professor Anderson measured the strength of the right and left arms of eleven young men. The average strength of the right arms was one hundred and eleven pounds; of the left arms, ninety-seven pounds. The men practiced special physical exercises with only the right hand for one week. Tests of both arms were again made, and, while—as would be expected—the average strength of the right arm had increased six pounds, that of the unexercised left arm had also increased—seven pounds! The part of the brain connected with the performance of these exercises not only developed the muscles that were actually put into action, it also affected the other muscles that it correspondingly controlled. This could come about only by the brain sending blood and nervous force to the various muscles.

Studies at other universities have shown that exercise without proper thought does little to develop muscles. While conversely, very little exercise, but with the mind directing it, will practically rebuild the body.

It has been further found that exercise involving competition and a lively interest does far more good than merely engaging in mechanical movements, performed without interest. For instance, while it may aid in the stimulation of ideas, walking was shown to be a poor form *of exercise* for those who like to mull things over a lot, as the activity is so purely automatic that it is not sufficient to draw enough blood from the brain, which goes on solving and ruminating over intellectual problems as the person walks. A brisk walk or run, on the other hand, set within a definite time period that requires concentration on one's movements and one's pace, sends the blood to the legs and builds them up.

Exercising before a mirror, watching the muscles swell with the different motions, was also found to aid in their development, because of the corresponding mental activity that was being engaged by the act of watching—noticing—oneself.

In his now famous experiments on dogs by the Russian scientist and 1904 Nobel Prize winner, Prof. Ivan Pavlov proved conclusively that secretion of the gastric juice in the stomach does not, as previously supposed, take place automatically when saliva is secreted or when food enters the stomach. On the contrary, gastric juice is secreted when a dog is made to anticipate that it is to be fed with a much-loved food, as raw meat—*even if the meat is not given to it; even if food is given to it but is not allowed to pass into the stomach of the dog, but bypasses it by a slit made for that purpose!* Pavlov demonstrated the part played by the mind in what had theretofore been considered a merely mechanical, physical function. He demonstrated that psychological attitude is of great importance to physiological performance.

Lastly, experiments at the University of Chicago and at Stanford University have seemed to show that thought produces phenomena similar to those of electricity, that the particles of living matter change from positive to negative and negative to positive by the influence of thought. This makes the old comparison of thought to a "telegram from the brain" all the more apt, and further enlarges our conception of what the miraculous mind can do in changing bodily conditions.

It seems now that there should be little doubt as to the answer to the question, Cannot this same miraculous power of thought upon bodily functions be called upon to change our *mental* habits, our *characters . . . the destiny of our lives?*

CHAPTER 22
Self-Motivation by Self Suggestion

S toutly assert that there is a place for you in the world, and that you are going to fill it.

Thoughts are forces, and by them we create ourselves and our conditions. They are constantly sculpting, molding our characters—fashioning our lives.

Some one has said, "All human duty is boiled down into this, learn what to think and think it."

The next time you are in a discordant mood, when you feel cross and crabbed and out of sorts with everybody, when little things nettle you and you cannot get along with those around you, when instead you seem to be antagonizing others, when your brain is confused and you feel that you can not control yourself; try this experiment: Leave whatever you are doing, and go out of doors. Walk a few blocks, or, if possible, slip out into the country and determine that you will drive out of your mind everything that fights against harmony and mental balance. Think of beautiful, harmonious things, pleasant things. Resolve that whatever comes, you will be cheerful and poised, that you will not let little nagging things make a fool of you, that you will keep your mental instrument in tune.

You will be surprised to find how well it will pay you to take time to put yourself in tune. No matter when you get out of tune, stop whatever you are doing, and *refuse to do another thing until you are yourself*—until you are back on the throne of your mental kingdom.

I have a friend who has helped himself wonderfully by talking to himself about his conduct. When he feels that he is not doing all that he ought to, that he has made some foolish mistake or has failed to use good sense and good judgment in any transaction, when he feels that his stamina and his ambition are deteriorating, he goes off alone to the country, to the woods if possible, and has a good heart-to-heart-talk with himself something after this fashion:

"Now, young man, you need a good talking-to, a bracing-up all along the line. You are going stale, your standards are dropping, your ideals are getting dull, and the worst of it all is that when you do a poor job, or are careless about your dress and indifferent in your manner, you do not feel as troubled as you used to. You are not making good. This lethargy, this inertia, this indifference, if you're not very careful, will seriously cripple your career. You are letting a lot of good chances slip by you, because you are not as progressive and up-to-date as you ought to be.

"Your ideals need rubbing up. They are getting dim. In short, you are becoming lazy. You, like to take things easy. Nobody ever yet amounted to much who let his energies flag, his standards drop, and his ambition ooze out. Now, I am going to keep right after you, young man, until you are doing yourself justice. This sort of take-it-easy policy will never land you at the goal you started for. You will have to watch yourself very closely, or you will be left behind.

"You are capable of doing something much better than what you are doing. You must start out today with a firm resolution to make the returns tonight from your work greater than ever before. You must be a conqueror, and make this a red-letter day. Bestir yourself, get the cobwebs out of your head, brush off the brain ash. Think, think, think, to some purpose! Do not mull and mope like this. You are only half-alive! Get a move on, you!"

This young man says he hauls himself "over the coals," as he calls it, every morning when he finds that his standards are down and he feels lazy and indifferent—in order to force himself up to a higher standard and put himself in tune for the day. It is the very first thing to which he attends.

He constantly chides himself for inaction, indifference, laziness, lack of energy. "Now, John," he says to himself, "Brace up. Make this day count. Don't let any opportunity slip. Seize it, wring every possibility out of it. Don't shrink from responsibility, no matter how hard or disagreeable, if there is valuable discipline in it, if it will help to make you more efficient, more self-confident. Don't try to get out of anything which will help you, which will make you a stronger and larger man."

He forces himself to do the most disagreeable tasks first, and does not allow himself to skip hard problems. "Now, don't be a coward," he says to himself, "If others have done this, you can do it."

By years of stern discipline of this kind he has done wonders with himself. He began as a poor boy living in the slums of New York with no one to take an interest in him, encourage, or push him. Though he had little opportunity for schooling when as a small boy, he has given himself a splendid education, mainly since he was twenty-one. For many years he took up one study after another during his spare evenings, holidays, and odd moments—conquering and becoming proficient in each in its turn, until he has made himself a well-educated and broadly-read man. I have never known anyone else who carried on such a vigorous campaign in self-victory, self-development, self-training, self-culture as this young man has.

If you find yourself not achieving to the level of your desire, call a halt and say to yourself, "Now, haven't I given about enough of the years of my life to worry and anxiety? For years I have been robbed of my sleep, have been made miserable a large part of my time by these detestable enemies of my comfort, my welfare, my prosperity, my health and my happiness.

"Now, _____[your name], isn't it about time you called a halt on all this miserable business? For a quarter of a century or more you have been a slave of worry, a miserable victim of anxiety. You have lived in constant terror of the expectancy of bad business, hard times, probable panics. There has hardly never been in your adult life in which you have enjoyed the peace of mind, the satisfaction, and the contentment that is the birthright of every human."

There is no fate or destiny which puts one person down and another up. There is no power which parcels out good things to a favored few, and gives you and me inferior things.

"It is not in our stars, but in ourselves, that we are underlings."

Good things come to those who can take them by force of purpose and tenacity of determination.

When doubts and fears set in, keep your mind filled with the thoughts which uplift and encourage.

Motivate yourself past those doubts and fears by unstinting self-talk. Remind yourself that you regardless of whatever difficulties you have encountered in life thus far, you have passed through.

Do this, and you will have discovered one of the great secrets of the power of your thoughts to move you toward your goals.

CHAPTER 23
Heart-To-Heart Talks
and Affirmations

y words are spirit and they are truth; and they shall not return to me void; but shall accomplish that whereunto they were sent.

How many of us grasp the real significance of this Biblical utterance? Or of this other: "And the word was made flesh and dwelt among us"? How many of us ever think that our own words, our uttered thoughts are living forces and are made flesh? Yet it is literally true that they are being outpictured in our body, are chiseling our physique, shaping our faces, molding our expression to their likeness. What we think and say reappears not only in our expression, but also in our physical condition, in our health, good or bad, according to the nature of our thoughts and words. Every word we speak is an indestructible force, because it affirms a thought, a sentiment, an emotion, a motive, which never ceases to exert its power.

Jesus evidently recognized that words are real forces, for He said, "Heaven and earth shall pass away, but my word shall not pass away."

Material things might pass away, but His word was a force which could never cease to exercise its power.

All through the Bible the power of the word is emphasized. "The Word was made flesh and dwelt among us," "The Word was with God, and the Word was God," "He sent His Word and healed them."

There is a mysterious power in the spoken word, in the vigorous affirmation of a thought, which registers a profound impression on the subconscious mind, and the silent forces within us proceed to make the word flesh, to make the thing we affirm a reality. There is a tremendous constructive power in registering your vow, in vigorous, determined affirmation, backed by a persistent, dogged endeavor to bring about the thing we desire.

A very striking proof of this was afforded in the European war, in the awful conflict at Verdun in 1916. As stated in a telegraphed report from a high French officer, the fundamental secret of French resistance to the terrific German onslaught was psychological. It was, he said, auto-suggestion on a vast scale. General Petain replaced doubt and discouragement with iron determination when throughout the entire army flashed his expressed resolution that the Germans should not get through the French lines—"*Ills ne passeront pas.*" (They shall not pass.) All of the soldiers were so hypnotized by the constant repetition of the phrase "*Ills ne passeront pas,*" that no idea save that of resistance could enter their heads.

There is no doubt that it trebled and quadrupled the resisting power of the army. The mighty suggestion of invincibility in the words was literally the decisive factor in the battle. The repetition of "They shall not pass," was what enabled the infantry to undergo unexampled bombardment and then rush forward with the bayonet as eagerly as fresh troops. The confidence of victory seen even in captured Frenchmen amazed their German captors.

The French officer's report further stated that a surgeon in the dressing station close to the front said that the most remarkable thing about the wounded was their general attitude of determination. In some cases, the surgeon said, the faces seemed fixed with an expression of ferocious resolution. Many of those suffering from shell shock and those only partially conscious would repeat at intervals of their delirium, *"Passeront pas, passeront pas."*

All of the soldiers at Verdun were obsessed by this one dominating idea to the exclusion of everything else. "The Germans shall not pass." A correspondent at the front said: "I saw a regiment coming back to rest after six days in the trenches. The soldiers all seemed animated by a spirit of intense determination and iron resolution. When asked their opinion of the battle, the general reply was just this: *'The Germans shall not pass.'*"

And the Germans did not pass.

Suppose you should instill in your subconsciousness regarding the entrance into your mind of destructive thoughts, motives and emotions—those bitter enemies of your prosperity and happiness—a grim resolution such as the French soldiers at Verdun registered regarding the Germans? What would happen? If whenever enemy thoughts or emotions tried to get entrance to your mental kingdom you said grimly to them, "You shall not pass. I will not allow in my mind any enemies of my success and happiness," do you think it would be possible for them to get by? Why, of course they couldn't. It would be impossible. And if you should iterate and reiterate the same grim resolve—"You shall not pass"—regarding hindering habits, regarding every temptation that makes an appeal to you, why, my friend, this would revolutionize your life.

Words are the clothes of our thoughts. Every word we speak, even uttered thought, is power for good or ill. We must remember that it is what we put into the word that gives it its meaning, and determines its quality and its force.

Your words are messengers of life or death to yourself and to others.

We can take a word and think love into it, think service into it, think friendliness into it, and it will create a corresponding feeling in the one it is addressed to. Or we can take the same word and think hatred into it, think jealousy into it, think envy into it, and hurl it out and arouse antagonism, jealousy, hatred or envy in another mind.

Everything depends upon the thought behind the word. It is the mental attitude that gives the word its real meaning.

Words have put civilization where it is today. The word wedded to the thought has built everything that we have achieved.

There is a force in spoken words which is not stirred by going over the same words mentally. Words spoken aloud arouse slumbering energies within us which thinking does not stir up; when vocalized they make a more lasting impression on the mind—just as we are so much more impressed and inspired by listening to a great lecture or sermon than we would be if we read the same words in print; or how *seeing* things in nature makes a more lasting impression upon the mind than *thinking* about them. A vividness, a certain force, accompanies the spoken word—especially if earnestly, vehemently uttered—which is not conveyed in merely thinking about what words express. If you repeat to yourself aloud, vigorously, even vehemently, a firm resolve, you are more likely to carry it to reality than if you merely resolve in silence.

We can talk to our inner self and know from experience that it will listen to and act on our suggestions. After all, we are constantly sending suggestions or commands to this inner self. We may not do so audibly, but we do so silently, mentally. Unconsciously we advise, we suggest, we try to influence it in certain directions. Now, by consciously, audibly addressing it, in heart-to-heart talks with ourselves, we will equally find that we can very materially influence our habits, our motives, our methods of living. In fact, the possibilities of influencing the character and the life by this means are practically limitless.

Many people have killed character enemies, peace and happiness enemies, have doubled and quadrupled their self-confidence, have strengthened tremendously their initiative, their executive ability, have literally made themselves over, by heart-to-heart talks with themselves.

I know a man who has so completely changed his timid, self-effacing nature by talks with his inner self that no one would dream that only a few years ago he was so shy, so extremely sensitive, that he would blush scarlet if attention were called to him in any gathering, and he would avoid people in every possible way.

Five years ago no amount of money would have induced this man to get up in a public meeting, even to put a motion or to make the simplest statement. I think he would have fainted away at the mere calling of his name in a public place. Not only had he no confidence whatever in himself, but he had a haunting obsession that he was a fraud. Although a perfectly honest, earnest, hard-working man, with good intentions toward all, he could not help feeling that in some way he was not genuine, and that sometime something would happen to show him up in his true light.

For years he suffered untold tortures from his foolish imaginings about himself. Conscious that he had ability, but cursed with weaknesses that made it in many ways unavailable, his life was headed towards failure, when he accidentally came across a which told him of the miracles possible through the practice of audible self-encouragement. He began immediately to carry out the suggestions of the book and made a daily habit of heart-to-heart talks with himself. In a very short time he was conscious of a great improvement in his feelings, his mental attitude, and his spirits. Others soon began to notice an improvement in his manner and bearing. Now, he presides at public meetings without the slightest feeling of self-consciousness. His painful shyness has vanished; he can stand any amount of criticism and denunciation without a sign of sensitiveness or embarrassment.

There is no fault, no weakness, great or small, which will not succumb to persistent, audible auto-suggestion. Not only this, but it tends to arouse slumbering qualities within us which mere thinking does not stir up or waken.

We all need stirring up. There is gunpowder enough in us to make a tremendous explosion if we could only get the spark to the giant powder that is sleeping within us.

If you are doubting, fearful of failure, or poverty, you can reinforce your courage and strengthen your confidence in yourself by daily heart-to-heart talks with your inner self, by the frequent affirmation of the positive assertions "I must," "I can," "I will." There is no better suggestion than Emerson's for stiffening the will and the power to do: "Nerve us with incessant affirmatives." And incessant affirmatives will nerve us.

The perpetual affirmation of the power to achieve one's ambition, of one's grim determination to win out in life at any cost; the affirmation of prosperity, of success, the constant assertion of confidence in one's self, of the belief in one's ability to do the thing that one has set one's heart on, will nerve a weak will and brace up a wavering purpose as nothing else can.

If you are not satisfied with your progress so far, if you are not growing bigger and broader, something is holding you back, hindering you from making your ideal real. Find out what it is and then remove it by audible self-treatments.

The best way to find what is your stumbling block is to have a frequent heart-to-heart talk with yourself. Look into your own soul and take an account of your personal stock, your success and failure qualities. Analyze yourself as you would a friend you were anxious to help—whose strong and weak points you could see clearly.

Get by yourself where you can be absolutely alone and examine yourself something after this fashion, putting the questions aloud, and addressing yourself by name:

"Now (James or Ann, or whatever your name is) what is the trouble with you? Why do you not get along faster? Are you locking up your ambition or has it not yet been awakened? Why are you not doing as well as you would like? Why are you plodding along in mediocrity while those all about you with no better chances, perhaps infinitely poorer chances than yours, are getting on by leaps and bounds? There, must be some reason for this? Do you lack vitality, energy, or are you not using what you have? Have you some weakness, defect or peculiarity which is holding you down? Are you the victim of a weak link in the chain of your character which is nullifying all your efforts in other directions? Where is the trouble? You must do all you can to put your finger on it and correct it."

Write out a list of the qualities that make a strong, courageous, successful character and their opposites—those that make a weak, timid, unsuccessful one—and examine yourself to see what is your rating in the list. Call them off aloud—faith, courage, self-confidence, ambition, enthusiasm, perseverance, concentration, initiative, cheerfulness, optimism, thoroughness, etc. Ask yourself if you possess these splendid qualities, or if you incline to their opposites.

Don't be afraid to face your weak points, to call your faults by their right names. Bring them into the light, see them for what they are, and then grapple with them. *You cannot afford to be less than you feel that you should be and can be, to have your life spoiled by some defect which you can overcome.*

When you have gone over the specific character qualities ask yourself these broader questions; always visualizing and addressing yourself by name:

"What are you here for? What do you mean to the world? What message does your life bring to it? What do you stand for? What do you represent? Do you realize that you were sent here with a message for humanity? Are you delivering it—persistently, determinedly, without grumbling, whining, or shirking? *What are you giving to the world?* Are you dreaming of the big thing you *might* do tomorrow, or are you doing the little things which you *can do today,* giving *yourself* as you go along—giving, if you have nothing else to give, encouragement, inspiration, helpfulness to those on the way with you?"

Probe yourself in this manner until you get a good line on yourself, a fair estimate of yourself; until you know both your strength and your weakness; until you can see with clear eyes the things that are keeping you back, the lack in your nature that is handicapping you, the weakness that is cutting down the average of your ability by ten, twenty, fifty or even seventy-five percent. Then vigorously attack your enemies—the enemies of your success, of your efficiency, of your happiness. Constantly stoutly affirm your complete mastery over them, their powerlessness to dominate your life and ruin your career.

By heart-to-heart talks of this sort with yourself you can change your whole nature, revolutionize your career. Whether it is faith, courage, initiative, cheerfulness, whatever it is you lack, assume the quality you wish to possess, affirm positively that it is already yours, exercise it whenever possible, concentrate on it, and you will be surprised how quickly you can acquire the desired.

A prominent music master in New York who trained opera singers advised a girl with great musical ability—but who lacked self-confidence and self-assertion—to stand before a mirror every day and, assuming a magnificent pose, say to herself, "I, I, I," with all the emphasis and power she could muster. He coupled this by telling her to simultaneously imagine that she was the then leading singer of the day. He told her that as she affirmed herself and constantly played the role, she would acquire the habit of self-confidence, which would be worth everything to her. "Assume your art boldly and fearlessly," he told her, "and hold yourself with a dignity and power corresponding with the character." She followed his advice literally, and it proved to be worth more to this timid girl than scores of music lessons—increasing her confidence in herself wonderfully, and curing her of her shyness and timidity.

I am a great believer in the building power of affirmation; in the possibilities in persistently affirming the thing I am determined to do, in strengthening qualities in which I am weak, in building character, in making life noble.

The habit of *claiming as our own, as a vivid reality that which we desire,* has a tremendous magnetic power. There is a mysterious power in the spoken word, in the stalwart affirmation of a thought, which registers a profound impression on the subconscious mind—where the silent forces within us proceed to make the word flesh, to make the thought we affirm a reality.

"As the rain cometh down, and the snow from heaven, and returned not hither," says Isaiah, "but watered the earth and maketh it bring forth and bud, that it may give seed to the sower, and bread to the eater: So shall my word be that goeth out of my mouth: it shall not return unto me void, but it shall accomplish that which I please, and it shall prosper *in the thing* whereto I sent it."

Great things are done under our repeated conviction of our ability to do whatever we undertake. But many of us seldom ever give thought to the words we utter, to the reality that our uttered thoughts are living forces and are made flesh. Yet those words are continually being manifest in our bodies, shaping our faces and expressions, and molding our destinies to their likeness.

Those immersed in material things and who live only to make money, for example, *believe* they will make it—*know* that they can make it; *affirm* that they will make it. They do not say to themselves every morning, "Well, I do not know whether I can make anything today. I will try. I may succeed and I may not." They simply and positively asserts that they can do what they desire—and then start out to put into operation plans and forces which will bring it about.

When you assert yourself, assert the spiritual "I," the divinity in you, not the physical "I," the flesh of you. This would be mere egotism, and it is not asserting your egotism that will benefit you. This will only hurt you. But asserting the reality, the divinity of yourself will do everything for you.

Remember: "And the word was made flesh." First comes the spirit—then the flesh.

Your divine is your creative self, and when you assert the reality of this self, not the outward or bodily personality, you are asserting omnipotence, omniscience—you are asserting a power that can do things.

If we could only realize the creative power of affirmation, of assuming that we are the actual embodiment of the thing we long to be or to attain—not that we simply possess all the qualities of good, but that because the thought of them has arise from within us, because our thought of them are the expressions brought to consciousness of our inherent aspirations, we are these qualities—what lives we would live!

Affirmation is a living, vital force. The Bible owes much of its strength to this force. It is a book of affirmations, of strong, positive statements. But for this fact it would long ago have lost its power.

There is no parleying, no arguing, no attempt by the sacred writers to prove the truth of what they say. They merely assert, affirm dogmatically that certain things happened, and that certain other things would happen. Had they attempted to prove the authenticity of what they wrote, endeavored to convince the reader that they were honest men making genuine statements, they would have aroused doubts. But there is no appeal to sympathy, no appeal to the readers' credulity, no appeal for confirmation, no posing for effect, only unrelenting positiveness, persistent affirmations. They simply state facts and affirm principles. Every line breathes dominance, superiority and confidence. In this lies their tremendous power. There is no sentimental imploring even in the Lord's Prayer. It demands. It is "give us," "lead us not," "forgive us," etc.

In your talks with yourself, be like the Biblical writers. Don't wobble, or "think," or "hope." Say stoutly, "I am," "I can," "I will," "It is." Constantly, everlastingly affirm that you will become what your ambitions indicate as fitting and possible. Do not say, "I shall be a success *sometime*," say "I am a success now. Success is my birthright." Do not say that you are going to be happy in the future. Say to yourself, "I was intended for happiness, made for it, and I am happy now." Say with Walt Whitman, "'I, myself, am good fortune.'" Assert your actual possession of the things you need; of the qualities you long to have. Force your mind toward your goal; hold it there steadily, persistently, for this is the mental state that creates. This is what causes the word to be made flesh. The negative mind, which doubts, wavers, fears, creates nothing. It cannot send forth a positive, confident assertion.

We are constantly letting loose mighty thought forces, emotion forces, word forces which are forever multiplying and expressing themselves in the universal energy, which are forever fashioning our conditions. We are rich or poor, successful or unsuccessful, happy or unhappy, noble or ignoble, according to our use of our thought and word forces. The outer registration in the flesh, in *all* material circumstances and things, corresponds with the inner thought and the decisive positive word.

But remember it is the life, the driving power of the spirit, that gives the word its power. If you don't mean what you say, if you don't live the meaning into your words, they are mere idle breath.

You must *believe* what you affirm. If you affirm "I am health; I am prosperity; I am this or that," but do not believe it, you will not be helped by affirmation.

Remember, it is the life in your affirmations—your heart-to-heart talks—the *spiritual life*, that does the healing through the words which the intellect suggests. Just as faith without good works is of no avail without the spirit, your words, without the life behind them, are cold and ineffectual.

People who affirm by saying that "If God willing," or "If Providence so wills" they will then do this or that, little realize how the doubt expressed by the "if" takes the edge from their positiveness, and tends to produce negative minds.

The intensity of your affirmation of your confidence in your ability to do what you attempt is definitely and directly related to the degree of your achievement. To confront life's vicissitudes, we often need great projectile—power: It is easier to force a huge shell through the steel plates of a ship when projected with lightning speed from a cannon than to try to push it through slowly.

When you long for anything that it is right for you to have, affirm in perfect confidence that the thing is already yours; claim it as a reality. No matter whether you feel like it or not, affirm that you *must* feel like it, that you *will* feel like it, that you *do* feel like it—that whether you are doing so now or not, you have it within your capacity to do your best.

Then, do what you can on the material plane to make it yours, and soon you will reap what you have sown in thought and in positive creative affirmation.

Make your affirmations again and again, and do not wait for an opportunity to begin the thing you want to do. Make your opportunity. The power of affirmation will work miracles for you.

You will find that, just in proportion as you increase your confidence in yourself by the affirmation of what you are determined to be and to do, your ability will increase. No matter what other people may think or say about you, never allow yourself to doubt that you can do what you will to do. Boldly, confidently assert that there is a special place for you in the world, an individual role which only you can fill, and that you are going to fill it. Train yourself to expect great things of yourself. Never admit, even by your manner, that you think you are destined to do little things all your life.

Stoutly, constantly, everlastingly affirm that you will become what your ambitions indicate as fitting and possible. Do not say "I shall be a success sometime," say, "I am a success. Success is my birthright." Do not say that you are going to be happy *in the future*. Say to yourself, "I was intended for happiness, made for it, and I am happy."

Always stoutly affirm your ability to conquer.

Resolve every morning that you will be prosperous, that your destiny is prosperity.

The following strong, positive affirmations by C. D. Larson, are very suggestive and would make a splendid daily exercise:

"I will become more than I am."

"I will achieve more because I know that I can."

"I will recognize only that which is good in myself; that which is good in others."

"When adversity threatens, I will be more determined than ever in my life to prove that I can turn all things to good account."

"I will wish only for that which can give freedom and truth, which can add to the welfare of others."

"I will always speak to give encouragement, inspiration and joy."

"I will work to be of service to an ever-increasing number; and my ruling desire shall be to enrich, ennoble and beautify existence for all who may come my way."

Every day, impersonate someone you admire for his or her prosperity thinking. No matter if you make mistakes at first, stick to your resolve to be prosperous once and for all. Continually reinforce yourself throughout the day with positive affirmations.

But remember, if you do not act with the same grim resolution in making good your words as the French soldiers did at Verdun, they will be worse than useless. If you don't mean what you say, if you don't live the meaning into your words, they are mere idle breath. You might just as well be saying "I'm a successful playwright," yet not even be writing a play; or having written one, leave it in your desk drawer.

Give people the suggestion of invincibility. This will be worth more to you than a large amount of money without it.

Deciding to talk to yourself may at first seem silly to you, but you will soon get accustomed to it and feel its beneficial effects. Remember, you are already talking to yourself every minute of the day. Now you want to control the words you are telling yourself. Now you want to practice prosperity-empowering affirmations faithfully every day, throughout the day, and just before retiring at night. They will, if backed up by earnest effort to make your words true, do wonders in bringing about the desired results.

You will think more highly of yourself, you will have more self-respect, more self-confidence; you will believe more in yourself, you will have more assurance, more confidence in your ability, you will stand higher in your own estimate in every way. This does not mean that you will become egotistical or conceited, but simply that you will know yourself and your possibilities better, and be able to use to better advantage all the power and talent within you.

We all have the power to be prosperous. We were not born to be anything less. Does not every child come into this world eager to embrace it? experience it? be filled by it?

Don't be disappointed if you do not get immediate relief. Continue to talk to yourself in a confident manner, especially upon retiring, always affirming your ability to overcome your weakness, whatever it may be, and you will conquer it. Your will power will assist you, but conviction is a thousand times stronger than will power, and the constant affirmation of the ability of the power within you to overcome the thing which handicaps you will finally help you to conquer.

Always encourage yourself; always talk up, never down. In every possible way establish confidence in yourself, because a great self-faith is a powerful force, a creative force.

"According to your faith be it unto you."

PART III

THE POWER
OF THOUGHT IN
CREATING HEALTH

CHAPTER 24
The Power of the Mind Over the Body

t he body is but a servant of the mind.

Dominated by a great idea, the weak become strong, the timid brave, the vacillating resolute.

"I am sorry to learn that you are so sick that you cannot possibly be in your accustomed place tomorrow morning, Miss Hysee," said a minister's wife consolingly, according to the Chicago *Tribune*, "and I have hurried over to say that you need not feel the slightest uneasiness about the solo you were to sing in the opening anthem. Mr. Goodman and the chorister have arranged that Miss Gonby shall take the part, and. . . ."

"What?" screamed the popular soprano of the Rev. Dr. Goodman's church choir, and at once sat bolt upright in bed. "What! The old maid with the cracked voice try to sing my solo? Never!" With one hand she tore the bandage off her head, with the other she swept the medicines from the side table to the floor. "Tell Dr. Goodman and the chorister," she said, in a voice that rang through the house like the silvery tones of a bell, "to notify Miss Gonby she needn't mangle that solo. I'll be there."

When Mary I, a Roman Catholic, became queen of England and had Hugh Latimer—the Bishop of Worcester—and Nicholas Ridley— the bishop of Rochester who participated in compiling the *Book of Common Prayer*—burned at the stake for refusing to renounce their Protestantism, and Latimer and Ridley, as well as hundreds of others, went to the stake rejoicing, the spectators wondered at the smiles of ineffable peace which illumined their faces above the fierce glare of the flames, at the hymns of praise and thanksgiving heard amid the roar of crackling fire.

A butcher in New York, suffering terrible agony, was brought into a drug store. Investigation showed that he had slipped and fallen from a stepladder upon a sharp meat-hook upon which he was trying to hang a side of beef. He groaned in distress while his clothing was removed. He was pale and almost pulseless, and could not be moved without suffering great pain. But it was found that the hook had only pierced his clothing, the man being totally uninjured. When he learned this, his sufferings ceased at once. The pain which had been real to him wash caused wholly by his imagination.

Physicians reported a case a few years ago of a poor woman in Paris who was bitten by a dog near Notre Dame, and taken to the Hotel Dieu, where the wound was cauterized. Months afterward a student met her in the street and expressed surprise to see her alive. He told her that the dog which bit her was mad. The poor woman was seized immediately with spasms of the most violent kind. A doctor was summoned at once, but he could do nothing, and she soon died.

Dr. Chalmers, riding on a stagecoach by the side of the driver, said, "John, why do you hit that off leader such a crack with your lash?" "Away yonder there's a white stone; that off leader is afraid of that stone; so by the crack of my whip and the pain in his legs I want to get his idea off from it." Dr. Chalmers went home, elaborated the idea, and wrote "The Expulsive Power of a New Affection."

You must drive one idea by putting a new idea into the mind.

Lord Byron, when a boy, was warned by a fortuneteller that he should die in the thirty-seventh year of his age. That idea haunted him; and in his last illness he mentioned it as precluding all hope of his recovery. His physician said that it repressed the energy of spirit so necessary for nature in struggling with disease.

Every physician of experience and every reader of medical history must have been impressed many times with the power of a mind thus dominated and swayed by an idea or sentiment, a conviction or a resolution, to ward off disease or pain, or arrest its progress. On the other hand, they must have been equally impressed by the power of fear, or adverse convictions, to render the body more susceptible to contract disease or to hasten its development, even to fatal termination. Every physician knows that courageous people, with indomitable will, are not half as likely to contract contagious diseases as the timid, the vacillating, the irresolute.

Napoleon used to visit the plague hospitals even when the physicians dreaded to go, and actually put his hands upon the plague-stricken patients. He said the man who was not afraid could vanquish the plague.

Seneca had an almost fatal disease, but he said, "The thought of my father, who could not have sustained such a blow as my death, restrained me, and I commanded myself to live." And he did live.

Sir Walter Scott, at fifty-five, was deeply in debt. But, though far from being well, he was determined to pay every dollar. This resolution gave new courage to every faculty of the mind and every function of the body, and they rushed to the rescue under the stimulus. Every nerve and fibre said the debt must be paid, and it was paid.

It is difficult for a disease to get a foothold in a body where such an imperious will reigns supreme. It arrests the development of disease and often even defies death.

"No, we don't get sick," said an actor, "because we can't get sick. [Opera singer Adelina] Patti and a few other stars can afford that luxury, but to the majority of us it is denied. It is a case of 'must' with us; and although there have been times when, had I been at home, or a private man, I could have taken to my bed with as good a right to be sick as any one ever had, I have not done so, and have worn off the attack through sheer necessity. It's no fiction that will power is the best of tonics, and theatrical people understand that they must keep a good stock of it always on hand."

A tight-rope walker was so ill with lumbago that he could scarcely move. But when he was advertised to appear, he summoned all his will power, and traversed the rope several times with a wheelbarrow, according to the program. When through he doubled up and had to be carried to his bed, "as stiff as a frozen frog."

It is well known that men are often severely wounded in battle by shot or shell, yet during the excitement they are totally unconscious of pain or of any serious injury to themselves, until, perhaps, they discover their blood-soaked clothing, or some one tells them that they are shot. Then, as soon as the excitement abates, the very consciousness of their condition, with the power of the imagination to exaggerate, causes them to collapse. But, while the mind was intensely occupied, they did not feel the bullet or the piece of shell.

Every emotion tends to sculpture the body into beauty or into ugliness. Worrying, fretting, unbridled passions, petulance, discontent, every dishonest act, every falsehood, every feeling of envy, jealousy, fear—each has its effect on the system, and acts deleteriously like a poison or a deformer of the body.

"The time will come," says Humboldt, "when a sick man will be looked upon with the same abhorrence with which we now regard a thief or a liar, for the reason that the one condition is as much under the subjugation of mind as the other, and as susceptible of correction as the other." While this is an extreme view, there is no doubt the mind does have a powerful influence over the body.

Sir John Lubbock says in *The Pleasures of Life*: "It is said that the celebrated physiognomist, Campanella, could so abstract his attention from any sufferings of his body, that he was even able to endure the rack without much pain. Whoever has the power of concentrating his attention and controlling his will can emancipate himself from most of the minor miseries of life. He may have much cause for anxiety, his body may be the seat of severe suffering, and yet his mind will remain serene and unaffected; he may triumph over care and pain."

The *Youth's Companion* says, in substance, that the mysterious power of mind over the body has given rise to a new department in science, and that scientific experiments have recently been made in order to investigate what is called the psycho-physical—or, in simpler language, the soul-physical—phenomena. It has been discovered that there is a great chemical difference between that sudden, cold perspiration of a person under a deep sense of guilt and ordinary perspiration—and that the state of the mind can sometimes be actually determined by chemical analysis of the two: When brought in contact with selenic acid, the former produces a pink color which cannot be obtained from ordinary perspiration.

Anger changes the chemical properties of the saliva to a poison dangerous to life.

It is well known that sudden and violent emotions have not only whitened the hair in a few hours, but have caused death and insanity. One of Stanley's men was so overjoyed when Stanley announced that they were nearly through their hardships in the jungles of Africa, and were approaching the opposite ocean, that he went crazy and plunged into the wilderness, never to be seen again.

Professor James of Harvard, an expert in the mental sciences, says, "Every small stroke of virtue or vice leaves its ever so little scar. Nothing we ever do is, in strict literalness, wiped out." We look with pity and distrust upon those who vitiate their vitality, pollute and ruin their bodies by alcohol, while we ourselves may be changing our own bodies into hideous forms by what seem to us "innocent sins": A fit of anger may work a greater damage to the body and character than a drunken bout. Hatred may leave worse scars upon a clean life than the bottle. Jealousy, envy, anger, uncontrolled grief may do more to wreck the physical life than years of smoking. Anxiety, fretting, and scolding, may instill a more subtle poison into the system than the cigarette.

There are many ways of ruining the body besides smoking or getting drunk. Running for the train may injure the heart more than the tobacco habit. The lack of self-control, yielding to vulgar indulgences, and illicit imaginings, often injure lives infinitely more than the things which are popularly denounced. A sulky dog and a bad-tempered horse wear themselves out with half the labor that kindly creatures do. An ugly cow will not give down her milk, and a sour sheep will not fatten. Truly the great Hebrew seer enunciated a wonderful chemistry when he said, "As righteousness tendeth to life: so he that pursueth evil pursueth it to his own death" (Prov. 11:19).

No one thing contributes more to health or success than a strong, vigorous will. It is a perpetual health tonic, physically and mentally. It braces the system, enabling it to endure hardships, disappointments, and disease. It is a balance wheel; it unifies and steadies all the movements and functions of the body and mind, and wards off the destructive shocks which often wrench unbalanced minds from their orbits, producing discord instead of harmony. The will power is the great executive in the republic of the brain; and if this ruler be weak and vacillating, there will be no order or harmony in mind or body. This executive rules with an iron hand, with a grasp upon all the faculties which secure regularity and order and harmony both in the physical, the mental, and moral realm. A weak ruler cannot execute even good laws, and uncertainty and anarchy must ever reign in his dominion.

"Give me a great thought that I may quicken myself with it," the German philosopher, clergyman, and critic, Herder, said to his son as he lay near death. Newton, while at Cambridge, would sit up all night on some difficult mathematical problem, and would seem refreshed in the morning by his great triumph.

Next to the power of the will to ward off disease or maintain health is the might of conviction or belief. This is powerfully illustrated in an example I refer to again later, in the chapter "Why Grow Old?" The British medical journal *Lancet* once reported the case of an English lady who was abandoned in love when she was quite young and became insane. She lost all consciousness of the passage of time. Nothing could persuade her that she was still not living during the time period of her courtship with her lover. Though in fact he had left her, she stood by the window day after day and month after month, waiting for his return. The conviction that she was still young kept her from growing old in appearance. Americans who saw her a few years ago declared that she was not over twenty years of age, and yet she is seventy-five: What a power this suggests that there is in mind to carry youth into age, if we only knew how to use it!

Fear often kills even the robust, while courage is a great invigorator.

An English criminal, blindfolded and laid upon a table by physicians, was made to believe that he was bleeding to death, when only warm water was trickling from his arm, which was slightly scratched, but not enough to draw blood. The man died in a short time from fear. Could the bandage have been removed one instant, so that he might see that the vessel contained water instead of blood, he would have recovered immediately.

In Philadelphia several medical students agreed to experiment upon a companion. On meeting him, each would ask him what was the matter, adding that he looked very sick, or some similar remark. The young man went to bed sick and in a few days died.

Another man in a hospital was made to believe that a patient had just died of cholera in the same bed he was occupying. The alleged symptoms of the man who had died were described minutely, and soon similar symptoms were manifested by the listening patient, and he died, although the whole story was a fabrication.

A man in Providence, R. I., while engaged in putting down a carpet in July, 1891, drank from a goblet in which tacks had been placed, and, on being told of this fact, was at once afflicted with great pain from a tack lodging in his throat. He tried in vain to remove it, but the swelling increased, inflammation set in, and he consulted a doctor. The latter sent him for treatment to a hospital, where a careful examination showed that no tack had lodged there. The pain at once disappeared, and the man felt no further annoyance from the mythical tack.

In Marshall College, Aberdeen, I think it was, the students made the janitor believe they were going to execute him. They bound him, blindfolded him, laid his head upon a block, and quickly drew a wet cloth across his neck when, to their amazement, they found that he was dead.

Not long ago a prisoner was to be executed in France, and although he did not show the slightest signs of fear until he came in front of the ghastly instrument of death, yet, when he glanced upward at it, he turned deathly pale and at the same time his body became apparently lifeless. He was lifted upon the bascule, where he lay for twenty awful seconds, when the knife fell. The blood did not spurt eight or ten feet as is usual in such cases. The physicians found the heart filled with coagulated blood, which proved that he was dead before the knife fell.

The captured Texans in the Santa Fe expedition had marched until they seemed nearly dead from exhaustion. Yet upon being told that any one who should prove unable to walk would be shot, they set off at a good pace, which they kept up all day.

Ambroise Paré, describing the comet of 1520, says, "This comet was so horrible and dreadful that it engendered great terror to the people, so that many died, some with fear, others with illness."

A poor fellow once went to hang himself, but finding by chance a pot of money, he flung away the rope and went hurriedly home. The man who had hid the gold, upon finding it missing, hanged himself with the rope which the other man had left.

Success is a great tonic, and failure a great depressant.

The successful attainment of what the heart longs for, as a rule, improves health and happiness.

I have known hunters completely exhausted by a day's tramp, perhaps in rain or snow without any results, and scarcely able to put one foot ahead of the other, who became instantly so transformed at the sight of the long-looked-for deer or moose that they forgot their hunger, their fatigue, and were as lively as boys. The change of mental attitude enabled them to tramp again for hauls without rest and yet without fatigue.

Generally we not only find our treasure where our heart is, but our health also. Who has not noticed those of indifferent health, perhaps even invalids, and those who lacked energy and determination, suddenly becoming roused to a realization of unthought-of powers and unexpected health upon attaining some signaled success? The same is sometimes true of persons in poor health who have suddenly been thrown into responsible positions by death of parents or relatives, or who, upon sudden loss of property, have been forced to do what they had thought impossible before.

Every pure and uplifting thought, every noble aspiration for the good and the true, every longing of the heart for a higher and better life, every lofty purpose and unselfish endeavor, reacts upon the body, makes it stronger, more harmonious, and more beautiful.

Emperor Dom Pedro, while lying sick in Europe, received a telegram from his daughter acting as regent, saying that she had "signed a decree, totally, universally, and forever abolishing slavery in Brazil." The reaction from the news that the dream of his life was realized restored him completely.

A great horse tamer, said that an angry word would sometimes raise the pulse of a horse ten beats in a minute. If this is true of a beast, what can we say of its power upon a human being, and especially upon a child? Indeed, anger in the mother may poison her nursing child, causing illness and even convulsions. What then is the influence of a mother's passions upon *the fetus'* life?

The *Scientific American* reports the case of a lady in Bridgeport, Conn., who called a physician to extricate her false teeth which she had swallowed. When the physician arrived the muscles of her throat were in violent spasm, and she was apparently choking to death. Eminent physicians consulted and agreed to resort to tracheotomy. But one of the physicians felt something under the edge of the bed, which, upon examination, proved to be the missing molars. When the patient saw them the convulsions ceased immediately.

Madame Bernhardt, the famous actress, says: "I have never played *Phaedre* without fainting or spitting blood; and after the fourth tableau of *Theodora*, in which I kill Marcellus, I am in such a nervous state that I return to my dressing-room sobbing. If I do not weep I have a hysterical fit which is much more disagreeable to those around me, and more dangerous to the vases and other things near at hand."

Sir Humphry Davy cured a man of paralysis by inserting a thermometer in his mouth to take the temperature, the patient supposing it to be an appliance to cure that disease.

Persons who have been bedridden for years, and lifelong invalids who were considered almost helpless, have risen from their beds when the house was on fire, and have not only helped to rescue others, but have helped to clear the house of furniture and valuables. Physicians who have been convinced that bedridden patients have been laboring under a delusion have often cured them by resorting to giving an alarm of fire, or applying to their flesh a red-hot poker, thus forcing them out of bed and sometimes out of the house.

Cross, crabbed, fretful individuals, even when suffering agony are sometimes completely changed by a call from some genial friend or by the news of some good fortune. The excruciating pain is banished, the face lightens, and a pleasant smile takes the place of a scowl. The person is completely transformed, yet the change has been only a mental one, and has come from no medicine or treatment.

Bulwer advises us to refuse to be ill, never to tell people we are ill, never to own it ourselves. Illness is one of those things which one should resist on principle. Never say you are weak if you wish to be strong, or fatigued if you would be perpetually fresh. All these discordant pictures of the mind have an influence on the body.

Instead of bracing ourselves against disease by expelling every discordant thought, and barring every avenue of possible approach, as we would guard our homes against thieves or contagion, we render ourselves an easy prey to the enemy by watching for the symptoms of the very disease we fear, and dwelling upon, and picturing in the mind, the physical features of the malady. Thus the power to resist the disease is lessened. Instead of fighting the thousand enemies which dog our heels from the cradle to the grave, we put ourselves into sympathy with them, and invite their approach by rendering ourselves more susceptible.

Every one knows the depressing influence of fear upon patients with certain diseases, especially heart disease. The action of the heart is weakened, and the vitality is lowered by concentrating one's mind upon that organ.

Who can estimate the woe, the anxiety, the suffering, caused by fear, in all its variety of forms?

"Where are you going?" asked an Eastern pilgrim on meeting the Plague one day. "I am going to Bagdad to kill five thousand people," was the reply. A few days later the same pilgrim met the Plague returning. "You told me you were going to Bagdad to kill five thousand people," said he, "but instead you killed fifty thousand." "No," said the Plague. "I killed only five thousand, as I told you I would; the others died of fright."

A Philadelphian consulted a physician for what he feared was a hopeless case of heart disease, but found instant relief when he discovered that the rasping sound which he heard at every deep breath was due to a little pulley in his patent suspenders.

Fear and anxiety destroy the red blood globules; and if they are reduced below a certain proportion, disease and death ensue. Many have lost their lives by because they were brought up with the conviction perpetually thrust upon their minds that they must die of whatever disease their parents did.

How many, for example, have the conviction that they have inherited the seeds of some terrible disease, such as cancer. They have been told, "Now be careful, you know that your mother went this very same condition." And their conviction is then often coupled with the fact that their physician has told them that this condition is liable to show itself soon after the age of forty. It is like sending someone to a prison or to the gallows because his or her parent committed robbery or murder. As a result, the person is cruelly robbed of any resisting power the mind may have, and so the person lives expectantly looking for the symptoms of this disease—and an ordinary sore often then develops into an ulcer.

Sudden shocks to the nervous system are destructive of health and harmony.

The hair of an English banker became white in three days after he met with great financial reverses. A German physician was crossing a bridge when he saw a boy struggling in the water below. He rushed into the stream and seized the drowning boy, only to discover that it was his own son. His hair turned white in one day. Marie Antoinette's black hair turned white a few days before her execution. Captain P of Vermont, captured by the British in 1813 on the Canadian frontier, was put under guard and told that he would be shot in the morning. His jet-black hair turned white during the night.

Good news will elate you correspondingly, but by a similar process.

Watch the sick in the hospital ward and notice the faces beam with gladness, or cloud with sorrow, as the physician passes from bed to bed, and reveals in a smile, a perplexed look, or a shake of his head, hope or despair for the patient. How eagerly each watches the doctor's face for a ray of hope! If the fevered patients get encouragement, their parched tongues immediately moistens, their eye brightens, and their hot, dry skin becomes moist and cool. No drug could have wrought such magic as that one ray of hope. Nothing has touched the patient—an idea, a sentiment only—and yet he or she is completely transformed. Yet if the doctor but shake his or her head in doubt, the secretions stop, and the cold, clammy sweat appears. Despair settles over the patient's face. All the centers of life's energy are depressed.

A flaw in the thought will appear in the statue. Raphael could not paint the face of Christ with Judas for a model. Phidias could not call an angel from the marble while be had a fiend in his mind.

We can never accomplish anything great without a high ideal, and can we expect to gain that exquisite poise, that rhythmic pose which we call health, and which a thousand conditions must be met to produce, while we have a defective ideal in the mind. The mind devours everything that is brought to it—the true, the false, the good, the bad—and it will produce soundness or rottenness, beauty or deformity, harmony or discord, truth or error, according to the quality of the food we give it.

"As a man thinketh in his heart, so is he."

The body is molded and fashioned by the thought. If you were to try to make yourself beautiful, you would not begin by contemplating ugliness. Nor would you try to make yourself graceful by practicing awkwardness. We can never gain health by contemplating disease any more than we can reach perfection by dwelling upon imperfection, or harmony through discord.

We should *keep a high ideal of health and harmony constantly before the mind*; and we should fight every discordant thought and every enemy of harmony as we would fight a temptation to crime. Never affirm or repeat about your health what you do not wish to be true. Do not dwell upon your ailments nor study your symptoms. Never allow yourself to be convinced that you are not complete master of yourself. Stoutly affirm your own superiority over bodily ills, and do not acknowledge yourself the slave of an inferior power.

Something of the miraculous power of Christ, no doubt, was due to his superior moral, mental, and physical harmony. He seems to have been sent into the world to show *the possibilities of a perfect personhood*, eliminated of inherited or acquired weaknesses, which so limit and cripple other lives. There was a superb harmony in his moral and mental as well as spiritual touch which banished the physical discord of disease. He demonstrated the superiority of a perfect physical system over the petty ills and discords which haunt the inferior physique; the superiority of mind over matter, the supremacy of a rounded manhood over the discords and limitations of inferior development. He showed that a healthy body tends to make a healthy soul, and that a healthy soul tends to produce a harmonious body. He illustrated the uplifting, purifying, and sustaining power of the mind over the body.

Physicians tell us that perfect *health is impossible to the self-dissector*—those who are constantly thinking of themselves, and studying themselves, and are forever on the alert for the least symptom which indicates disease.

Those without will power, those who are vacillating, uncertain, do not possess their very selves—even physically—and are much more susceptible to disease and physical infirmities than those with a strong will. The former have no hold, no grip upon themselves. They are blown hither and thither by everybody's advice, taking every patent medicine recommended or advertised, impairing rather than strengthening themselves by useless drugging.

There is no faculty more susceptible to training, none which responds more readily to drill, than the will power, although it is seldom trained in school or college. No faculty can do more for us in forming habits which bless or curse, but it is seldom cultivated. It holds our success or failure in its grasp—our happiness or misery—but we often allow it to run wild.

There is a divine remedy placed within us for many of the ills we suffer: The mind is the natural protector of the body.

If we only knew how to use our power of will and mind to protect ourselves, many of the physicians would be out of employment—and many of us would be able to carry youth and cheerfulness with us into the teens of the second half of our lives.

CHAPTER 25
Thought Causes
Disease and Health

I t is not necessary to appeal to scientific experiments alone to prove the control of the mind over health and disease. Everyday experience gives ample demonstration. Striking and interesting incidents by the hundred have been collected and published by physicians, but a few will suffice.

For example, someone dies of "shock." What does that mean? Simply that some sudden and powerful thought has so deranged the bodily mechanism that it has stopped. Fright—that is, *a thought of fear*—stopped the heart's action. Excitement set it beating so hard that a blood-vessel burst in the head.

Or, a loved one dies and the thought of grief prevents nutrition, repair of waste, and the performance of other bodily functions dependent on normal mental condition, and the person pines away and dies from some a condition the enfeebled body could not resist—from no disease at all but the sick and mourning thought.

At one time, a trolley wire in London broke and fell into the street with sputtering fire. A young lady, seemingly as well as any one, was about to board the car, but, on seeing the accident, fell dead. Nothing had touched her. She had suffered no harm. She simply thought she was in danger, and thought so intensely that something gave way and separated her spirit from her body. A mind more composed, less easily startled, would have saved her life.

A beautiful young lady was struck in the face by a golf stick. It broke her jaw, but that was healed in a few weeks. However, a scar was left that marred her beauty. The idea of disfigurement so preyed upon her mind that she shrank from meeting people, and melancholia became habitual. A trip to Europe, expensive treatment by specialists, did no good. The idea that she was marred and scarred took all joy from her life, all strength from her body. She soon could not leave her bed. Yet no physician was able to find any organic disease.

These are strange stories, no doubt, but each illustrates what diseased thought can do in overcoming perfectly healthy bodily functions.

Fright and grief have often blanched human hair in a few hours or a few days. Ludwig, of Bavaria, Marie Antoinette, Charles I of England, and the Duke of Brunswick are historic examples, and every little while modern instances occur. The supposed explanation is that strong emotion has caused the formation of chemical compounds, probably of sulphur, which changed the color of the oil of the hair. Such chemical action is caused by thought, instead of gradually by advancing years. On the other hand, sickness and disease have been known to give way before strong thought of any kind: excitement, alarm, or great joy.

Benvenuto Cellini, the 16th century Italian sculptor, when about to cast his famous statue of Perseus, now in the Loggia dei Lanzi, at

Florence, was forced by a sudden fever to go home and to bed. In the midst of his suffering, one of his workmen rushed in to say: "O Benvenuto, your statue is spoiled, and there is no hope whatever of saving it." Dressing hastily, he rushed to his furnace, and found his metal "caked." Ordering dry oak wood brought, he fired the furnace, fiercely working in the falling rain, stirred the channels, and saved his metal. In telling of this incident, Cellini said, "After all was over, I turned to a plate of salad on a bench there and ate with a hearty appetite and drank, together with the whole crew. Afterward I retired to my bed, healthy and happy, for it was now two hours before morning, and slept as sweetly as though I had never felt a touch of illness." His overpowering idea of saving his statue not only drove the idea of illness from his mind, but also drove away the physical condition and left him well.

It is related of Muley Moluc, the Moorish leader, that, when lying ill, almost worn out by incurable disease, a battle took place between his troops and the Portuguese. Roused by the crisis of the fight, he rose from his litter, rallied his army, led them to victory, and then instantly sank exhausted—and expired.

Whence comes the power which enables a frail, delicate woman, invalid for years, unable to wait upon herself, with hardly strength enough to walk across the floor, to rush upstairs and to drag out sleeping children from a burning home? Whence comes the strength which enables such a delicate creature to draw out furniture and bedding from a house on fire? Certainly no new strength has been added to the muscle, no new strength to the blood, but still she does what, under ordinary conditions, would have been impossible for her. In the emergency she forgets her weakness, she sees only the emergency. The danger of her the loss of children and home stares her in the face, and it is this changed condition of the mind, not changed blood or muscle, that gives her the needed energy. The muscle has furnished the power, but the conviction of the ability to do the thing was first necessary. The fire, the danger, the excitement, the necessity of saving life and property, the temporary forgetfulness of her supposed weakness—these were necessary to work the mind to the proper state.

Evidence of this power of mind over the body is made manifest to us in many ways. The wonder is that humanity—and in particular the medical profession—has been so long recognizing this, and to this day is still undecided in its acceptance.

One of the highest medical authorities, for example—Dr. William Osler, summoned by King Edward VII from Johns Hopkins University to be Regius Professor of Medicine at Oxford University—wrote in the *Encyclopedia Americana*:

"The psychical method has always played an important, though largely unrecognized, part in therapeutics. It is from faith, which buoys up the spirits, sets the blood flowing more freely and the nerves playing their part without disturbance, that a large part of all cure arises. Despondency, or lack of faith, will often sink the stoutest constitution almost to death's door; faith will enable a spoonful of water or a bread pill to do almost miracles of healing when the best medicines have been given over in despair. The basis of the entire profession of medicine is faith in the doctor, his drugs, and his methods."

At the same time, Dr. Smith Ely Jelliffe, of Columbia University, wrote in the same encyclopedia:

"Unquestionably the oldest and yet youngest therapeutic agent is suggestion. The power to heal by faith is not the special property of any sect or class, nor the exclusive right of any system. Belief in gods and goddesses, prayer to idols of wood, of stone, of gossamer fiction, faith in the doctor, belief in ourselves engendered from

within or without—these are all expressions of the great therapeutic value for healing that resides in the influence of mental
states on bodily functions. These will not move mountains, they
cannot cure consumption; they do not influence a broken leg, nor
an organic paralysis; but suggestion, in its various forms, may be,
and is one of the strongest aids to all therapeutic measures. Of
its abuse by designing hypnotists, blackmailers, clairvoyants, and
a motley crew of parasites, space does not permit particulariza-
tion. The human mind is credulous—it believes what it wants or
wills to believe—and the use of suggestion in therapeutics is one
of great power for good and for evil."

In this statement Dr. Jelliffe is being ultra-conservative, for he
would have certainly admitted that the knitting of a broken bone
is vitally affected by the state of mind of the patient, which has to
do with all the functions of breathing, digestion, assimilation, and
excretion. And a sturdy resolution has, with proper conditions of climate and hygiene, aided in the recovery from the milder stages of
consumption, while even the stagnation of paralysis has been stirred
into life by violent shocks to the mind and nervous system.

Long ago, Sir James Y. Simpson said "The physician knows not,
and practices not the whole extent of his art, when he neglects the
marvelous influence of the mind over the body."

We are, by now, familiar with the effects certain thoughts can
have on our emotions—our passions—but we have yet fully accepted,
studied, or incorporated into our medical practice or personal lives
the effects that our thought can have on disease (the production of it),
health (the restoration of it), or death (the cause of it). When we do one
day fully accept, study, and incorporate into our lives and medical
practice the role of thought on health and disease, we will grow in
heretofore unimagined proportions—as individuals and civilization.

CHAPTER 26
Strengthening Deficient Faculties

few people are well-balanced, well-rounded. A great many have splendid ability in certain lines, good education, fine training, and yet have some deficiency in their make-up which cripples the whole life and dwarfs the results of their utmost industry.

Many of us have some little, contemptible weakness which offsets our strong qualities and ruins their effectiveness.

How humiliating it is to be conscious that one has dragged up to maturity some such weakness or deficiency without realizing it, or at least without having it remedied. The deficiency is slight, perhaps, and yet if it cripples life, if it mars achievement, if it is a perpetual humiliation, if it submits us to a thousand embarrassments and keeps us from rising in the world, what a terrible misfortune it is!

What a pity to see a giant in possibility tied down by some little, contemptible weakness which cripples what might have been a magnificent career! If parent or teacher would only point out to a child a weakness which, perhaps, will be fatal if not remedied, and teach it how to guard against it, how to strengthen the defective quality by mental exercise, what a tremendous help it would give to the child, perhaps preserving it from failure.

If you are conscious of a mental weakness, a deficient faculty, using a little concentration, thinking in the opposite direction, and dwelling upon the perfect faculties or qualities you desire would soon put you in a normal condition. And it is normal thinking that makes the normal life.

If, for example, melancholia, taking too serious a view of things, is your fatal weakness, you can entirely remedy this condition in a little while by perpetually concentrating the thought upon the bright, cheerful, sunny side of things. If you persist in this, after a while you will seldom have a depressing, gloomy thought. When you do, fling it out of your mind. Thrust it out as you would the thief from your house. Just because a burglar gets into your room, is that any reason why you should let him stay there?

Shyness, too, sometimes becomes a disease; but it is a disease of the imagination only, and can be easily overcome by driving the thought of it out of the mind and holding the opposite thought; by just making up your mind that you are not being watched by everybody, that people are too busy about their own selfish aims and ambitions to be watching you.

If you leave your weak faculties alone—do not exercise them, do not try to enlarge them—how can you expect to strengthen, correct, them? You cannot acquire a symmetrical body by simply exercising the arms. The same is true of the mental faculties. Those which are not used deteriorate.

If you long for a thing and strive for it with all your might persistently enough and long enough, you cannot help approximating it; you must get what you wish in some degree.

If, for example, you wish to become wiser in some area, and your call for wisdom is loud enough and persistent enough, you will become wise.

If you wish health, then say health, think health, hold the picture of yourself in health before your mind as the sculptor holds that of the statue to be carved from the marble. Hold the idea of health persistently, and you will create health.

Do you wish relief from poverty? Hold the idea of having plenty to use, the idea of enjoying not hoarding, the idea of blessing not oppressing, and prosperity will as surely come to you as a rose from a bud.

"Affirm that which you wish, and it will manifest in your life."

Consequently, every time you nurse a weakness thought or harbor a thought that depresses you, you make friends with it and invite it to stay. When you dwell upon the dark side of things, then you are encouraging everything which is darkening your life and hampering your career.

If you hold persistently in the mind the picture of the faculty which is the opposite of the one you think is deficient, you will soon bring about the desired results.

If, for example, you long for a beautiful character, claim it, assume it, stick to it with all possible tenacity, and you will not only prepare the mind to receive it, but will also increase the power of the mind to attract it.

We all know that in some way, somehow, most people get the things they long for and struggle for persistently. And even if they do not get all that they desire, they approximate much nearer to it, get much more of it than they would if they did not claim it stoutly and struggle for it persistently. We have the ability to change our attractive power, to increase it or diminish it, just in proportion to the in tensity of our yearning for it and assuming it as our birthright.

Many people become morbid in dwelling upon the thought that they are peculiar in some respect. They think they have certain tendencies or peculiarities—inherited or otherwise acquired—and are always looking for the appearance of these tendencies or peculiarities in themselves. This is just the way to make them appear! For what we encourage in the mind or hold there persistently, we get. These people continually increase the unwanted by worrying about it and dwelling upon its sad effects on themselves. They become sensitive about their idiosyncrasies. They never like to speak of or hear of them, and yet the very consciousness that they possess them takes away their self-confidence and mars their achievement.

More often than not, the majority of these abnormalities and peculiarities are simply imaginary or are exaggerated by imagination. It is just that they have been nursed and brooded over as possibilities so long that they become real to the sufferers. The remedy lies in doing precisely the opposite: dwelling on the perfect qualities, and ignoring any possible shortcomings.

The mere assumption of a desired quality with all your will-power, and the determination to possess it which knows no retreat, are wonderful helps in achieving the things you long for. By holding the desired quality-thought persistently in your mind, you will soon no longer think thoughts of any quality which you now consider a deficiency. It will soon disappear, and you will gain confidence and that which you desire.

Do not be afraid of claiming and repeating over and over again the qualities you long to attain or the object of your ambition. Keep your desires in the forefront of your thought. Resolve that you will possess these things and will accept nothing else, and you will be surprised to see how rapidly you will make yourself a magnet to draw the things you yearn for.

CHAPTER 27
Our Mental Friends and Foes

We can make our minds art galleries of beauty or chambers of horror; we can furnish them with anything we please.

A thousand times better to allow thieves to enter your home and steal your most valuable treasures, to rob you of money or property, than to allow the enemies of your success and happiness—discordant thoughts, disease thoughts, sick thoughts, morbid thoughts, fear thoughts, jealous thoughts—to enter your mind and steal your comfort, rob you of that peace and serenity without which life is a living tomb.

We think in mental images. They always precede the physical realities. The mental pictures are copied into the life, etched upon the character. The whole physical economy is constantly translating these images, these mental pictures, into life, into the character.

We sometimes see the power of thought strikingly illustrated when a great sorrow or a disappointment or a heavy financial loss in a short time so changes the personal appearance of people that their friends scarcely recognize them.

The value of our life output will depend very largely upon the degree with which we can keep ourselves in harmony by keeping from our minds the multitude of enemies which kill initiative and neutralize efficiency through destructive friction.

Most of us fail to appreciate the difference between the influence of diverse thoughts or suggestions. We all know how a cheerful, optimistic, encouraging idea gives a thrill of well-being, how it rejuvenates, recreates. We feel its tingle to the tips of our fingers. It permeates and quickens as an electric shock of joy and gladness; it brings with it fresh courage, hope, and a new lease of life.

We each build our own world, make our own atmosphere. We can fill it with difficulties, fears, doubts, and despair and gloom, so that the whole of life will be influenced to gloom and disaster; or he can keep the atmosphere clear, transparent and sweet by dispelling every gloomy, envious, malicious thought.

Those who can keep their thoughts right can substitute hope for despair, courage for timidity, decision and firmness for hesitancy, doubt or uncertainty. Those who can keep out the enemies of his success by filling their minds with friendly thoughts, optimistic, courageous, hopeful thoughts, have a tremendous advantage over those who are the victims of their moods: the slaves of the "blues," discouragement, doubt. Those who can master their thoughts can accomplish more with five talents than those who cannot master his moods can with ten.

Whatever you do or do not do for a living, resolve that no morbid, discordant, sick thoughts shall get access to your mind.

What a tremendous amount of wear and tear, wrenching, rasping, aging friction we could prevent, if we had only been taught as children always to shut the doors of our minds to all tearing down, destructive, enemy thoughts, and to hold in the mind ideas that uplift and encourage, that cheer, gladden and refreshen, encourage and give hope! I have known instances where gloomy, melancholy thoughts sapped the life of more vitality and energy in a few hours than weeks of hard work would have taken out of the man.

To get rid of our thought enemies requires constant, systematic, persistent effort. We cannot accomplish anything worthwhile without energy and determination. We can only expect to keep the enemies of our peace and prosperity out of the mind by energetically resisting them, driving them out of consciousness, locking the door of the mind against them.

Ideas, thoughts, like everything else, a tract what is akin to them. The thoughts which dominate in the mind will tend to drive out their opposites. Optimism will drive out pessimism. Cheerfulness will tend to drive out despondency; hope, discouragement Fill your mind with the sunshine of love, and all hatred and jealousy will flee. Those dark, mental shadows cannot live in love's sunshine.

You cannot affirm too often or too vigorously the idea that you were made in the image of perfection, love, beauty, and truth; made to express these qualities and not their opposites. Say to yourself: "Every time an idea of hatred, malice, revenge, discouragement, or selfishness comes into my mind, I have done myself an injury. I have struck myself a blow that is fatal to my peace of mind, my happiness, my efficiency; all these enemy thoughts cripple my advance in life. I must destroy them immediately by neutralizing them with their opposites."

Persistently keep your mind filled to overflowing with good thoughts, generous, magnanimous, charitable thoughts; love thoughts, truth thoughts, health thoughts, harmony thoughts—and all the discordant thoughts will have to go. Two opposite thoughts cannot exist in the mind at the same moment. Truth thoughts are the antidote for error; harmony, for discord; and good, for evil.

Love, charity, benevolence, kindliness, and goodwill towards others all arouse the noblest feelings and sentiments within us. They are life-giving, uplifting. They make for health, harmony, power. They put us in tune with the Infinite.

CHAPTER 28
Mental Self-Thought Poisoning

e very thought or emotion vibrates through every cell in the body and leaves an influence like itself.

The body is but a mass of billions of cells so closely tied together and interrelated that they are instantly affected by every vicious thought, mood, or unfortunate conviction.

The normal law of our lives is wholeness. Discord of any kind—ill health, disease, weakness—is abnormal, foreign to our real selves, to the truth of our being.

The time will come when we shall listen to the cry of the cells, suffering from disease and discord of our negative thoughts and attitudes, just as we now listen to the cry of a child, and we shall antidote the discord with the balm of soothing, healing thoughts. We shall speak harmony, peace, health to the discordant cells until disease is neutralized and harmony reigns.

In early phonograph records of our great singers, the slightest error—a note a little too sharp or flat—was faithfully reproduced. In just the same way every mistake, every sidestep from virtue, every slip, every blunder we make in life is faithfully recorded in our cells. The phonograph would only say the words that were on the record. You must make a recording upon your cells which has on it the words, the, sentiment, you want them to repeat.

Few people realize that they are constantly running thoughts through their minds and indulging in emotions and passions which are disease producers. Every evil feeling towards another is a little disease producer. Every discordant thought, feeling, or emotion must pay the penalty in the physical manifestation of some physical discord.

Since we know that whatever we hold in the mental attitude will be reproduced in the body, how comparatively easy and scientific character-building and self-building should become! Even thoughts, ideals, sentiments, and emotions which are only mechanically assumed, still become faithfully outpictured in our lives.

Whatever we think about a great deal, we tend to become like. How easily we can pick out of a crowd the one in whom dominant thoughts have dwelt long upon sacred things!

Did you ever realize that it is possible to read in your face and manner the record of your thoughts; that your face is a bulletin board upon which is advertised what has been going on in your mind for years?

It was a saying of Swedish scientists and mystic, Emanuel Swedenborg that "a man writes his life in his physique; and thus the angels discover his autobiography in his structure."

You may have supposed that your thoughts were secret; but the fact is that they are all displayed upon your face bulletin. In reality, we can hide nothing, for we radiate the truth of ourselves. What we think is written on our countenance.

Right thinking and right living make a right life. The body, being a product of the mind, must necessarily be like it.

It is well known that inflammation or trouble of any kind anywhere in the body is aggravated by concentrating the mind upon it or worrying about it.

Many people make robust health impossible by holding the sickly thought, the thought of their weakness, the picture of diseased tissues somewhere in the body, and, of course, their general health corresponds with this diseased model, for the thought furnishes the pattern which is reproduced in the body.

We cannot be physically vigorous until we hold the vigorous thought.

Always try to realize that truth, health, and harmony are not something far away from you, but are always with you, in you. Realizing their presence as an actual present fact will help you wonderfully.

Just try the experiment of thinking of yourself as an absolutely perfect being, possessing superb health, a magnificent body, a vigorous constitution, a sublime mind, and capable of standing any amount of strain.

Never allow yourself to have a defective, crippled, dwarfed ideal of yourself; never entertain such an imperfect health model for an instant, for these mental patterns of yourself will gradually begin to be reproduced in your physical condition.

Your ideal, your conviction of your health, your thoughts, emotions, moods, and mental attitudes, send a constant succession of vibrations through every cell, every organ, and through all the functions of the body. There is a perpetual succession of these impulses through the entire mass of the millions of cells.

If we scratch with a nail or some other hard substance on the end of along piece of timber, the sound waves are transferred through the entire length. Every cell in the huge timber feels the vibration and passes it on. So, every thought, emotion, every sense of fear, worry, jealousy, hatred, that enters your mind instantly makes itself felt through every cell in your body, and affects it according to its own nature.

We are beginning to learn that the cells of the stomach and of all the other organs are but an extended brain, so to speak, and that they are very seriously affected by anything which affects the brain. Hence all the bodily functions refuse to do good work when the mind is disturbed, just as the mental faculties refuse to give up their best when they are in discord.

It is very unfortunate that there is such a deep-seated conviction in the human race that the mind is *confined* to the brain cells alone. There is every evidence that there is intelligence in cells all through the body.

Many interesting experiments have been made to prove this theory. If we slice a bit of tissue, which, of course, is all cells, from any part of the living body and put it upon a slide of the microscope where there is the least trace of nitroglycerin, the cells quickly, instinctively, shrink from contact with the powerful chemical, drawing themselves back as far as possible from the poisonous substance, which they evidently regard as their fatal enemy.

On the other hand, if we bring it in contact with some harmless drug such as capsaicin, instead of shrinking they rush towards it and give every evidence that they seek it.

If we put opium in contact with these cells they vibrate rapidly as though in a fatal tremor, and quickly succumb to its influence and become narcotized.

We find this power of selection even in the lowest forms of animal life, such as the amoeba, the simplest form of one-cell structure. Even where there is no brain structure whatever the cell recognizes its enemies, from which it tries to make escape and to seek a hiding-place.

The whole body is a mass of cells, and this is why the cells in any part of the body, when disarranged or diseased, respond so quickly to mental treatment. It is because there is intelligence in them, because they are a part of the mind themselves. They have a mental quality, and the combined mentality of the brain cells and all the other cells in the body can restore any group of cells in any organ or tissue when they begin to shrink and shrivel, as in old age, or when they become diseased.

Mind is the great healer, the great restorer. It is the *mind* within and back of the cell structure that, by virtue of the thoughts it holds, restores lost balance and heals disease.

The organs are susceptible to mental influence. Structural changes in the different organs are often due to chemical changes in their development through the influence of mentally poisonous thoughts, emotions, or attitudes.

I know a man who so poisons his system in a few minutes by a hot temper that he does not get over it for days. Jealousy will so poison the system as completely to change the nature of its victim in a very short time. There is nothing which will burn out the life cells and ruin harmony and efficiency quicker than the violent indulgence of the explosive passions. Indigestion or dyspepsia often follow fierce domestic quarrels. Five minutes of hot temper may work such a havoc in the delicate cell life of the nervous system that it will take weeks or months to repair the injury—or it will never be repaired. Multitudes of people have died from heart trouble induced by uncontrolled passions.

Whenever there is any disturbance in the mind from any cause there is starvation in the tissues of the body, because perfect nourishment is impossible when discord is present anywhere. The digestive organs—the liver and stomach for instance—are so dependent upon harmony that when there is the slightest mental disturbance they can not act normally, and digestion is interfered with. And we all know how quickly our digestion is affected by our moods, our mental processes, our mental attitude. A sudden shock caused by a telegram or letter containing bad news will often completely arrest the entire digestive processes, which will not be resumed until the mind is again in comparative harmony.

If we could examine the stomach after a severe mental shock from bad news, we should find the natural flow of digestive fluids from the digestive follicles suspended; the follicles would be parched and feverish and for the time absolutely deprived of their digestive power.

So closely is the digestive apparatus connected with the brain that an accident of any kind, or great fear, will instantly stop all of its processes, just as though they had received an, imperative command to cease working.

The finding of disgusting things mingled with our food will often so affect our stomachs that we can not eat anything for some time afterwards. Our sensation of hunger departs instantly and the very thought of food nauseates us. Just think of the tremendous power thought must have to cause this instantaneous revulsion and complete cessation of all the digestive processes!

Correspondingly, it does not follow that just because you eat a great deal that you are properly nourished. It often happens that owing to the impairment of the efficiency of the digestive fluids—through mental from poisoning mental discord—many of the tissues, even when there is plenty of food in the digestive organs, suffer seriously from starvation.

During fits of anger and jealousy, acute worry, or when one is suffering from fear, the gastric juices, for example, become deficient in digestive essentials, become diluted, and hence can only partially digest the food. They are entirely lacking in some of the ingredients which are absolutely necessary to perfect digestion and assimilation.

When gastric juice is secreted under unfavorable conditions, during mental depression, when the person is suffering from fear, worry, jealousy, revenge, anger, or hatred, it is of a very inferior quality. There is something lacking; it is not a perfect digestive fluid. The chemical proportions are not normal, and, in fact, there is often actual poison present.

Some people so poison themselves mentally during their meals that they can not digest their food. It is a dangerous thing to quarrel and to be angry and hateful at any time, but especially so during meals. Whatever you do, do not take your troubles to the table with you, for there is nothing which will ruin digestion quicker than a troubled, worried mind.

However uncomfortable, unhappy, worried, or troubled you may be at other times of the day, it is absolutely imperative to keep as happy and as harmonious as possible during meals and the digestive hours; otherwise the gastric fluids will seriously lack the essential digestive element.

If you carry your worries to the table, bring surly, ugly moods to your meals, you are in fact poisoning everything they eat.

The circulation of the blood is also very seriously affected by all thoughts which depress and discourage.

Many people, after prolonged fits of anger or acute attacks of jealousy and fear, have colds, indigestion, or headaches.

Some have perpetual severe headaches, which are due to mental poisoning from violent fits of anger and the corresponding resultant general shock to the mental system, and also to impairment of nerve nutrition. Many suffer from perpetual selfishness-poisoning.

We are much more susceptible to disease when suffering from any sort of mental discord, discouragement, or the "blues," because of the cell damage due to the presence of chemical changes, the impairment of nutrition, imperfect digestion, and mental self-poisoning.

Why do we learn so quickly that on the physical plane hot things burn us, sharp tools cut us, bruises make us suffer, and endeavor to avoid the things which give pain, and to use and enjoy the things that give pleasure and comfort, while in the mental realm we are constantly burning ourselves, gashing ourselves, poisoning our brain, our blood, our secretions with deadly, destructive thoughts, moods, and emotions? How we suffer from these thought lacerations, these mental bruises, these burnings of passion—and yet we do not learn to exclude the causes of all this suffering!

Whatever improves the health of the mind improves the health of the body. The uplifting, inspiring, cheerful and optimistic thought is not only a great mental tonic, but a physical tonic also.

How can your body have resisting power to ward off disease when you are all the time acknowledging its weakness and inferiority? How can you expect harmony in your physical kingdom when you are constantly reflecting mental discord?

Never allow yourself to be convinced that you are not complete master of yourself. Stoutly affirm your own superiority over bodily ills, and do not acknowledge yourself the slave of an inferior power.

Nothing else will hasten the development of a disease so quickly as that attitude of mind which tends to lower the vitality by constantly looking for the thing we dread, always expecting and watching for every symptom which heralds it, because we are powerfully affected by the imagination, which builds all sorts of hideous predictions and forebodings out of the things we fear and dread.

This perpetual expectancy of something which is going to make us suffer and finally kill us has a terribly depressing influence, because it cuts off hope and expectancy—the very things we live upon.

Every physician knows what a tremendous healing, restorative force comes to a patient who has been in great danger when the patient is assured by a physician in whom the patient has great confidence that he or she is going to get well. The mere expectancy of relief from suffering through some noted specialist or a remedy in which the patent has great faith often materially affects the chemistry of the patient's body in all its physical processes, arouses the healing potencies, creative energies within, and completely changes the patient.

Indeed, there is often a very marked improvement in the patient immediately after taking the medicine in which he or she implicitly believes, even before it could possibly have been absorbed and assimilated in the system, showing conclusively that the expectancy, the faith, alone, did the work.

There is no doubt, on the other hand, that thousands of patients have been killed by the brutal plainness of physicians, when under cheerful, hopeful encouragement the patients might have recovered. Hope and cheer are infinitely better tonics than any drugs. In fact, there is little danger as long as the courage and cheerfulness of the patient can be maintained, for the reactive influence upon all the functions of the body is very powerful.

Faith has ever been the great miracle worker of the ages. It has endowed a spoonful of sugar water or a rabbit's foot carried in the pocket with marvelous healing powers.

Think of the tremendous curative force in the faith of the people who make pilgrimages of thousands of miles on foot to some shrine, often barefooted, and lacerating themselves because of their belief in the beneficence of it to heal! Think of the blind, superstitious faith to heal in those who sacrifice property—sometimes children; almost life itself—to get what they regard as the miraculous power of some sacred healing water—as of the Jordan or the Ganges rivers!

Those poor deluded people do not realize that there is no power whatever in these inanimate objects to give them health, but that they take the healing power with them in their faith—which they could just as well have exercised upon themselves at home.

The physical is often the outpicturing, the expression, of our mental condition; our health is often our objectified thought.

It will not be long before *mental* medicine will be recognized as a real science, infinitely more scientific than the present medical system.

For ages we have searched the earth for mineral and vegetable remedies which would cure our ills, when all the time, without knowing it, we have had stored our own brains, in the depths of our being, the sovereign panacea for all aches and pains—a divine harmony which would antidote virtually all our discords.

The coming physician will teach patients that life does not always depend upon chance or a cruel fate, but more often upon mental therapeutics.

Many regular physicians are gradually recognizing mental healing and employing it. A noted nerve specialist, for example, now instructs patients to thoroughly relax their muscles and nerves at certain periods each day and *imagine a vigorous life current flowing through their entire systems.*

There is more and more a tendency to use the mind cure *in a strictly scientific sense.* We are recognizing that it is not the drugs, but the mind which heals our wounds and hurts, restores us, and heals all our physical discord.

The more intelligent physicians are beginning to see that the healing of the body is brought about by connecting the patient with the life principle itself.

It is not difficult to shut out poisonous thoughts from the mind. All one need do is to substitute the opposite thought to that which produces the fatal poison, for it will always furnish the antidote. Discord cannot exist in the presence of harmony. The charitable thought, the love thought, will very quickly kill the jealousy, the hate, and the revenge thought. If we force pleasant, cheerful picture into the mind, the gloomy, "blue" thoughts, will have to get out.

When we shall have learned to shut out all the enemies of our health, of our digestion—the enemies which poison our blood and other secretions—when we shall have learned how to keep the imagination hopeful, our thoughts positive, our ideals bright; when we shall have learned the tremendous power that a great life-purpose has to systematize and purify our lives, then we shall know how to live.

When we shall have learned to antidote the hate thought, the jealousy thought, the envy, the revenge thought, with the love, the charity thought; when we shall have grasped the secret of antidoting all discordant thoughts with the harmony thought; when we shall have learned the mighty life-giving power in the holding of the right mental attitude and the awful tragedy and suffering which come from holding the wrong mental attitude, then will not only civilization go forward by leaps and bounds, but each of us as individuals.

The body and mind are one. Untold harm has come to the race through the belief that they are distinct. All the intelligence that is in us is distributed through the cells of the body. These cells are all specialists and all more or less intelligent, and the combined intelligence of all of the cells of the entire body forms the intelligence of the individual. It may be true that there is a higher development of intelligence in the brain cells, but there is a wonderful help in regarding your whole body as a brain, permeated with a certain Divine intelligence. When we become conscious that every cell in our body is a Divine thing, where all health and harmony and beauty and truth and love reside, we shall then know what it is to taste power.

CHAPTER 29
Imagination and Health

physicians tell us that susceptibility to illnesses and diseases often depends very largely upon the mental condition.

Not long ago a clergyman was sent to a hospital, suffering terribly, and so weak that he could scarcely hold up his head. He said he had swallowed several false teeth and the plate, and that he felt he horrible grinding and cutting of these in his stomach. The physician in attendance tried to talk him out of this idea, but to no purpose. A little while later a telegram from his wife informed him that the teeth had been found under the bed. Mortified and chagrined at having made such a fool of himself, the clergyman, free from his imaginary suffering, immediately got up, dressed himself, paid his bill, and went home without assistance.

Well-authenticated cases have been recorded by physicians where patients, who had a mortal fear of chloroform, went into syncope before a whiff of chloroform had been given. They became perfectly unconscious through the suggestion of their own minds.

I know of a physician who, while away from home on a fishing trip, was summoned to attend a patient who was suffering indescribable agony. The physician had no drugs with him, but knowing the power of suggestion, made small powders out of ordinary flour and gave instructions with the greatest care as to the exact time and spanner of taking. They were to be given every few minutes.

The patient was told that he was being treated by a noted physician, and his great faith in the physician and the remedy in a short time wrought a marvelous change in his condition. He said that he felt the effects of the medicine throughout his entire being. Flour and faith did the work.

In the medical report, after the great epidemic of yellow fever in Philadelphia, we find this reference to the remarkable healing balm in the spiritual influence of the great Dr. Rush: *"Dr. Rush's presence was a powerful stimulant; men recovered to whom he gave no medicine, as if his word was enough to turn the fever."*

The sick thought must go before the sick condition will depart. When the diseased thought goes, the body at once rebounds and becomes normal.

Recently, for example, I heard of a young lady who, while at the theater with her fiance, complained suddenly of feeling faint. Her fiance, a young doctor, took; something out of his pocket, and, giving it to her, whispered, "Keep this tabloid in your mouth, but don't swallow it." The young lady did as directed, and immediately felt better. Curious to know what the "tabloid" was, which, although it had not dissolved, had given her such relief, she examined it on her return home, and found—a small button!

Medical history shows that thousands of people have been made sick—or even died—as victims of their imaginations. They were convinced, they had diseases which in reality they never had. The trouble was not in the body but in the mind.

A short time ago I read a story about a young officer in India who consulted a great physician because he felt enervated from the excessive heat and long hours of service. The physician examined the man and then said that he would send his report to him the next day. The letter the patient received informed him that his left lung was entirely gone, his heart seriously affected, and advised him to adjust his business affairs at once. "Of course, you may live for weeks," it said, "but you had best not leave important matters undecided."

Naturally the young officer was dismayed by this death warrant. He grew rapidly worse, and in twenty-four hours his respiration became difficult and he had an acute pain in the region of the heart. He took to his bed, convinced that would never rise from it. During the night he grew rapidly worse and his servant sent for the doctor.

"What on earth have you been doing to yourself?" demanded the physician. "There was no indication of this sort when I saw you the other day."

"It is my heart, I suppose," weakly answered the patient in a whisper. "Your heart!" repeated the doctor. "Your heart was all right yesterday." "My lungs, then," said the patient.

"What is the matter with you, man? You don't seem to have been drinking."

"Your letter, your letter!" gasped the patient: "You said I had only a few weeks to live." "Are you crazy?" said the doctor. "I wrote you to take a week's vacation in the hills and you would be all right."

The patient, with the pallor of death in his face, could scarcely raise his head from the pillows, but he drew from under his bedclothes the doctor's letter.

"Heavens, man!" cried the physician. "This was meant for another patient! My assistant misplaced the letters."

The young officer sat up in bed immediately, and was entirely well in a few hours.

When I was in the Harvard Medical School, one of the best professors there, a celebrated physician, who had been lecturing upon the power of the imagination, warned the students against the dangers of imagining that they themselves had the disease about which they studied. The professor told me that he got it into his head that he was developing Bright's disease in his own system. This conviction became so strong that he did not even dare to have an examination made. He was so certain that he was in the grasp of this so-called fatal disease that he preferred to die rather than be told of his condition by another physician. He lost his appetite, lost flesh rapidly, and became almost incapable of lecturing, until one day a medical friend, astonished at the change in his appearance, asked what was the matter with him.

"I have Bright's disease," was the reply. "I am sure of it, for I have every symptom."

"Nonsense," said his friend; "you have nothing of the kind."

After a great deal of persuasion, the professor was induced to submit to an examination, and it was discovered that there was not the slightest evidence of Bright's disease in his system. He rallied so quickly that even in a day those who knew him noticed the change. His appetite returned, his flesh came back, and he was a new man.

We read and hear of these stories and believe them, yet few of us can see that their own perverted imaginations, our own discordant, discouraged thoughts are producing similar effects upon ourselves.

We are all at some time in our lives victims of the imagination. The conviction that we have been exposed to a terrible malady, to some incurable, contagious disease, completely upsets the entire system and reverses the processes of the various functions; the mind does not act with its customary vitality and power and there is a general dropping of physical and mental standards all along the line, until we become the victims of the thing we fear.

Sadly, then, we live our lives as an echo of Job: "For the thing which I greatly feared is come upon me, and that which I was afraid of is come unto me." And the rich power of thought to enrich our lives, impoverishes them.

Our lives move in the direction of our thoughts. Carefully watch how you think, and you will move in the direction of health, happiness, and prosperity of all kinds.

CHAPTER 30
How Suggestion Influences Health

Someone has said: "The mortalest enemy you can have is the friend who meets you and says: 'You are not looking well today; what's the matter?' From that moment you don't feel well. Your friend has blasted your hope and spread a pall over your brain."

The power of suggestion is strikingly illustrated by the fact that a hypnotic subject under control may, by the simply application of a cold coin to the skin, be made to believe that he or she is being burned, until an actual blister is raised.

If it is possible for a mere thought suggested by another to cause injury or illness, does it not seem reasonable to conclude that a suggestion could also equally cure? If it is possible, in other words, to make a hypnotic subject stagger and reel like a drunken person just by holding in mind the suggestion that a glass of pure water he or she drank was whiskey, it seems possible to produce all sorts of effects—positive as well as negative—by mental suggestion.

Some examples of the marvelous power of suggestion are given by Dr. Frederik Van Eden, a graduate of medicine at the University of Amsterdam and an advocate of the psychotherapeutic method of healing the sick, in his accounts of Professor Debove, of Paris, an authority in such cases.

"At his clinic in the hospital of St. Andral," Van Eden said regarding Debove, "he showed me how he could give a patient a glass of water, telling him that it was wine; and how the patient took it for wine. I saw how he told a man that a cold silver spoon was glowing hot, and how the man dropped it with every token of burning pain. How he gave another a book and said: 'Look at it; it's all white paper! all blank! . . . Now blow on it. Look again!—it's all portraits, all portraits! Now blow again!—all landscapes and pictures! Look!' And the man saw everything in great amazement, and even described the landscapes and portraits which nobody saw but himself. 'Well, I never saw magic like this,' said the man.

"'I'll do better,' said Debove. 'Shut your eyes. When you open them, I have no head.' And as the man looked up he stared at the professor with a wild, scared look. 'Well,' said Debove, 'how do you like me without my head?' And the poor man struck his own head with a violent blow and said, 'For sure, I have gone mad!'"

In support of these seemingly incredible accounts, I have seen an experiment tried on a horse to make him believe he was sick. He was covered with blankets, rubbed with medicines, pitied and petted until he lost his appetite, and could not be induced to eat or drink. Another perfectly sound horse was, in a short period of time, so similarly convinced of his having a defect—by the holding up of his foot, feeling of it, bandaging it and rubbing it with liniment—that he actually limped when he attempted to walk, as of he were truly lame.

It is well known that the fears, the anxieties, and the worries of parents have a great deal to do with the diseases of their children.

In a home which I visited recently, the mother kept telling her little boy how ill he looked, asking him how he felt, and giving him doses of this and doses of that. At least half a dozen times during the evening she asked the different children of the family how they felt, if they had a headache or a cold. She was worried all the time about them; afraid they would get into drafts, go outdoors bareheaded, or get their feet wet. She was constantly warning them to avoid these things, and telling them that if they didn't they would get croup, or pneumonia, or something terrible would happen to them. She kept the picture of physical discord constantly in the minds of her children. The result was that some member of the family was sick most of the time. The mother said she could not go out much, because there was so much sickness in her family!

The father was almost as bad as the mother in worrying about the health of the family. He would call his little boy to him, feel his pulse, tell him his skin was hot, that he was feverish. He would look at his tongue and remark that he was a sick boy. The result was the boy actually thought himself sick and had to go to bed.

Think of children being brought up in such an atmosphere of fear and anxiety and disease picturing, constantly warned of danger and cautioned all the time not to do this or that, until they begin to think there are very few things that a person *can* do with safety! They grow up with a terrible fear of disease that becomes a perpetual nightmare.

How little parents realize the harm they do in projecting their own discordant thoughts and fears into their children's receptive minds, thus tending to develop in the child the very thing the parents are presumably trying to avoid!

We are beginning to appreciate the marvelous power of suggestion to uplift or depress the mind. Recently, for example, I heard a very intelligent woman say that she was forced to take to her bed for the greater part of a day because of the depressing influence of a magazine story she had just read. The story was written by a famous writer. It was strong, but brutal. It appealed to what was morbid in her mind and completely prostrated her.

It is common for medical students to become ill through the horrible suggestions of the dissecting rooms, and the depressing influence which comes from the constant study of disease conditions.

On the other hand, the constant mental contact with cheerful, hopeful, health thoughts, tends to reproduce the corresponding qualities in the body.

Most of us know what a glorious uplift and stimulus we have received when ill, from a call from one who is cheerful and optimistic—one who injects hope and courage into us. And we know how we dread to have others call on us when we are ill, because they rob us of hope and leave us in such a dejected mood by their long faces and pessimistic minds.

The mind of a sick person is in more or less a helpless, subjective, negative condition, and is very susceptible to thought influences, good or bad. A positive, creative attitude gives the mind the power of resistance, which protects it from its enemies. Imagine, therefore, what an uplift it would be to a patient if the attending physician, nurse, and visiting relatives, and friends were all trying to radiate hope, good cheer, and courage.

I once knew two physicians in hospitals in Boston who illustrated this point. One was an extreme optimist with a keen sense of humor. He was always cracking jokes with the patients, cheering them up, and telling funny stories. The whole atmosphere of the wards was entirely changed after he had passed through them. His bright, cheerful face and sunny optimism gave the patients a great uplift.

The other physician was morose, stern, silent, profound, a man of great learning but of few words and who seldom smiled. If he found a patient not looking well, he did not hesitate to tell the patient so—and that the patient appeared to be losing ground!

This physician always said what he thought, even when it, was cruel. The sick person in his care, thus discouraged, would often immediately lose heart and collapse.

Physicians little realize how *implicitly* patients pin their faith to them and how closely they watch their faces for signs of encouragement, a ray of hope.

Some conscientious physicians think they should always tell the patient exactly how things are, that it is the patient's right to know, especially when in extreme danger. Now there might be reason in this if the physician were omniscient, if the physician never erred in a diagnosis, and if he or she could measure with exactitude every force acting in the patient. But even the most learned physicians feel that they know comparatively little about the human mechanism. They know that patients often recover after eminent physicians in consultation have given up all hope. Why should they not give the patient the benefit of a doubt, especially when they know the power of a depressing thought or unfavorable verdict on one in an extremely weak condition? Do physicians owe their patients a greater duty than to help them all they can to recover? And is there any greater healing power than in hope, in confidence?

The influence of the strong mind of the physician on the weak, discouraged, exhausted patient is far-reaching, and knowing this, the physician should give the patient as much mental uplift and hope as possible. There are times when a physician owes a patient an infinitely greater duty than to tell him or her the truth—or to put things more precisely, what the physician believes to be the truth.

The power of suggestion on expectant minds is often little less than miraculous. Invalids who think they have been robbed of their chances in life and who has suffered for years, often become all wrought up over a new remedy which is advertised to do marvels. They are in such an expectant state of mind that they are willing to make any sacrifice to obtain the remedy. And when they get it, they are in such a receptive mood that they often respond quickly to the suggestion and think it is the medicine they have taken that has worked the magic.

Religious history is full of examples of people who have been cured by going to famed springs, by bathing in sacred waters, or streams supposed to have great curative qualities.

People who go to health resorts attribute their improvement to change of air or to the waters they drink, when, as a matter of fact, it has probably been wrought by change of environment, change of mental suggestion, as much as by the change of air or water.

Buoyancy of mind, courage, hope, and cheerfulness are factors that far outweigh drugs in the cure of the sick, and should be encouraged in every possible way. The trouble with us is that we do not realize the omnipotent remedies that lie within our own minds.

The Bible assures us that "perfect love casteth out fear," and fear is one of the most potent sources of discord and disease.

Those who lives close to God (good), who abide in His love, fear nothing—they are not worried or anxious, because they feel always the protection of omnipotent Power and infinite Wisdom.

A few, passages from the Scriptures will show how freely and fully abundant life, health, strength—all good things—are promised to those who heed the words of God, who love Him and put their faith in Him.

Attend to my words For they *are* life unto those that find them, and health to all their flesh.—Prov. 4:20–22

They that wait upon the Lord shall renew *their* strength; they, shall mount up with wings as eagles; they shall run, and not be weary; *and* they shall walk, and not faint.—Isaiah 40:31

He sent his word and healed them.—Psalm 107:20

I cried unto thee, and thou hast healed me.—Psalm 30:2

His flesh shall be fresher than a child's.—Job 33:25

For I will restore health unto thee, and I will heal thee of thy wounds.—Jer. 30:17

Behold, I will heal thee.—II Kings 20:5

Then shall thy light break forth as the morning, and thine health shall spring forth speedily.—Isaiah 58:8

I *am* the Lord that healeth thee.—Exodus 15:26

There shall be no more death, neither sorrow, nor crying, neither shall there be any more pain; for the former things are passed away.—Rev. 21:4

"Neither shall any plague" (discord or harm) "come nigh thy dwelling"—Psalm 91:10

Let thine heart keep my commandments; For length of days, and long life, and peace, shall they add to thee.—Prov. 3:1–2

When we are thoroughly entrenched in the conviction of our unity with the All-good; when we realize that we do not take on health from outside by acquiring it, but that we *are* health; that we do not absorb a bit of justice, here and there, but that we *are* justice; that we do not take on truth, a little here and a little there, but that we *are* truth itself—principle—then we shall really begin to live.

I believe that most people are conscious of a power deep in their nature which would remedy all their ills if they only knew how to get hold of it. We all feel that there is something divine in us, something in the flesh that is not of it, a power back of the flesh that will ultimately redeem us and bring us into the state of blessedness which we instinctively feel is the right of the children of the King of kings. The great end of life is to train ourselves to find this creative, rejuvenating, life-giving force and to apply it to our everyday life.

CHAPTER 31
Health Through Right Thinking

few people realize how largely their health depends upon the nature of their thinking. You cannot hold ill-health thoughts, disease thoughts, in the mind without having them outpictured in the body. *The thought will appear in the body somewhere,* and its quality will determine the results—sound or unsound, healthful or unhealthful. As it is impossible for a person to remain absolutely pure who habitually holds pictures of impurity in the imagination, so it is just as impossible to be healthy while holding the disease thought. There cannot be harmony in the body with disease in the mind.

We can never gain health by contemplating disease any more than we can reach perfection by dwelling upon imperfection, or harmony by dwelling upon discord.

We should keep a high ideal of health and harmony constantly before the mind; and we should fight every discordant thought and every enemy of harmony as we would fight a temptation to crime.

Never affirm or repeat about your health what you do not wish to be true. Do not dwell upon your ailments nor study your symptoms. Physicians tell us that perfect health is impossible to the self-dissectors—those who are constantly thinking of themselves, studying themselves, and are forever on the alert for the least symptom of disease.

Librarians report that there is an astonishing demand among, readers for medical books. Many who imagine they have some particular disease often develop a morbid curiosity or desire to read everything they can get hold of that bears upon the subject. When they find, as they do frequently, that some of the symptoms of the disease they are reading about coincides with their own, the conviction is still more deeply fastened in their minds that they have this disease. The strength of this conviction is often their greatest hindrance to a cure.

I know people in delicate health who habitually hold in their minds sick and discordant thoughts. They are always thinking and talking of their ailments. They virtually gloat over their symptoms—watch them, study them, look for them, until they have what they expect: for like produces like; it cannot produce anything else. A reversal of the thought—thinking of health instead of disease, and holding in mind the health picture instead of the disease picture—would cure many an invalid without medicine. Healthy thought is the greatest panacea in the world.

Many people not only cripple their efficiency, but keep themselves sick or in a condition of semi-invalidism or diminished power, by holding constantly in their minds negative suggestions as indicated by such expressions as "Oh, I do not feel well today," "I feel miserable," "I am weak," "I am half sick," "My food does not agree with me," "I did not sleep well last night, and I know I shall not be good for much today."

If you are constantly saying to yourself, "I am wretched, weak and sick," "I am running down all the time," how can you expect to become strong and well? Has it not now become accepted wisdom that according to our word it will be done unto us?

Health and vigor will never come to you if you perpetually harp upon your weakness and pity yourself because of your poor health. Health is integrity. Health is wholeness, completeness. If you talk anything else, you will get it.

Imagine yourself an attorney pleading the cause of your health. Summon up every bit of evidence you can possibly find. Do not give away your case to your opponent. Plead it vigorously with all the strength you can command.

You will be surprised to see how your body will respond to such mental entreaty; such robust, vigorous, healthy affirmative argument.

I know of a case where a physician in passing through a ward thoughtlessly said to the nurse, in a voice loud enough for the patient to overhear, "That man cannot live." The young man happened to know enough about the power of the mind as a restorative to assert himself, saying to the nurse with great emphasis, "I *will* live." He got well.

We do not realize how we weaken ourselves and destroy our powers of disease resistance by harboring the sick, the disease thought, by holding in the mind the idea of physical weakness and debility.

The time will come when right thinking will be the great preventive medicine and when physical discord will be looked upon as a possible indication that one has weakened in thought—as it is now looked upon entirely as an indication that one has weakend physically.

I believe the time will come when disease will not be able to fasten itself upon those whose thought is pure, clean, and strong, because this quality of thought is healing. The time will come when greed and all forms of selfishness will be looked upon as a disease which we pay very dearly for in the outpicturing of some physical discord.

People little realize what price they pay in physical suffering for their selfishness.

We cannot think ill-health, we cannot hold the thought of disease, we cannot harbor convictions that this disease or that is lurking in the system—that there are seeds of disease within us only waiting for an opportunity to develop and destroy us—without seriously impairing the harmony of the body and its efficiency.

Every discordant thought, every thought of ill-health, all the vivid pictures of unfortunate physical conditions held in the imagination, all the horrible ghosts of fear—the things we dread and are anxious about—all the passions of anger and hatred, jealousy and envy, greed and selfishness, affect the integrity of all physical functions.

The mind is the health sculptor, and we cannot surpass the mental health pattern. If there is a weakness or a flaw in the thinking model, there will be corresponding deficiencies in the health statue.

So long as we think ill-health and doubt our ability to be strong and vigorous, so long as we hold the conviction of the presence of inherited weaknesses and disease tendencies so long as the model is defective—perfect health is impossible.

Life and health follow thought.

We should lay a foundation for our health just as we establish anything of importance—by studying and adopting the sanest and the most scientific methods. We should think health, talk health, hold the health ideal, just as a law student thinks law, talks law, reads law, and lives in a law atmosphere.

The same power that created us repairs us. If we could only harmonize our lives with this principle, we would reach our highest efficiency, our greatest possible happiness—the only truth of our being.

PART IV

THE POWER
OF THOUGHT
IN CREATING
HAPPINESS

CHAPTER 32
Don't Get The Worry Habit!

Worry has caused more failures, more broken hearts, more blasted hopes, than any other one thing since the days of the world. It has forced genius to do the work of mediocrity.

Work kills no one, but worry has killed its multitudes. It is not *the doing* of things which injures us so much as *the dreading to do them*—not only in performing them mentally over and over again, but in anticipating something disagreeable in their performance.

No one can utilize one's normal power who dissipates their nervous energy in useless anxiety. Nothing will sap one's vitality and blight one's ambition or detract from one's real power in the world more than the worrying habit. Worry has disqualified many a man from paying their debts by sapping their energy, ruining their health, and impairing their productive capacity.

Did you ever hear of any good coming to any human being from worry? Did it ever help anybody to better his or her condition? Does it not always—everywhere—do just the opposite by impairing the health, exhausting the vitality, lessening efficiency?

What would be thought of business people who would keep in their service employees *known* to have been robbing them for years, stealing a little here and a little there every day? Yet do we not all keep in our *mental* business house, at the very source of our power, a thief infinitely worse than one who merely steals money or material things—a thief who robs us of energy, saps our vitality, and bankrupts us of all that makes life worthwhile.

Do we not pity the pagans who lacerate themselves in all sorts of cruel ways in their worship? Yet many of us constantly torment ourselves by all sorts of mental instruments of torture. We borrow trouble; endure all our lives the woe of crossing and recrossing bridges weeks and years before we come to them; do disagreeable tasks mentally over and over again before we reach them; anticipate our drudgery and constantly suffer from the apprehension of terrible things that never happen.

Worry not only saps vitality and wastes energy, it also seriously affects the quality of our work. It cuts down ability. The mental faculties must have perfect freedom before they will give out their best. A troubled brain cannot think clearly, vigorously, and logically. Attention cannot be concentrated with anything like the same force when the brain cells are poisoned with anxiety as when they are fed by pure blood and are clean and unclouded.

The brain cells are constantly bathed in the blood, from which they draw their nourishment. When our blood is loaded with the poisons of fear, worry, anger, hatred, or jealousy, the protoplasm of our delicate cells becomes hard and is materially injured.

Is it not strange that people will persist in allowing little worries, petty vexations, and unnecessary frictions to grind life away at such a fearful rate that old age stares them in the face in middle life?

Worry not only us *look* older, it actually *makes* us older. It is a chisel which cuts cruel furrows in the face. I have seen a person so completely changed by a few weeks of anxiety that the whole countenance had a different expression and the individual seemed almost like another person.

You can kill worry thoughts easily when you know the antidote; and this you always have in your mind. You do not have to go to a drug store or a physician for it, it is always with you—always ready. All you have to do is to substitute hope, courage, cheerfulness, serenity, for despondency, discouragement, pessimism, anxiety. Nothing else will so quickly drive away worry as the habit of cheerfulness, of making the best of things, of refusing to see the ugly side of life. Opposite thoughts will not live together. The presence of one excludes the other.

When you feel fear or anxiety entering your thought, just fill your mind instantly with courage, hope, and confidence.

Refuse to let any enemies of your happiness and success camp in your mind.

Drive out the whole brood of vampires.

CHAPTER 33
The Source Of True Contentment

When will we learn that happiness is as legitimate a product of our thought, our effort, our aims and ambitions, our mental attitude, our outlook upon life, as the correct answer to a mathematical problem is the result of scientific procedure? Somehow most of us seem to think that happiness can only be *found* just as people find gold—that there is a great deal of luck about it.

Undoubtedly, ambition stands in the way of more people's contentment and happiness than almost anything else. The foolish determination to do what others do, to get ahead of others and to be able to live as they do, to have the luxuries and comforts of people who are better off than they—this over-vaulting ambition is one of the great happiness enemies.

It is a false ambition which keeps us pulling and hauling and straining to do something which somebody else has done, not because we need it ourselves, not because it would add a particle to our comfort or real welfare, or because it is really worthwhile, but because we are eaten up with the canker of an over-vaulting ambition—the desire to outshine others, to outdo them, to get ahead of them, to live a little better off than they, to have a little better home and in a little better part of the town, to dress our children a little better, to surround ourselves with more luxuries. But when all is said and done, are these things really helpful, are they really worthwhile?

Growth, enlargement of life, enrichment of one's nature—these are the things that are worthwhile. It is the ambition to be true to oneself, to stand for more in the community, to push one's horizon of ignorance farther and farther away from oneself, to think a little higher each day, to think a little more of oneself, to have a little more faith in oneself and in everybody else, to be of real use in the world, which, if achieved, will bring contentment and true happiness.

Everywhere we see one-sided, unbalanced individuals—mere dwarfs people they could be—who have starved their social and aesthetic faculties, their mental growth, in their restless strife to put a little more money into their purse. They are always *getting ready* to live, neglecting the present, focusing their eyes upon the future—always straining for something yet to come, and never half appreciating what they have or enjoying as they go along.

The majority of people seem to think they can purchase happiness. But no one has yet been able to bribe real happiness. There is one price for it, and the poor may gain it as well as the rich.

The great majority of people in this world have an idea that happiness consists in the satisfaction which comes from gratified desires. But this is always a delusion: The satiety of desire is always followed by a reaction, an ever-increased call for more gratification. The appetite for gratification overpowers all possibility of satisfaction. The more it is indulged, the more imperious the craving The appetite survives even when the victim is exhausted. The thirst can never be quenched.

How often we hear people give expression to the thought that they don't get much out of life. This very spirit of trying to see how much they can *get out of life* is what causes them to get so little. It is the people who put the most *into* life who get the most out of it. It is the people who give the most to life who get the most out of it. But to many people, life seems something to plunder instead of to cultivate to the utmost. A farmer might as well sit still and see how much can be gotten out of the farm without sowing and planting.

Put love, cheerfulness, and unselfish service into life, then you will not go around complaining that you get so little out of life, that the world has no reward to offer you.

It will do you no good to chase all over the world trying to find happiness. If you do not carry it with you, you will never find it. History is strewn with wrecks of those who pursued happiness desperately all their lives, and never once caught up with it, while multitudes of others who never thought much about happiness, but were intensely busy with their duties, busy trying to provide for the home and those dear to them and to make life a little easier, a little more comfortable, for those about them, were surprised to find that it came to them unsought.

Life has its full measure of happiness for every one of us if we would only make up our minds to make the very most of every opportunity that comes our way, instead of longing for the things that come our neighbor's way.

How many of us are like the buttercup that grew in the field beside the daisy. The buttercup was discontented and envied the daisy—"for daisies grow so trim and tall"—and she always had a longing to wear a frill around her neck too. A robin who was flying by heard her lamentation and told her how foolish she was to want to be a made-up daisy instead of her own bright self. He told her to

"Look bravely up into the sky
And be content with knowing
That God wished for a buttercup
Just here where you are growing!"

Did you ever stop to consider that in all probability you are living right at this moment as truly as you ever can live, that you are just now going through the only sort of life you may ever experience on this earth?

Every day, stop for a few minutes and empty your mind of envy and jealousy. Thrust out your ambition of forever desiring what others have and appreciate what is your own, instead. Real happiness comes from the cultivation, the development, of the highest that is in us.

The world is full of happiness, and there is always plenty to go round, if we are only willing to take the kind that comes our way.

CHAPTER 34
The Aesthetic Mind

everything in life is loaded with some special meaning, but will only give up its secret to the soul that responds to it; the soul that has an affinity for it. Music does not awaken response in the deaf ear but only in those who have the musical sense. The sweetest organ does not appeal to those who have no appreciation of the laws of harmony and melody. It only speaks to those who have a spiritual responsiveness which can interpret its divine meaning. What a treasury of intellectual joys, which infinitely surpass all the pleasures of the senses or the joys which come from material things, is revealed by the opening of the door of thought! No matter how poverty-stricken one's environment may be, no matter what misfortunes, failures, distressing conditions surround an individual, it is possible—through the training of our thoughts—to rise out of discords of an inhospitable environment into a heaven of unspeakable joy.

As Lovelace, in prison, wrote to Althea . . .

Stone walls do not a prison make

Nor iron bars a cage;

Minds innocent and quiet take

That for an hermitage.

The sources available to an aesthetically trained mind are inexhaustible.

If we have a good mind, well developed toward aesthetic sensibilities, we ought never to have a dull moment. If things are disagreeable, if people bore us if our surroundings are uncongenial, we can lift ourselves out of it all and in an instant be in the world of our ideals. No power can keep us from enjoyments of the mind, said Epictetus.

And yet, what school or college has ever taught the marvelous possibilities of creating one's own ideal world?

What luxury, greater than that of one possessed of the greatest wealth, one can find in the development of the mind for beauty.

If you think your life has so little for you, you have not learned the secret of extracting from life its joys, beauties, truth, and loveliness. The soul that loves beauty can feast on it everywhere. There is not a nook or corner where it does not exist. Think of the marvels which the microscope reveals to the scientist, the wonderful mysteries which the telescope brings to us from the depths of the universe!

What you can abstract from life, is just a question of how you train your mind and form your habits of thought—your ability to extract beauty from your environment, which otherwise you may think so commonplace, dry, lean.

The things we were never trained to see or enjoy, would, if we were taught to see them, greatly revolutionize our lives. What the most intelligent of sees is as nothing compared to what so often passes us by, unseen.

No matter which way we turn, there are marvels of design, of beauty, which a whole lifetime of study could never exhaust.

No doubt we would more fully appreciate our opportunities could we realize what a blind person would give just for a glimpse of the world that we see around us. What would such a person not give to have his or her eyes opened even but for a few moments and be able to see what we see? To be see the flower which we so often see? The landscape? To look into human faces and watch the play of thought, sentiment, and mood upon their countenances? What would all this mean to one without sight? Yet how little we ourselves appreciate this privilege.

Suppose a human being could be endowed with omnipotence, the omniscience, the magic power and the wisdom, to create a world which in every particular would be a paradise, a world which would be absolutely perfect in every respect; to evolve a plant life which would give the greatest possible joy and satisfaction to human beings; create fruits, vegetables and all else which would give the most intense pleasure to the human palate. In other words, suppose this human being should be endowed with the God-like qualities to create a world which could satisfy every yearning and every longing of his soul. Could such a person equal the marvelous creations which have already been provided for every human being?

So why is it that our lives are so often so very lean, so aesthetically poverty-stricken, so pinched, so limited, so blighted, when they might be so grand, so magnificent, so sublime?

The love of the beautiful is a fundamental quality of the human mind. It first manifest itself in the decoration of the so-called savage, and has become an increasing passion with the progress of civilization.

Merely to exist was not the object of our creation, but to live sublimely, magnificently Surrounded as we are with the real sources of happiness—costless, limitless—many of us allow our finer senses to atrophy and turn to money as the primary source of happiness. But putting money into the purse is pretty poor sort of business compared with putting beauty into the life, cultivating the sublime, the magnificent in our natures.

The joy of living lies not with us but within us. It is the power to appreciate, to make our own the aesthetic joys that are free to all, which raises us from the multitude, who, owning more than we, are like "dumb driven cattle," that walk and sleep and feed but know only the things that minister to the grosser appetites.

From those who have been trained to think, to extract the honey of life from all sorts of sources, those who have been trained to use their ears and to see things, the mere lack of money can take little away. Circumstances have scant power to rob such a person of a good life. Although a pauper in material things, such a person can be a millionaire in beauty, a billionaire in cheerfulness nobility of character.

Beauty is a refining, elevating, saving force. The love of the beautiful is an indication of superiority, of a superior mentality. It indicates that the possessor has risen out of the basement of life into the upper stories.

The power of material things to bestow happiness, to bring joy into the life, is tremendously exaggerated.

The mind trained to see beauty—"the splendor in the grass, [the] glory in the flower"—will bring to us the best there is in the universe.

CHAPTER 35
Holding The Beauty Thought

by acquiring the perpetual habit of holding in mind the beauty thought—not the thought of mere superficial beauty, but that of heart beauty, soul beauty—someone with even the homeliest face, the ugliest expression, can be thought of as beautiful by every one who knows him or her.

The basis of all real beauty is a kindly, helpful heart and a desire to scatter sunshine and good cheer everywhere—and this disposition, shining through one's face, makes it beautiful.

I know men and women, however, who have dwelt upon what they consider their unfortunate plainness for so long that they have seriously exaggerated it—deforming themselves mentally far more so than they were physically. They are not half so plain as they think they are, and were it not for the fact that they have made themselves very sensitive and self-conscious about it, others would not notice it at all. In fact, if they could get rid of their sensitiveness and be natural, they could, with the merest effort, make up in sprightliness of thought, in cheerfulness of manner, in intelligence, and in helpfulness, what they lack in physical beauty—attaining everything, and more, that those whose physical features are admired, attain.

I have known, for example, a girl whose extreme plainness of features and awkwardness of manner so pained her as she approached womanhood that she almost despaired of ever making anything of herself, and even contemplated suicide. She was so convinced that she was a target for cruel remarks, and became so impressed with the conviction that she was not wanted anywhere, and that she was continually being insulted, that she resolved to make one supreme effort to redeem herself from her handicap. She resolved that she would make people love her, that she would attract them instead of repelling them; that she would take such an unselfish interest in them that they could not help loving her. She determined to develop those beautiful heart qualities which would more than compensate for mere physical beauty.

She began to sympathize with people and to take thought of their welfare. Wherever she went, if she saw any one who was ill at ease or looked troubled or friendless, she immediately took such a deep interest in that person that she won the person's friendship at once.

She began to cultivate her mind in every possible way in order to make herself interesting, bright, cheerful, and hopeful. She cultivated optimism, radiating good cheer from every pore and soon noticing that the people who formerly shunned her began to flock around her.

She not only succeeded in compensating for her physical deformity, which she had at once thought was fatal to her pleasure and her usefulness, but she developed a soul beauty that did not pass with years, and which was infinitely superior to that beauty of feature and form.

So popular did she become that the so-called pretty girls envied her.

The highest beauty—beauty that is far superior to the beauty of features—is within the reach of everybody. If you hold the beauty thought, the love thought, persistently in the mind, you will make such an impression of harmony, of sweetness, of soul beauty wherever you go, that no one will notice anything about you but beauty.

CHAPTER 36
The Divinity Of Ideals

When we begin to desire a thing, to yearn for it with all our hearts, we begin to establish relationship with it in proportion to the strength and persistency of our longing and intelligent effort to realize it.

The trouble with most of us is that we live too much in the material side of life and not enough in the ideal. We should learn to live mentally in the ideal which we wish to make real.

The habit of thinking and asserting things as we would like to have them, or as they ought to be, and of stoutly claiming our wholeness or completeness, supplies the pattern which the life-processes within us will reproduce. Keep constantly in your mind the ideal of the man or woman you would like to become. Hold the ideal of your efficiency and wholeness, and instantly strangle every disease image or suggestion of inferiority. Never allow yourself to dwell upon your weaknesses, deficiencies, or failures. Holding firmly the *ideal* and struggling vigorously to attain it will help you to realize it.

There is a tremendous power in the habit of expectancy, of believing that we shall realize our ambition; that our dreams will come true. There is no more uplifting habit than that of bearing a hopeful attitude, of believing that things are going to turn out well and not ill; that we are going to succeed and not fail; that no matter what may or may not happen, we are going to be happy.

There is nothing else so helpful as the carrying of this optimistic, expectant attitude—the attitude which always looks for and expects the best, the highest, the happiest—and never allowing oneself to get into a pessimistic, discouraged mood.

Believe with all your heart that you will do what you were made to do. Never for an instant harbor a doubt of it. Drive it out of your mind if it seeks entrance. Entertain only the friend thoughts or ideals of the thing you are determined to achieve. Reject all thought enemies, all discouraging moods—everything which would even suggest failure or unhappiness.

It does not matter what you are trying to do or to be, always assume an expectant, hopeful, optimistic attitude regarding it. You will be surprised to see how you will grow in all your faculties, and how you will improve generally.

When the mind has once formed the habit of holding the expectant thought, t will not be easy to form the opposite habit. A mind so trained would always be in a condition to exercise its maximum power and overcome inharmony, unkindness and the hundred and one enemies of our peace, comfort, efficiency, and success

The very habit of expecting that the future is full of good things for you, that you are going to be prosperous and happy, that you are going to have a fine family, a beautiful home, and are going to stand for something, is the best kind of capital with which to start life.

What we persistently express, we tend to achieve, even though it may not seem likely or even possible. If we always express the ideal, the thing we would like to come true in our lives, whether it be robust health, a noble character, or a superb career, if we vizualize it as vividly as possible and work with all our might to realize it, we give it the best chance to come to us.

Many of us, however, allow our desires and longings to fade out. We do not realize that the very intensity and persistency of desire increases our power to realize their dreams. Our constant effort in keeping our desires alive, increases our capacity to realize them.

It does not matter how improbable or how far away your goal may seem, or how unlikely the prospects may be. Visualize your ideal as best you can, as vividly as possible. Hold tenaciously to it and vigorously struggle to attain it, and it will gradually become actualized, realized your life. But a desire, a longing, a yearning held indifferently will vanish without realization.

But a note of caution: It is only when *desire crystallizes into resolve* that it is effective. It is desire *coupled with the vigorous determination to realize it* that produces the creative power. It is yearning, longing, and striving *together* that produce results.

We are constantly increasing or decreasing our efficiency by the quality and character of our thoughts, emotions, and ideals. *Think and say only that which you wish to become true.* People who are always excusing themselves constantly saying that they are tired, used up, played out, "all in"; that they are all out of kilter somewhere; that they are always unfortunate, unlucky; that fate seems to be against them; that they are poor and always expect to be; that they have worked hard and tried to get ahead but could not, little realize that in so speaking and thinking, they are etching picture-enemies of their peace, their happiness, and their success deeper and deeper into their consciousness, and are making it all the more certain that their doubts will be realized in their lives.

We are all the products of our own thoughts. Whatever we concentrate upon, that we are. The daily habit, of picturing oneself as a superb individual, sent to earth with a divine mission—*and with the ability and the opportunity to deliver it grandly*—gives you a marvelous confidence, an uplifting power, and perpetual encouragement.

Our ideals are great character-molders, and have a tremendous life-shaping influence.

What we believe is coming to us is a tremendous creative motive. The dream of home, of prosperity, the expectancy of being a person of influence, of standing for something, of carrying weight in our community—all these things are powerful creative motives.

Many people have an idea that it is dangerous to indulge their dreaming faculties, their imagination, very much, for fear that in doing so they will become impracticable. But these faculties are just as sacred as any others we possess. They were given us for a divine purpose—so that we could get glimpses our possible realities.

Our dreaming capacity gives us a peep into the glorious realities that await us further on. It is the evidence of things possible to us:

Building air castles should not be looked upon as an idle, meaningless pastime. Every real castle, every home, every building was an air castle first. Legitimate dreaming is creative; it is bringing into reality our desires; the things for which we long and hope.

Whatever comes to us in life we create first in our mentality. As the building is a reality in all its, details in the architect's mind before a stone or brick is laid, so we create mentally everything which later becomes a reality in our achievement:

Our visions are our plans of our possible life structure; but they will end in plans if we do not follow them up with a vigorous effort to make them real—just as the architect's plans will end in his drawings if they are not followed up and made real by the builder.

Do not give up your dream because it is apparently not being realized; because you can not see it coming true. Cling to your vision with all the tenacity you can muster. Keep it bright. Keep in an ambition-arousing atmosphere. Read the books which will stimulate your ambition. Get close to people who have done what you are trying to do, and try to absorb the secret(s) of their success.

Take a little time before retiring at night and get by yourself. Sit quietly and think and dream to your heart's content. Do not be afraid of your vision, or of your power to dream, for "without a vision the people perish." The faculty to dream was not given to mock you. There is a reality back of it. It is a divine gift intended to give you a glimpse of the grand things in store for you and to lift you out of the common into the uncommon; out of hampering conditions into ideal ones, and to show you that these things can become realities in your life. *Our glimpses into paradise are intended to keep us from getting discouraged by our failures and disappointments.*

There is a divinity behind our legitimate desires.

By the desires that have divinity in them, I do not refer to the things that we want but do not need. I refer to the legitimate desires of our souls for the realization of full, complete self-expression; for the weaving of the pattern of our highest transfiguration.

The bird does not have an instinct to fly South in winter without a real South to match it. Non do we have our heart yearnings, our soul longings, for a larger, completer life, for an opportunity for a full expression of our possibilities, without a reality to match them.

There is material in each of us to realize our ideals. If we will only mentally hold our perfect pattern, our perfect ideal, persistently, so that it becomes our dominant mental attitude, it will soon be woven into our lives and we will become what we dream.

CHAPTER 37
The Sundial's Motto

On a famous sundial it is written: "I record none but hours of sunshine." Every human life would be beautified by making this a life motto.

What a great thing it would be if we could only learn to wipe out of our memories forever everything unpleasant, everything which brings up bitter memories and unfortunate associations and depressing, discouraging suggestions! If we could only keep the mind filled with beautiful thoughts which uplift and encourage, the efficiency of our lives would be multiplied.

Are not some people so unfortunately constituted that they are unable to remember pleasant, agreeable things? When you meet them they always have some sad story to tell, something that has happened to, them or is surely going to happen. They tell you about the accidents, narrow escapes, losses, and afflictions they have had. They seldom mention the bright days and happy experiences. They recall the disagreeable, the ugly, the discordant. The rainy days make such an impression upon their minds that it seems that to them it rains all the time.

There are others who are just the reverse. They always talk of the pleasant things, good times, and agreeable experiences of their lives I know some of these people who have all sorts of misfortunes, losses, sorrows, and yet they so seldom speak of them or refer to them that you would think they never had had anything in their lives but good fortune, that they had never had any enemies, that everybody had been kind to them. These are people who attract us, the people we love.

The habit of turning one's sunny side toward others is a result of the practice of holding charitable, loving, cheerful thoughts perpetually in the mind; while the gloomy, sarcastic, mean character is formed by harboring hard, uncharitable, unkind thoughts until the brain becomes set toward the dark, so that the life can only radiate gloom.

Some people's minds are like a junk shop: They contain things of considerable value mixed with a great deal of rubbish. There is no system or order in them. These minds retain everything—good, bad, or indifferent. They can never bear to throw anything away, for fear it might be of service at some time, so that their mental storehouses are clogged with all sorts of rubbish. If these people would only have a regular house-cleaning and throw away all the rubbish, everything of a doubtful value, and systematize and arrange what is left, they would find their lives so much more improved: no one can do good work with a mind full of discord and confusion.

Get rid of the mental rubbish. Do not go through life burdened with non-essential, meaningless things. Everywhere we see people who are handicapped, doing everything to a great disadvantage, because they never will let go of anything. They are like the over-careful housekeeper, who never throws anything away for fear it may be of use in the future, and whose attic and woodshed, every closet and corner in the house, are piled up with rubbish which "might be wanted some time." The practice of throwing away rubbish of all kinds is of inestimable value.

Occasionally we come across minds that are like public cabs. Now you see in them a good-looking man or, woman—a beautiful charac-ter; a little later a drunkard or vicious woman. In other words, just as the cabbie who picks up customers without regard to whether they are good or bad, so this order of mind picks up all sorts of ideas, good, bad, and indifferent, without selection or choice. This sort of mind is like a sponge: It absorbs everything that comes near it. It is impossible for such a mind to be clean, pure, free from enemy thoughts, con-flicting thought currents, inharmonious vibrations or demoralizing influences.

One of the greatest accomplishments of the finest character is their ability to order their minds and to exclude from them all the enemy thoughts—thoughts that bring friction and discord into life, thoughts that depress, that stunt, that darken.

No mind can do good work when clouded with unhappy or vicious thoughts. The mental sky must be clear or there can be no enthusi-asm, no brightness, clearness, or efficiency in our mental work.

If you would do the maximum of which you are capable, keep the mind filled with sunshine, with beauty and truth, with cheer-ful, uplifting thoughts. Bury everything that makes you unhappy and discordant, everything that cramps your freedom, that worries you, before it buries you.

The mental temple was not given us for the storing of low, base, mean things. It was intended for the abode of the gods, for the trea-suring of high purposes, grand aims, noble aspirations.

It is a shame, and will some time be looked upon as a disgrace, for a human being bearing the stamp of divinity to be dominated by base, unworthy, demoralizing thoughts. The time will come when one will be as much ashamed of harboring a disagreeable, discordant, contaminating thought as he would feel if he were caught stealing. When we once get a true perception of ourselves, of our grandeur, dignity, and infinite possibilities, we will not allow ourselves to be dominated by the mental enemies which now dog us from the cradle to the grave.

No one has learned the art of true living until he or she has trained the mind to forget every experience from which one can no longer derive any advantage, every thought that will hinder one's progress and make one unhappy. No matter how great a mistake you have made, it should be forgotten, buried *forever*. Don't keep digging it up. You have already learned the lesson there is in it for you. The only good use you can make of an unfortunate mistake is to make it a starting-point for something better.

What is there to be gained by harboring injuries, by dwelling upon misfortunes, by morbid worrying over our failures? Did it ever pay to harbor slights and imagined insults?

There is only one thing to do with a disagreeable thought or experience, and that is get rid of it; hurl it out of your mind as you would a thief out of your house. You cannot afford to give shelter to enemies of your peace and comfort:

If you have hard feelings, unkindly thoughts toward others, if you are trying to "get even" with some one who has injured you or if you are suffering from jealousy, envy, or hatred, dispel these killing emotions, these discordant feelings, as vicious enemies: Say to yourself: "This is not humane; these are the thoughts for the base, the degraded; they are not the sort of thoughts for one who is trying to stand for something in the world."

So long as you harbor the hatred thought, the jealous thought, the revenge, worry, anxiety, or fear thought, you must suffer—just as one with gravel in a shoe must suffer until he or she removes the stone.

We cannot harbor any grudge, any hatred against another without suffering a frightful loss in our own nature. It coarsens, animalizes, brutalizes us. On the other hand, the holding of the kindly feeling, the love thought, the helpful, charitable, magnanimous thought, ennobles the life, beautifies the character, enriches the nature.

Our mental attitude gives its color to our lives. We are like our ideals.

Do not go about nursing some fancied wrong or insult or grudge against somebody, cherishing unkind feelings toward any one. Such thoughts poison the brain. They sting and corrupt. Bitterness in the heart is like a leaven, which works its way through the entire system. The constant dwelling upon bitter things saps your vitality and lessens your ability to do something worth while. These are enemies of your youthfulness, of your happiness and success. You cannot afford to have them festering in your heart and tormenting your mind.

Do not remember anything disagreeable which can cripple your efficiency or mar your work. Just wipe it out of your memory, no matter how much it may hurt your pride to do so. Your, great aim should be progress, and you cannot afford to have a lot of rubbish clinging to you which keeps you back or hinders your speed in your life race. You need all your energy, every ounce of power you possess, for the race. Preserve your strength for the main issues. Make every ounce of force tell.

Why should we remember the unkind things people say of us? If we practiced the art of forgetting these things we should learn to love where we once hated, to admire where we despised, to help where we hindered, to praise where we criticized.

A woman who had great sorrows and afflictions said, "I made the resolution that I would never sadden any one with my troubles. I have laughed and told jokes when I could have wept. I have smiled in the face of every misfortune. I have tried to let every one go away from my presence with a happy word and bright thought to carry with them. Happiness makes happiness, and I myself am happier than I would have been had I sat down and bemoaned my fate."

When you were in the dumps, "blue" and discouraged, worried and almost ready to give up the struggle for the thing you were trying to reach, did you never meet some sunny jovial, humorous character, through whose influence it seemed that the whole world was changed in a few minutes—the whole atmosphere cleared of bogies and haunting skeletons—and you caught the contagion of the humor and good cheer, and were another person? This was due only to your change of thought, the new suggestions held in your mind. It was only a question of the expulsive power of a stronger motive, affection, or idea. If we only knew the philosophy of this expulsive power of a stronger, higher motive to drive out the weaker or the lower, we could quickly clear the mental atmosphere of all the clouds of doubt and despair, of all worry and anxiety and uncertainty by substituting their opposites If we did not harbor in the mind the things that are not good for us, they would not make such a lasting impression upon us In fact, they would not get hold of us. It is the harboring of them, turning them over and over, thinking of them, that entrenches them in the mind.

The way to get rid of error is to keep the mind full of truth; the way to get rid, of discord is to keep saturated with harmony, the love thought.

Make up your mind to be large, generous, and charitable, to forget slights or injuries, not to harbor malice.

Harmony is the creative force. Protect yourself from insidious enemies of mind and body. Keep yourself in harmony by always living in the light of hope and truth, where ghosts and hideous shadows cannot live. Train yourself in the knowledge that truth and beauty, joy and gladness, harmony, goodwill thoughts, health thoughts, will kill their opposites—that they have the same effect upon them that water has upon fire.

PART V

THE POWER OF THOUGHT TO CREATE PROSPERITY

CHAPTER 38
How To Attract Prosperity

a poor woman who had all her life previously lived in the back country, moved to a progressive little village where, to her great surprise, she found that her new home was lighted by electricity. She knew nothing about electricity, had never even seen an electric light before, and the little eight candle power electric bulbs with which the house was fitted seemed very marvelous to her.

Later, a man came along one day, selling a new kind of electric bulb and asked the woman to allow him to replace one of her small bulbs with one of his new style sixty candle power bulbs—just to show her what it would do. She consented, and when the electricity was turned on she stood transfixed. It seemed to her nothing short of magic that such a little bulb could give so wonderful a light, almost like that of sunlight. She never dreamed that the source of the new flood of illumination had been there all the time, that the enormously increased light came from the same current which had been feeding her little eight candle bulb.

We smile at the ignorance of this poor woman, but the majority of us are far more ignorant of our own power than she was of the power of the electric current. We go through life using a little eight candle power bulb, believing we are getting all the power that can come to us, all that we can express or that destiny will give us, believing that we are limited to being eight-candle-power bulbs. We never dream that an infinite current, a current in which we are perpetually bathed, floods our lives with light, with a light inconceivably brilliant and beautiful, if we would only put on a larger bulb, make a larger connection with the infinite supply current. The supply wire we are using is so tiny that only a little of the great current can flow through, only a few candle power, when there are millions flowing past our very door. An unlimited supply of this infinite current is ours for the taking, ours for the expressing.

Multitudes are getting no more from the vast resources at their command than this woman was getting from the electric current. They seem to think that if they are expressing four candle, or eight candle power, that it is all the infinite supply can give them, or all that they were intended to have. It never occurs to them that the trouble is not in the current itself, but in the small bulbs they are using.

But we must keep the current open or the supply will be cut off.

The law of supply is scientific. It will not act unless all the necessary conditions are fulfilled. Simply believing in a new philosophy and still keeping your old life doubts and fear habits, living in your old thought habits of lack and poverty, inefficiency, will not bring prosperity. If you don't believe you will prosper and you don't practice what you believe, you will get no results. If you would reap its fruits you must obey the law of supply, the law of abundance, the law of prosperity.

Prosperity never comes by merely wishing or longing for it. Keeping your mind fixed on it, simply thinking of prosperity, will never bring it to you. This is only the first step. You must cling to your prosperity thought, your prosperity ideal, but you must also back it up with scientific methods, the practical common-sense methods which all prosperous people employ.

You could dream of abundance and prosperity all your life and die in the poorhouse, if you do not back up your dream with efficient, business-like methods. That is, you must be methodical, orderly, systematic, accurate, thorough, industrious. You must do everything to a finish. You must fling your energy, your heart into your business, your profession, your work, whatever it is.

If you are determined to turn your back upon poverty and face toward prosperity, however your actual conditions may contradict this; if you really believe that you were not intended for poverty, but that on the contrary the good things, the beautiful things of life are for you, the life glorious and not the pauper or the drudge life; then you are opening your mind to the inflow of the prosperity current.

Imagine the entire universe, the great cosmic ocean of creative intelligence, packed with all the riches, all the glorious things, the magnificent possibilities the human mind can conceive, and then try to picture what it would mean to you if by some magic you could call out of this universal supply anything which would match your desires, your heart's longings.

You will say, doubtless, that such a thing is too silly to contemplate for a moment. Yet, haven't human beings been doing this very thing since the dawn of civilization, all up through the ages?

Every discovery, every invention, every improvement, every facility, every home, every building, every city, every source of transportation, every new technology, has been fashioned out of this vast cosmos.

How?

By thought force.

Everything we use, everything we have, every achievement is preceded by a mental vision, a plan. Someone's imagination first pictured the thing he or she wanted to do. He or she kept visualizing this mental conception, never stopped thinking about it, mentally creating and recreating it, until the efforts to match the vision with reality drew to that person the thing that he or she had been concentrating on.

We all imagine that we, of ourselves, create these things. We do not. We simply work in unison with the creative energy of the universe, drawing out of the vast invisible cosmic ocean of supply.

But we must do our part or there will be no realization for us. Just as the first step in an architect's building is the plan, so must we first make a plan or picture of the thing we desire.

The architect first sees in the mind's eye all the details of the building to be erected—even before drawing the plan on paper. He or she mentally sees the real building long before there are any materials on the spot for its construction. The plan has come out of the invisible, out of the fathomless ocean of possibilities which surrounds us.

In a like manner, all of our wants and desires can find their fulfillment in this unlimited supply.

This is a marvelous revelation, the significance of which most of us have not grasped. Only here and there are there those who utilize it in their daily living. But science is recognizing it. Edison says all scientists feel that *"about and through everything there is the play of an Eternal Mind."* They are recognizing that this is the first great Cause.

It is difficult to realize that every instant, under the impulse of Eternal Mind, miracles are leaping out from the cosmic ocean of energy into objectivity to meet our wants, to supply all our needs. Most of us are not able to grasp the idea that there is wealth and beauty and unthinkable luxuries waiting here. And because of this we do not materialize the things we desire.

It is one of the most marvelous things that we actually live, move, and have our being in this invisible ocean of limitless creative material, and that all we have to do to attract what we want is to hold the right mental attitude toward it and do our best on the physical plane to match it with its reality.

Do you doubt it?

Consider the following then: Noah might have lighted the Ark had he known enough. The force was there just as today.

When we once get it firmly fixed in our minds that in this invisible world of possibilities is everything which matches every legitimate desire and ambition, and that our own will come to us if we visualize it intensely enough, persistently enough, and do our best to make it real, we will no longer live in poverty and misery.

The idea of opulence, however, must be implanted firmly in the subconscious mind—just as everything else which we desire to bring about, to draw out of the universal supply, must be impressed upon our subconscious minds by registering in them our vow, our determination—until our unwavering dedication to our goal becomes a fixed motive or actuating principle.

Whatever we wish to bring about in the actual, we must first establish in the subconscious mind by the constant, positive, affirmative attitude toward our desire.

With such resolve, and hope, and expectation, and confidence, poverty is still, admittedly, not a very comfortable state, but there is no despair in it, there is no real pain in it, there is not much real distress, because hope sees the goal beyond the darkness—it gives a light that dispels the gloom of limitation by showing a vista of good things in process of realization. It is the poverty which is accompanied by despair, which sees no light ahead and forces men and women to drudge on day after day without prospect of relief or hope of betterment that grinds the life out of its victims. This is the poverty that kills the spirit, that destroys the buoyancy of life, the gladness and the joy, which are the birthright of every human being.

What a pity it is that in this land of opportunity and plenty that our government should not have institutions conducted by experts for the treatment of poverty sufferers—those who are obsessed with the idea that their poverty is unavoidable. These people are just as much in need of prosperity treatments as the patients in hospitals are in need of health treatments. They have only lost their way on the life path and are facing the darkness instead of the light, facing towards the poverty goal instead of the prosperity goal. Their mental attitude needs changing so it will point toward success instead of toward failure, toward comfort and plenty, opulence, instead of poverty and limitation. Mental prosperity treatments would kindle a new hope in their discouraged minds, and expectancy of good things would take the place of despair. A new light would come into the eyes of those poor people; and if these prosperity treatments were administered to poverty sufferers in every country of the globe the world would take on a different appearance.

But there is no need for those of you now suffering from poverty to wait for the coming of that time to be cured. Anyone can apply the law and treat himself or herself for prosperity.

Mental laws are clear and simple. We know that the fear thought attracts more fear, the worry thought more worry, the anxious thought more anxiety, the hatred thought more hatred, the jealous thought more jealousy, and the poverty thought more poverty. This is the law of attraction. Like every other law, it is unalterable.

The poverty disease can be cured only by its antidote—the prosperity thought. You carry within you this antidote to the poison of poverty, of lack, of pinching, dwarfing limitation. It is the prosperity thought. Use it, and cure yourself. Kill the poverty germ.

Picture yourself as prosperous. Obey the law of opulence by holding the ideal of opulence in your mind. Saturate yourself with the prosperity thought, the thought of abundance.

I was recently talking with a man who only a few years ago was so poor that he and his wife and children were reduced to a diet of bread and crackers without butter. They couldn't pay even the cheapest rent or buy themselves comfortable clothing. In fact, they were rapidly heading toward the ranks of the "down and outs." Today they are living in luxury, in a sumptuous hotel.

They own a beautiful car, and have all they need to make life comfortable. They do not appear like the same people who but a comparatively short time ago were in a condition of semi-starvation.

Whence the change? Did some one leave them a fortune, or did they find a gold mine? No, nothing of that sort at all. They simply realized that their poverty was of their own making, that the cause of their miserable condition was entirely mental. And there and then they turned their backs on their despair environment and resolved that, no matter what appearances were, they would face the light and struggle toward it. As a result they began in a very short time to attract better things.

The whole family has now taken a new lease of life. The expression of despair and misery has gone out of their faces, and is replaced by the light of hope and joy. There is just the difference in their appearance and condition between despair and gladness, between the hope and expectation of more of the good things which belong to them, and the fear of want, the misery of grinding limitations.

Psychology is teaching us that all forms of discouragement, despondent thoughts, thoughts of doubt, of fear, of worry, must be kept out of the mind, for the mind cannot create while these enemies are in possession of the mental kingdom. We are finding that in order to create, to build, we must bold a constructive mental attitude all the time, that we must keep all negatives, all thoughts of discouragement, despondency, of possible failure out of the mind. We are learning through psychology that we can produce only that which we concentrate upon, that which we constantly think of; that only that which is dominant in our mind, whether it is beneficial or injurious, will be reproduced in our lives.

Your mental attitude will lead you into the light or hold you in darkness. It will lead you to hope or despair, to a glorious success or a miserable failure, and it is entirely within your own power to choose which it shall be.

Successful people are—and perhaps without always consciously being aware of it—constantly giving themselves prosperity treatments, success treatments, by encouraging themselves, by making their minds positive, so that they will be immune from all negative, discouraging, poverty, thought currents.

Holding the success thought, the prosperity ideal, constantly dwelling upon one's successful future, expecting it, working for it, these are, whether you know it or not, prosperity treatments.

Every time you indulge in discouraging and gloomy, despondent thoughts, every time you allow yourself to get down in the dumps or in the blues, you are tearing down what you have been trying to build up by your success treatments, by holding the prosperous thought. Your attitude is hostile to prosperity, and your very atmosphere blights and strangles it. It is as if you are saying to yourself, "I long to have you, Mr. Prosperity, but I don't believe I ever will. You were evidently not intended for me, for everything I do ends in failure. There must be some strange fate that is keeping me from the success and prosperity I want. I really never expect to be prosperous, although I am working hard to get you, Mr. Prosperity."

When we get lost in the woods, we cannot tell the direction in which we are facing, because we have lost the points on the compass.

Unless we can see the sun and recover our bearing, we will walk around in a circle, thinking we are going in a straight line in the right direction. But we make no advance, because we aren't facing our goal. After a while, when we find that we are not getting toward any opening and don't know how long we will wander about in a circle, we get discouraged.

Millions of us are lost in the dense woods of wrong thought. We are not traveling toward the goal of prosperity. We see no light, no way out of the woods, and we lose courage. We are turned about mentally, and don't know it.

CHAPTER 39
Poverty a Mental Disability

p overty itself is not so bad as the poverty thought. It is the conviction *that we are poor and must remain so that is fatal.* It is the attitude of mind that is destructive—the facing toward poverty and feeling so reconciled to it that one does not turn about face and struggle to get away from it with a determination which knows no retreat.

So long as you carry around a poverty atmosphere and radiate the poverty thought, you will be limited.

You will be but a poor person while you think poverty—just as, relatedly, you will be a failure while you think failure thoughts.

If you are afraid of poverty, if you dread it, if you have a horror of coming to want in old age, it is more likely to come to you, because this constant fear saps your courage, shakes your self-confidence, and makes you less able to cope with hard conditions.

The mind is a magnet, and a magnet must be true to itself: it must attract things like itself. If your mind is saturated with the fear thought, the poverty thought, then no matter how hard you work, you will attract poverty.

You walk in the direction in which you face. If you persist in facing toward poverty, you cannot expect to reach abundance. When every step you take is on the road to failure, you cannot expect to reach the success goal.

Holding the poverty thought keeps us in touch with poverty-stricken, poverty-producing conditions—the constant thinking of poverty, talking poverty, living poverty, makes us mentally poor. This is the worst kind of poverty.

I have never known a person to be successful who was always talking about business being bad. The habit of looking down, talking down, is fatal to advancement. Those who are always thinking of their hard luck and failure to get on, can by no possibility go in the opposite direction, where the goal of prosperity lies.

If you would attract good fortune you must get rid of doubt. As long as that stands between you and your ambition, it will be a bar that will cut you off. You must have faith. No one can make a fortune while convinced that he or she can't. The "I can't" philosophy has wrecked more careers than almost anything else. Confidence is the magic key that unlocks the door of supply.

When we lose the confidence that we can rise, improve ourselves, then every other success quality gradually leaves us, and life becomes a grind. We lose ambition and energy and become less and less capable of conquering poverty.

A young man of remarkable ability, who has an established position in the business world, recently told me that for a long time he had been very poor, and remained so until he made up his mind that he was not intended to be poor, that poverty was really a mental disease of which he intended to rid himself. He formed a habit of daily affirming abundance and plenty, of asserting his faith in himself and in his ability to become a man of means and importance in the world. He persistently drove the poverty thought out of his mind. He would have nothing to do with it.

He would not allow himself to think of possible failure. He turned his face toward the success goal—turned his back forever on poverty and failure.

He says that he used to pinch in every possible way in order to save in little ways. He would eat the cheapest kind of food, and as sparingly as possible. He would rarely get on a bus or streetcar, even if he had to walk for miles.

Under the new impulse he completely changed his habits. He resolved that he would go to good restaurants, get a comfortable room in a good location, and would try in every way to meet cultured people, and to form acquaintance's with those above him who could help him.

The more liberal he has been, the better he has been to himself in everything which could help him along, which would tend to a higher culture and a better education, the more things have come his way. He found that it was his pinched, stingy thoughts that shut off his supply.

Although he is now living well, he says that the amount he spends is a mere bagatelle compared with the larger things that come to him from his enlarged thought, his changed attitude of mind.

Nine-tenths of the people in the so-called industrialized, advanced countries who complain of being poor and failures are headed in the wrong direction, headed away from the condition or thing they long for. What they need is to be turned around so that they will face their goal, instead of turning their backs on it by their destructive thinking and going in the other direction. The Carnegies, Rockefellers, Vander-bilts, think prosperity, and they get it. They don't anticipate poverty, they don't anticipate failure, they know they are going to be prosperous and successful because they have eliminated all doubt of *not being so* from their minds.

Doubt is the factor which kills success, just as the fear of failure kills prosperity. Everything is mental first, whether failure or success. Everything passes through our consciousness before it is a reality.

That is why stingy, narrow minds do not attract money. If they get money they usually get it by parsimonious saving—like Ebenezer Scrooge—rather than by obeying the law of opulence. It takes a broad, liberal mind to attract money. The narrow, stingy mind shuts out the flow of abundance.

It is the hopeful, buoyant, cheerful attitude of mind that wins. Optimism is a prosperity builder; pessimism a prosperity killer.

Optimism is the great producer. It is hope, life. It contains everything which enters into the mental attitude which produces and enjoys prosperity.

No matter if you have lost your property, your health—your reputation even—there is always hope if you keep a firm faith in yourself and look up.

As long as you radiate doubt and discouragement, you will be a failure.

If those of you who believe that your opportunity has gone by forever, that you can never get on your feet again, only knew the power of reversal of your thoughts, you could easily get a new start.

But before you can live in a new world, you must believe in it.

I know a family whose members completely reversed their condition by reversing their mental attitude. They had been living in a discouraging atmosphere so long that they were convinced that success was for others, but not for them. They believed so thoroughly that they were fated to be poor that their home and entire environment were pictures of dilapidation and failure. Everything was in a rundown condition. There was almost no paint on the house, no carpets on the floors, and scarcely a picture on me wall—nothing to make the home comfortable and cheerful, All the members, of the family looked like failures. The home was gloomy, cold, and cheerless. Everything about it was depressing.

One day the mother read something that suggested that poverty was largely a mental disease, and she began at once to reverse her thinking habit—to gradually replace all discouraging, despondency, failure thoughts with their opposites.

She assumed a sunny, cheerful attitude, and looked and acted as if life were worth living.

Soon her husband and children caught the contagion of her cheerfulness, and in a short time optimism took the place of pessimism.

The husband changed his habits. Instead of going to his work unshaven and unkempt, with slovenly dress and slipshod manner, be became neat and tidy. He braced up, brushed up, cleaned up, and looked up. And the children followed his example.

The result of all this was that it brought about what many people would call "good luck." The change in the mental attitude, the outlook toward success and happiness instead of failure, reacted upon the father's mind, gave him new hope and new courage, and so increased his efficiency that he was soon promoted, as were also his sons. After two or three years of the creative, inspiring atmosphere of hope and courage, the entire family was transformed—as was the house! It was repaired—renovated within and without.

We must play the part of our ambition. If you are trying to be prosperous, you must play the part. If you are trying to demonstrate opulence, you must play it—not weakly, but vigorously, grandly. You must *feel* opulent. You must *think* opulence. You must *appear* opulent. Your bearing must be filled with confidence. You must give the impression of your own assurance, that you are large enough to play your part and to play it superbly.

Suppose the greatest actor or actress living were to have a play written for him or her in which the leading part was to represent a character in the process of making a fortune—a great, vigorous, progressive character, who conquered by his or her very presence. Suppose this actor, in playing the part, were to dress like an unprosperous character and walk on the stage in a stooping, slouchy, slipshod manner, as though he or she had no ambition, no energy or life— no real faith that he or she could ever make money or be a success, shuffling around the stage with an apologetic, shrinking, skulking manner, as much as to say, "Now, I do not believe that I can ever do this thing that I have attempted; it is too big for me. Other people have done it, but I never thought that I should ever be rich or prosperous. Somehow good things do not seem to be meant for me. I am just an ordinary person. I haven't had much experience and I haven't much confidence in myself, and it seems presumptuous for me to think I am ever going to be rich or have much influence in the world."

What kind of an impression would he make upon the audience? Would that actor or actress give confidence, radiate power or forcefulness, make people think that that kind of character could create a fortune, could manipulate conditions which would produce money? Would not everybody say that that character was a failure? Would they not laugh at the idea of that character conquering anything?

If you talk poverty, think poverty, live poverty, assume the air of a pauper, dress like a failure, how long do you think it would take you to arrive at the goal of prosperity?

Our mental attitude toward the thing we are struggling for has everything to do with our gaining it. If you want to become prosperous, you must believe that you were made for prosperity and happiness.

Erase all the shadows, all the doubts and fears, and the suggestions of poverty and failure from your mind. When you have become master of your thought, when you have once learned to dominate your mind, you will find that things will begin to come your way. Discouragement, fear, doubt, lack of self-confidence, are the germs which have killed the prosperity and happiness of tens of thousands of people.

If it were possible for all the poor to turn their backs on their dark and discouraging environment and face the light and cheer, and if they should resolve that they are done with poverty and a slipshod existence, this very resolution would, in a short time, revolutionize civilization.

Every human being from childhood on should be taught to *expect* prosperity, to believe that the good things of the world were intended for him or her.

Wealth is created mentally first; it is thought out before it becomes a reality. Those who decide to become physicians, talk medicine, read medicine, study medicine, and think medicine until they become saturated with it. They do not decide to become a physician and then put themselves in a legal atmosphere—read law, talk law, think law.

In a like manner, if you want success and abundance, you must think, walk, and talk success—you must think, walk, and talk abundance.

Stoutly deny the power of adversity or poverty to keep you down. Constantly assert your superiority to your environment. Believe that you are to dominate your surroundings, that you are the master and not the slave of circumstances.

Resolve with all the vigor you can muster that since there are plenty of good things in the world for everybody, you are going to have your share, without injuring anybody else or keeping others back. It was intended that you should have a competence, an abundance. Prosperity is your birthright, and you should resolve to reach your divine destiny.

Poverty is an abnormal condition. It does not fit any human being's constitution. It contradicts the promise and the prophecy of the divine in a person. There is not a single indication in our wonderful mechanism that we were created for a life of poverty. There is something larger and grander for us in the divine plan than perpetual slavery to the bread-winning problem.

No one can do their best work—bring out the best thing in themselves—while they feel want tugging at their heels, while they are hampered, restricted, and forever at the mercy of pinching circumstances.

The very poor, those struggling to keep the wolf at bay, cannot be independent. They cannot always afford to live in decent locations— and surely not in healthful houses. They cannot order their lives. Often they cannot even afford to express their opinions or have individual views.

Praise it who will, poverty in its extreme form is narrowing, belittling, contracting, ambition-killing—an unmitigated curse. There is little hope in it, little prospect in it, little joy in it. It too often develops the worst in people, and kills love between those who would otherwise live happily together.

It is difficult for the average human being to be a real man or real woman in extreme poverty. When worried, embarrassed, entangled with debts, forced to make a dime perform the proper work of a dollar, it is almost impossible to preserve that dignity and self-respect which enable a person to hold up his or her head and look the world squarely in the face. Some rare and beautiful souls have done this. Amidst dire poverty, they have given us examples of noble living that the world will never forget. But how many has poverty's lash driven to the lowest depths?

Poverty is more often a curse than a blessing, and those who praise its virtues would be the last to accept its hard conditions.

I wish I could fill every youth with an utter dread and horror of it; make them feel its constraint, its bitterness, its strangling effect—the way it can make one feel less of oneself.

There is no disgrace in unpreventable poverty. We respect and honor people who are poor because of ill-health or misfortune which they cannot prevent.

What we denounce is preventable poverty—that poverty which is due to the lack of effort, to wrong thinking, or to any preventable cause.

The trouble is that many of poverty's victims today have no confidence that they can get away from poverty. They hear so much about the poor person's lack of opportunities, that the great money combinations will compel nearly everybody in the future to work for somebody else; they hear so much talk of the grasping and the greed of the rich, that they gradually lose confidence in their ability to cope with conditions and become disheartened.

I do not overlook the heartless, grinding, grasping practices of many of the rich, or the unfair and cruel conditions brought about by unscrupulous political and financial schemers, but I wish to show the poor person that, notwithstanding all these things, multitudes of poor people do rise above their iron environment—and that there is hope.

The mere fact that so many continue to rise, year after year, out of just such conditions as you may think are fatal to your advancement—if you are currently struggling financially—ought to convince you that you also can conquer your environment.

Poverty begins in the mind. The majority of poor people in out cities remain poor because, tragically, they are mental paupers to begin with. They don't believe they are ever going to be prosperous. Fate and conditions are against them, they believe—they were born poor and they expect to always be poor: this is their unvarying trend of thought, their fixed conviction. Go among the poor in the slums and you will find them always talking about poverty, bewailing their hard luck, the cruelty and injustice of society. They will tell you how they are ground down by the upper classes, kept down by their greedy employers, or by an unjust order of things which they can't change They think of themselves as victims instead of victors, as conquered instead of conquerors.

The worst thing about poverty, then, is the poverty thought—the conviction that we are poor and must remain so.

Holding the poverty thought keeps us in poverty-stricken and poverty-producing conditions.

When you make up your mind that you are done with poverty forever; that you will have nothing more to do with it; that you are going to erase every trace of it from your dress, your personal appearance, your manner, your talk, your actions, your home; that you have set your face persistently toward better things and that nothing on earth can turn you from your resolution, you will be amazed to find what a reinforcing power will come to you, what an increase of confidence, reassurance, and self-respect.

The very act of resolving that you will have nothing more to do with poverty; that you will make the best possible out of what you do have; that you will put up the best possible appearance; that you will clean up, brush up, talk up, look up, instead of down—hold your head up and look the world in the face instead of cringing, whining, complaining—will create a new spirit within you which will lead you to the light. Hope will take the place of despair, and you will feel the thrill of a new power, of a new force coursing through your veins.

If you feel that you are down and out and everything about you looks bleak and discouraging, just try the experiment of turning squarely about and facing the other way—toward the sun of hope and expectancy—leaving all shadows behind you.

Cut off all currents of poverty thoughts, of doubt thoughts. Tear down from the walls of your mind all gloomy, depressing pictures, and hang up bright, hopeful, cheerful ones.

Remind yourself that thousands of people before you and around you in this country have *thought* themselves away from a life of poverty by getting a glimpse of this great principle: that we tend to realize in the life what we persistently hold in the thought and vigorously struggle toward.

CHAPTER 40
Making Yourself a Prosperity Magnet

every human being is a magnet, the attractive power of which may be developed in any desired direction. Each one can so direct this power that he can draw to himself whatever he wills.

Before your life can be really effective you must make yourself a magnet for the things that will make it so. You must learn how to attract, how to draw to yourself all that will help you to succeed in your work, that will enable you to attain your ambitions.

If poverty is holding you down, you can conquer it by making yourself a prosperity magnet. We are living in the midst of a stream of inexhaustible supply. It is one's own fault if he does not take from this stream whatever he needs.

What we get in life we get by the law of attraction. Like attracts like. Whatever you may have managed to get together in this world you have attracted by your mentality. You may say that you have earned these things, that you have bought them with your salary, the fruit of your endeavor. True, but your thought preceded your endeavor. Your mental plan went before your achievement.

The mere changing of your mental attitude will very soon begin to change conditions. Your decision to face toward prosperity hereafter, to cultivate it, to make yourself a prosperity magnet will tend to draw to you the things that will satisfy your ambition.

The text "He that hath a bountiful eye shall be blessed" (Prov. 22:9) is the expression of a fundamental truth. The pictures you make in your mind's eye, the thoughts you harbor are day by day building your outward conditions They are real forces working ceaselessly in the unseen, and the more you think and visualize favorable conditions the more you increase your power to realize them. You make yourself a magnet for the thing you desire. This is a psychological law.

If you want to become a prosperity magnet you must not only think prosperity but you must also turn your back resolutely on poverty. Begin today. Don't wait for tomorrow or next day. If you don't look, prosperous assume a prosperous appearance. Dress as far as possible like a prosperous man or woman, walk like one, act like one, think in terms of prosperity. A mental healer could not cure a cancer by holding in mind a picture of the hideous disease, with all its horrible appearances and symptoms. The healer must eliminate all this from his or her mind. He or she must see his patient whole, clean, healthy—free from all disease.

The same thing is true if you want to be prosperous: you must hold the prosperous thought, the prosperous picture in your mind. You must refuse to see or recognize poverty. You must not acknowledge it in your manner. You must erase all marks of it, not only from your mental attitude, but just as far as possible from your appearance. Even if you are not able to wear fine clothes at first, or to live in a fine house, you can radiate the hope and expectancy of the glorious inheritance which is your birthright, and -everything about you will reflect this light.

Prosperity begins in the mind. You must lay its foundations in your thoughts, surround yourself with a prosperity atmosphere. In other words, you will build into your environment, into your life, whatever dwells in your mind.

We hear of some people that "they are always lucky"; "everything seems to cone their way." Things come their way because there are invisible thoughts forces radiating from their minds toward the goal they have set for themselves. Things fall in line and come our way just in proportion to the force and velocity of the thought forces we project.

Thinking better things might be called the first aid for those who want to be prosperous.

To picture yourself as prosperous, living in a comfortable home, wearing good clothes, surrounded with the refinements of life, in a position to do your best work in the service of mankind, this is to put yourself into the current that runs success-ward.

It is a strange thing that most of us believe the Creator will help us in everything but our financial troubles. We seem to think that it is in some way almost sacrilegious to call upon Him for money to meet our needs. We may ask for comfort, for solace in our afflictions, for the assuaging of our griefs and the healing of our diseases, but to implore God to help us to pay the rent, to pay off the mortgage on the home or the farm, does not seem quite right.

Yet we know perfectly well that every mouthful of food we eat, the material for the clothing we wear and for the houses we live in every breath we breathe must come from this Divine Source, of infinite supply. If the sun were to be blotted out, or to cease to send its magic rays to the earth, in a few days there would not be a single living thing on the globe. Not a human being, not an animal could exist without it. Not a tree, not a plant, not a flower, no fruits, no vegetables, no grass, nothing green, no vegetable life, would be possible. Without the sun's energizing power all, life would cease on this planet. It would be as cold, barren and lifeless as on the moon. In a like manner, everything we have comes from the creator, and without the supply which flows from His abundance we could not live a single instant. Why should we not, then, look to this great Source for our money supply?

The truth is we were all intended to live the life abundant. Never for a moment harbor the thought that anything can come to you but prosperity, for this is your birthright; and because it is, you should demand it.

Turn your back on poverty. Make up your mind that you will never again have anything to do with it, that you will not encourage it by dwelling on and visualizing poverty suggestions. Face toward prosperity. Think of and plan for prosperous conditions; struggle toward prosperity with all your might and you will draw it to you.

Suppose you are poor and live in a humble home, just have a talk with your spouse and children, and make up your minds that you will all focus on your objective—improved conditions—that you will face the other way, toward prosperity instead of poverty. Tidy up your little home and make it as neat and cheerful as possible. Do the same with your dress and general appearance. Keep yourself better groomed; look up brace up, brush up, struggle up. Surround yourself with an atmosphere of hopefulness and show everybody by the new light in your eyes the light of hope and expectancy of better things, that there is a change in you. Your neighbors will notice it. They will see a change in your home and your family. The change in the mental attitude of yourself and family, through facing toward the light instead of darkness, toward hope instead of despair, will make a tremendous change in your whole outlook on life.

In this way you are making yourself a prosperity magnet, you are radiating thought waves of hope, of ambition, of determination. Your new mental attitude is expressed in an erect carriage, in squared, thrown back shoulders, in a neat, clean appearance—even though the clothing be old and threadbare—in a winning, forceful, magnetic countenance. You are thus establishing the conditions of success. The positive prosperity thought flows out like a wireless current and connects itself with similar thought currents. Hold the prosperity conviction, work steadily toward your object; see opportunity and success in your vista, determine to be somebody, hold firmly to the resolve, and your mentality will direct the invisible magnet of your personality to lift you higher and higher, to attract toward you others who will help you in the direction in which you are moving.

If you want a better position, more salary, money to pay off debts, or to get what you need, whatever it may be, cling with all the power of your mind to the thing you are trying to get, and never for a moment doubt you will get it.

As long as you keep yourself saturated with the poverty conviction you cannot rise out of poverty. You must think yourself out of it.

Abundance will never flow through pinched, doubting, poverty thoughts, any more than clear, crystal water can flow freely through foul, grease-clogged pipes. A right view-point must be your mental plumber to keep the connection open and free. Things of a kind attract one another. The poverty thought attracts more poverty, the fear thought more fear, the worry thought more worry, the anxiety thought more anxiety. On the other hand, the faith thought, trust thought, and the confidence thought attract things like themselves.

Poverty is a mental disease, and you carry the antidote to its poison in your mind. The prosperity thought is the natural antidote for the poverty germ. It kills it. The poverty thought cannot exist in the mind at the same moment with the prosperity thought. One will drive out the other. It rests with you which one you will harbor and encourage.

The trouble with us is that we have been in the habit of looking for a material supply when our first supply must be mental. We keep the supply avenues open or we close them with our thoughts, our convictions. We materialize poverty by our doubting thoughts, by our fears of it. We are just beginning to find that we get out of this world what we think into it and work out of it, that our thought plan precedes its material realization just as the architect's plan precedes the building.

Remember that prosperity cannot flow into your life while your mind is filled with poverty thoughts and convictions. We go in the direction of our thought and our convictions. By no law can you expect to get that which you do not believe you will get. Prosperity can not come to you if, you are all the time driving it away from you by your poverty thought.

You must think in a positive determined way that you are going to succeed in whatever you desire to do or to be before you can expect success. That is the first condition by which you make yourself a magnet for the thing you are after. It doesn't matter whether it is work or money, a better position or health, or whatever else it is, your thoughts about it must be positive, clean cut, decisive, persistent. No weak, wobbly, "*Perhaps* I may get it," or "*Maybe* it will come, *sometime*," or "I *wonder* if *I* shall *get* this," or "if *I* can *do* that" sort of thought will ever help you to get anything in this world.

When young John Wanamaker started with a pushcart to deliver his first sale of clothing, he turned on a positive current toward a merchant princeship. As he passed big clothing stores he pictured himself as a great merchant, owner of a much bigger establishment than any of those he saw, and he did not neutralize or weaken this thought current by all sorts of doubts or fears as to the possibility of reaching the goal of his ambition.

Most people think too much about blindly forcing themselves ahead. They do not realize that they can, by the power of thought, make themselves magnets to draw to them the things that will help them to get on. Wanamaker attracted to himself the forces that make a merchant prince. Every step he took was forward, to match the vision of his advance with its reality:

Marshall Field projected himself mentally out of a little country store into a clerkship in Chicago. Then he thought and worked himself out of this clerkship into a partnership. Still thinking and climbing upward, he next visualized himself at the head of the greatest merchandizing establishment in America, if not in the world. His mind always ran ahead. He was always picturing himself a little higher up, a little further on, always visualizing a larger business, and so making himself a magnet for the things he sought.

If John Wanamaker had been satisfied with himself at the start he would have remained in his first little store in Philadelphia, and thus cut off all possibility of becoming what he is—one of the greatest merchants the world has ever seen. If Marshall Field had stopped thinking himself higher up when the man he worked for in the little Pittsfield store predicted that he never would succeed as a merchant, he never would have been heard from But that man did not stop Marshall Field from thinking himself ahead. "On to Chicago, the City of Opportunity," he said to himself, and on and up he went until the little country merchant who predicted his failure was a Lilliputian by comparison.

The story of each of these men is, so far as the success principle is concerned, the story of every person who has ever succeeded in his undertakings. They may not have been conscious of the law underlying their methods, but they worked in unison with it, and hence succeeded.

The same thing is true of Andrew Carnegie, and of all the millionaires and self-made men and women among us who have raised themselves from poor boys to the ownership of colossal fortunes, or to commanding positions in some phase of the world's activities.

Any one who makes the accumulation of a fortune his or her chief goal, and who has grit, determination, willpower and sufficient faith in himself or herself to stick to his or her purpose, will get there. But sadly, long before many who have chosen such a goal have reached it, they will have dwarfed their ambitions and shriveled their souls.

To get away from poverty is one thing; to set one's heart on money as the ultimate good is another—and quite different—thing. There is a whole world of difference between so saturating one's mind with the thought of money and its acquisition that there is no room for any other aspiration, and the constant dwelling on the hopeless poverty thought, the incessant picturing yourself as a pauper until you are so convinced of poverty's hold on you that you destroy the very ability which should help you to get away from it.

People who are down and out financially are down and out mentally. They are suffering from a mental disease of discouragement and loss of hope. There ought to be institutions conducted by government experts for the treatment of these poverty sufferers, for they are just as much in need of it as are those in our hospitals. They need advice from mental experts. They have lost their way on the life path, and need to be shown the way back. They need to be turned about mentally, so that they will face the light instead of the darkness. They should be shown that they are stopping up their prosperity pipes, cutting off their source of supply by their pinching, poverty-stricken, limiting thought. Their whole mental attitude points toward failure, toward poverty, and by a natural law their outward conditions conform with the pictures they hold in mind.

What a revelation would come into your life if you will only eliminate from your mind for a single year the poverty thought; if you would erase from your mind poverty pictures and all the suggestions of grinding want that sadden and discourage; if, instead of expecting poverty, and all that the idea implies, you would go through one year expecting just the opposite—prosperity—visualizing, talking prosperity, thinking prosperity, acting as though you expected to be, as though you *were*, prosperous! Just this radical change of thought, this transposition of mental attitude; the persistent holding of the prosperous viewpoint for a year would not only change your whole outlook on life, but would revolutionize your material conditions.

Your ambition would grow; your new way of looking at life would give an upward tendency to your surroundings. Everything would take on a different appearance. There would be a new light in your face; expectancy of better things would give a glow of cheerfulness to your countenance. There would be a light in your eyes which never was there before. Working in the spirit of hope and expectancy of better things instead of that of discouragement and the fears of even greater poverty, you would forge ahead in a way that would astonish yourself.

There is much talk about our not yet having come close to tapping the world's natural resources. But of even greater consequence is that we have not yet tapped even a fraction of possibilities of any part of the world's *human* resources. Every inhabitant of the earth today is treading on secrets which would emancipate humanity from drudgery and allow it to live happily, instead of merely to mostly eke out a wretched subsistence as he it has done up to the present. Hitherto, in the great majority of cases, we have barely been existing on the husks of things.

Now we are beginning to taste the kernel, because we are coming into a knowledge of the powers locked up within ourselves. Here and there, people are mastering the law of opulence.

They are demonstrating that they can make themselves prosperity magnets, by thinking and working in conformity with the law of opulence, of abundance.

If every one of you reading these words who is suffering from the limitations and humiliations imposed by a grinding poverty would proceed to establish the prosperity habit along the lines suggested; if you would, by continually holding the prosperous thought, convince your subconscious self that you were made to be successful, that prosperity belongs to you; that it was never intended that you should live in poverty-stricken conditions, then you will have struck the very basic principle of prosperity.

Hold this victorious attitude toward life, and you will overcome all unfavorable conditions.

CHAPTER 41
Success and Happiness
Are for You

there is plenty of evidence that we were made for grand things, sublime things: for abundance and not for poverty. *Lack and want do not fit our divine nature.* The trouble, though, is that we do not have half enough faith in the good that is in store for us. We do not dare fling out our whole soul's desire, to follow the leading of our divine hunger and ask without stint for the abundance that is our birthright. Instead, if we ask at all, we ask little things, and we expect little things, pinching our desires and limiting our supply. Not daring to ask to the full of our soul's desire, we do not open our selves sufficiently to allow a great inflow of good things. We think in terms of limitation. We do not fling out our soul's desire with that abundant faith that trusts implicitly—and that receives accordingly.

The rose does not ask the sun for only a tiny bit of its light and heat, for it is the sun's nature to throw itself out to everything which will absorb it and drink it in.

The candle loses nothing of its light by lighting another candle.

We do not lose but increase our capacity for friendship by being friendly, by giving abundantly of our love.

One of the great secrets of life is to learn how to transfer the full current of the universal creative force to ourselves, and how to use this force effectively. If each of us will understand—grasp—this law of transference, we will multiply our efficiency a millionfold, because we will then be a co-operator, co-creator with the great creative force of life.

When we recognize that everything comes from the great Infinite Supply and that it flows to us freely, when we get in perfect tune with the Infinite, then all of the good things in the universe will flow to us spontaneously.

The trouble is that we restrict the inflow by wrong acts and wrong thoughts.

Do not be forever apologizing for your lack of this or that. Every time you say that you have nothing fit to wear, that you never have things that other people have, that you never go anywhere or do things that other people do, you are simply etching a despairing picture deeper and deeper. As long as you recite these unfortunate details and dwell upon your disagreeable experiences, your mentality will not attract the thing you are after, will not bring that which will remedy your hard conditions.

Your mental attitude, your mental picturing, must correspond with the reality you seek.

When you learn the art of seeing opulently, instead of stingily; when you learn to think without limits; when you learn how not to cramp yourself by limiting thought; when unfairness, a desire to take advantage of your brothers and sisters, is removed from your life; then you shall find that the thing you are seeking is seeking you—and that it will meet you half way.

Prosperity begins in the mind, and is impossible with a mental attitude which is hostile to it. We can not attract opulence mentally by a poverty-stricken attitude which is driving away what we long for. It is fatal to work for one thing and to expect something else. No matter how much one may long for prosperity, a poverty-stricken mental attitude will close all the avenues to it.

Opulence and prosperity can not come in through poverty-thought and failure-thought channels, for the weaving of the web is bound to follow the pattern.

We must think prosperity before we can come to it. It must be created mentally first.

How many of us take it for granted that there are plenty of good things in this world for others—comforts, luxuries, fine houses, good, clothes, opportunity for travel, leisure—but not for us? We settle down into the conviction that these things do not belong to us. And so, we put up bars between ourselves and plenty. We cut off abundance; we make the law of supply inoperative for ourselves by shutting your mind to it.

The limitation is in ourselves, not in life.

One of the greatest curses o f the world is the belief in the necessity of poverty. Most people have a strong conviction that some must necessarily be poor—and many believe that they were made to be poor. But there need not be a poor person on the planet. The earth is full of resources which we have scarcely yet touched. We have been poor in the very midst of abundance, simply because of our own limiting thoughts.

We are discovering that thoughts are things, that they are incorporated into life and form part of the character, and that if we harbor the lack thought, if we are afraid of poverty, of coming to want, this poverty thought incorporates itself into our very life texture and makes us the magnet to attract more poverty like itself.

It was not intended that we should have such a hard time getting a living, that we should just manage to squeeze along, to get together a few comforts, to spend about all of our time making a living instead of making a life. The life abundant, full, free, beautiful, was intended for us.

If we held the abundance thought that is our birthright, that we possess as children, then just as children, our living-getting would be a mere incident in our life-making.

Resolve that you will turn your back on the poverty idea and that you will vigorously expect prosperity; that you will hold tenaciously the thought of abundance, the opulent ideal, which is befitting your nature; that you will try to live in the realization of plenty, to actually feel rich, opulent. This will help you to attain what you long for. There is a creative force in intense desire.

The fact is that we live in the world of our making: We are creations, the results, of our own thoughts. We each build our own world by our thought habits. We can surround himself with an atmosphere of abundance, or of lack; of plenty, or of want.

We were made to aspire; to look up, not down. We were made for grand things, not to pinch along in poverty.

It is not life or circumstances, but the poverty attitude, the narrowness of our thought, that has limited us.

If we learn to trust implicitly that life is a source of Infinite Supply which always brings seed time and harvest, we shall never know what want is.

But most of us do not have half good enough opinions of our possibilities; do not expect half enough of ourselves. We do not demand the abundance which belongs to us, hence the leanness, the lack of fullness, the incompleteness of our lives. We do not demand *royally*, enough. We are content with too little of the things worth while. *It was intended that we should live the abundant life*, that we should have plenty of everything that is good for us. No one was meant to live in poverty and wretchedness. *The lack of anything that is desirable is not natural to the constitution of any human being.*

Hold the thought that you are one with what you want, that you are in tune with it, so as to attract it. Keep your mind vigorously concentrated upon it. Never doubt your ability to get what you are after, and you will move toward it.

Poverty is most often a mental disease. If you are suffering from it, if you are a victim of it, you will be surprised to see how quickly your condition will improve when you change your mental attitude. Instead of holding a limited, poverty image, turn about and face towards abundance and plenty, towards freedom and happiness.

Prosperity comes through a perfectly scientific mental process. Those who become prosperous *believe* that they are going to *be* prosperous. They have faith in their ability to make money. They do not start out with a mind filled with doubts and fears—all the time talking poverty, thinking poverty, walking like a pauper, and dressing like a pauper. They turns their faces towards the thing they are trying for and are determined to get, and will not admit its opposite picture in their minds.

There are multitudes of people in this country who work hard, but they have lost the hope, the expectation, of prosperity.

Some keep themselves poor by *fear* of poverty, allowing themselves to dwell upon the possibility of coming to want, of not ever having enough.

The terror of poverty, the constant worry about making ends meet, the fear of that awful "rainy day," not only will make you unhappy, it actually disqualify you from putting yourself in a better financial condition. In carrying around such thoughts, you are simply adding to a load which is already too heavy for you.

No matter how dark the outlook or how seemingly limited your environment, positively refuse to see anything that is unfavorable to you, any condition which tends to enslave you, anything that could keep you from expressing the best that is in you.

By what philosophy can we expect poverty thoughts, thoughts of lack and want, to produce prosperity? Our conditions will correspond to our attitudes and ideals. We tend to get what we expect, and if we expect nothing we get nothing. The stream cannot rise higher than its fountainhead; no one can become prosperous who expects, or half expects, to remain poor.

Do not say to yourself, "What's the use? The great business combinations are swallowing up the chances. Before long the multitude will have to work for the few. I do not believe I shall ever do anything more than make just a plain living in a very humble way. I shall never have a home and the things that other people have. I am destined to be poor and a nobody." You will never get anywhere with such ideals.

Those who expects prosperity *are constantly creating money in their minds, building their financial structure mentally.* There must be a mental picture of prosperity first. The building, after all, is first completed in all its details in the architect's mind. The contractor merely puts the stones, the brick and other material around the idea.

We are all architects. Everything we do in life is preceded by some sort of a plan.

It does not take as great a person to place the material around the idea as it does to *create* the idea, the mental picture.

This is not idle dreaming. It is mental planning, mental construction. The true dreamer is the believer, the achiever.

The poor man person is not the one who has little or no property, but the one who is poverty-stricken in ideas, in sympathies, in power of appreciation, in sentiment. The truly poor are those who are poverty-stricken in their opinions of themselves, of their own destinies, of their abilities to reach up—who commit the crime of self-depreciation.

It is *mental* penury that makes us poor.

The great achievers do comparatively little with their hands—they build with their thought. They are practical dreamers. Their minds reach out into the infinite energy ocean and create their opportunities—just as the seed reaches out into the infinite fertile soil around it and brings forth the tree.

To be prosperous we must put ourselves in the prosperous attitude. Parsimonious saving by cheese-paring efforts does not compare in effectiveness with the results of obeying the laws of opulence. We must think opulently. Our mental attitude towards the thing we are striving for and the intelligent effort we put forth to realize it will, in the final analysis, be the measure of our attainment.

We must feel opulent in thought. We must exhale confidence and assurance in our very bearing and manner.

We go in the direction of our concentration. If we concentrate upon poverty, if want and lack predominate in our thought, poverty-stricken conditions must result.

Before we can conquer outward poverty, then, we must conquer inward mental poverty.

PART VI

THE POWER
OF THOUGHT TO
PREVENT AGING

CHAPTER 42
How To Stay Young

many people look forward to old age as a time when, as a recent writer puts it, you have "a feeling that no one wants you, that all those you have borne and brought up have long passed out onto roads where you cannot follow, that even the thought-life of the world streams by so fast that you lie up in a backwater, feebly, blindly groping for the pull of the water, and always pushed gently, hopelessly back."

There is such a thing as an old age of this kind, but not for those who face life in the right way. Such a pathetic, such a tragic ending is not far those who love and are loved, because they keep their hearts open to the joys and sorrows of life, maintain a sympathetic interest in their fellow-beings and in the progress and uplift of the world, keep their faculties sharpened by use, and keep their minds constantly reaching out, broadening and growing.

We shudder at the thought of giving up of a large part of life that has potency for work, for action, and for happiness. But why should any one *look forward* to such a period? It is just this looking forward, the anticipating and dreading the coming of old age, that makes us old.

The creative forces inside of us build on our suggestions, on our thought models, and if we constantly thrust into our consciousness old age thoughts and pictures of decrepitude, of declining faculties, these thoughts and pictures will be reproduced in the body.

A few years ago a young man "died of old age" in a New York hospital. After an autopsy the surgeons said that while the man was in reality only twenty-three-years old he was internally eighty!

And what of birthdays? We celebrate birthdays and mark off each recurring anniversary as a red-letter day and fix in our minds the thought that we are a year older. All through our mature life the picture of death is kept in view, the idea that we must expect it and prepare for it at a certain time. The truth is the death suggestion has wrought more havoc and marred more lives than almost anything else in human history. It is responsible for most of the fear, which is the greatest curse of the race.

A noted physician says that if from childhood on, instead of hearing so much about death we were trained more in the principles of longevity, we would retain our youth very much longer, and would extend our lives to a much greater length than is now general.

The time should come when the custom of celebrating birthdays, of emphasizing the fact that we are a year older, that we are getting so much nearer the end, should be done away with. We should not be reminded so forcibly once in three hundred and sixty-five days that we have arrived at another milestone in age. Instead, we should know that the spirit is not affected by years. In our inmost souls, we should realize that there is a life principle within us that determines that old age is largely a question of mental attitude, and that we become what we are convinced we must become.

If you have arrived at an age which you accept as a starting point for physical deterioration, your body will sympathize with your conviction. Your walk, your gait, your expression, your general appearance, and even your acts will all fall into line with your mental attitude.

A short time ago I was talking with a remarkable man of sixty about growing old. The thought of the inevitableness of the aging processes appalled him. No matter, he declared, what efforts he might make to avert or postpone the decrepitude of age there would come a period of diminishing returns, and though he might fight against it, he would ever after be on the decline of life, going irrevocably toward the sunset, ever nearer and nearer to the time when he should be useless. "The conviction that every moment, every hour, every day takes me so much nearer to that hole in the ground from which no power in Heaven or earth can help, us to escape is ever present in my mind," he said. "This progressive, ever-active retrogression is monstrous. This inevitably decrepit old age staring me in the face is robbing me of happiness, paralyzing my efforts and discouraging my ambition."

"But why do you dwell on those things that terrify you?" I asked. "Why do you harbor such old age thoughts? Why are you visualizing decrepitude, the dulling and weakening of your mental faculties? If you have such a horror of the decrepitude, the loss of memory, the failing eyesight, the hesitating step, and the general deterioration which you believe accompany old age, why don't you get away from these terrifying thoughts, put them out of your mind instead of dwelling on them? Don't you know that what you concentrate on, what you fear, the pictures that so terrify you, are creating the very conditions which you would give anything to escape? If you really wish to stay the old age processes, you must change your thoughts. Erase everything that has to do with age from your mind. Visualize youthful conditions. Say to yourself, 'I cannot grow old in spirit, and that is the only old age to fear. As long as my spirit is youthful, as long as the youth in me lives, I cannot age.'"

The great trouble with those who are getting along in years is that they put themselves outside of the things that would keep them young. Most people after fifty begin to shun children and youth generally. They feel that it is not "becoming to their years" to act as they did when younger, and day by day they gradually fall more and more into old age ways and habits.

We build into our lives the picture patterns which we hold in our minds. This is a mental law. Consequently, when we have reached the time at which most people show traces of their age, we imagine that we must do the same. We begin to think we have probably done our best work, and that our powers must henceforth decline. We imagine our faculties are deteriorating, that they are not quite so sharp as they once were; that we cannot endure quite so much, and that we ought to begin to let up a little; to take less exercise, to do less work, to take life a little easier.

The moment you allow yourself to think your powers are beginning to decline, they will do so, and your appearance and bodily conditions will follow your convictions. If you hold the thought that your ambition is sagging, that your faculties are deteriorating, you will be convinced that those younger than you have the advantage of you, and, voluntarily, at first, you will begin to take a back seat, figuratively speaking, behind them. Once you do this you are doomed to be pushed farther and farther to the rear. You will be taken your own valuation. Having made a confession of age, acknowledged in thought and act and that in so far as work and productive returns are concerned, you are no longer the equal of those younger than you, others will naturally be preferred before you.

If people who have aged prematurely could only analyze the influences which have robbed them of their birthright of youth, they would find that most of the causes of their premature aging were a false conviction that they *must* grow old at about such-and-such a time. It is these aging thoughts and moods and passions make old men and women of many of us in middle life.

The laws of renewal, of rejuvenation are always operating in us, and will be effective if we do not neutralize them by wrong thinking. The chemical changes caused in the blood and other secretions by worry, fear, the operation of the explosive passions, or by any depressing mental disturbance, will put the aging processes in action.

We have the race belief that three score years, or three score years and ten, is a sort of measure of the limit to human life. This has crystallized into a race belief, and we begin to prepare for the end much in advance of the period fixed. As long as we hold this belief we cannot bar out of our minds the consequent suggestion that when we pass the half century limit our powers begin to decline. The very idea that we have reached our limit of growth, that any hope of further progress must be abandoned, tends to etch the old age picture and conviction deeper and deeper in our minds, and of course the creative processes can only reproduce the pattern given them.

Many people have what they call a premonition that they will not live beyond a certain age, and that becomes a focus toward which the whole life points. They begin to prepare for the end. Their conviction that they are to die at a certain time largely determines the limitation of their years.

Not long since, at a banquet, I met a very intelligent, widely read man who told me that he felt perfectly sure he could not possibly live to be an old man. He cited as reason for his belief the analogy which runs through all nature, showing that plants, animals and all forms of life which mature early also die early, and because he was practically an adult at fifteen he was convinced that he must die comparatively young. He said he was like a poplar tree in comparison with an oak: the one matured early and died early; the other matured late and was very long-lived.

So thoroughly was this man under the dominion of his belief that he must die early that he was making no fight for longevity. He did not take ordinary care of his health, or necessary precautions in time of danger. "What is the use," he said, "of trying to fight against Nature's laws? I might as well live while I live, and enjoy all I can, and try to make up for an early death."

Multitudes of people start out in youth similarly handicapped by a belief that they have some, hereditary taint, a predisposition to some disease that will probably shorten their lives. They go through life with this restricting, limiting thought so deeply embedded in the very marrow of their being that they never even try to develop themselves to their utmost capacity.

Just think of the pernicious influence upon a child's mind of the constant suggestion that it will probably die very young because its parents or some of its relatives did; that even if it is fortunate enough to survive the diseases and accidents of youth and early maturity, it is not possible to extend its limits of life much, if any, beyond a certain point! Yet we burn this and similar suggestions into the minds of our children until they become a part of their lives.

Our achievement depends very largely upon the expectancy plan, the life pattern we make for ourselves. If we make our plan to fit only one-half or one-third of the time we ought to live, naturally we will accomplish only a fraction of what we are really capable of doing. I have a friend who from boyhood has been convinced that he would not live much, if any beyond forty years, because both his parents had died before that age. Consequently, he expects to die by the time he is forty.

It is infinitely better to believe that we are going to live much longer than there is any probability we shall than to cut off precious years by setting a fixed date for our death simply because one or both of our parents happened to die about such an age, or because we fear we have inherited some disease, such as cancer, which is likely to develop fatally at about a certain time.

As a matter of fact the average length of life is steadily increasing. Formerly men and women grew old very much earlier than they do now, and they died much younger. To prepare for the future life seemed to be the chief occupation of our Puritan ancestors. They had very little use for this world and did not try to enjoy life here very much. They were always talking and praying and singing about "the life over there," while making the life here gloomy and forbidding. They forgot that the religion Christ taught was one of joy.

There is no greater foe to the aging processes than joy, hope, good cheer, gladness. These are the incarnation of the youthful spirit. If you would keep young, cultivate this spirit, think youthful thoughts; live much with youth; enter into their lives, into their sports, their plays, their ambitions. Play the youthful part, not half heartedly, but with enthusiasm and zest.

You cannot use any ability until you think, until you believe, you can. Your reserve power will stand in the background until your self-faith calls it into action. If you want to stay young you must act as if you felt young.

If you do not wish to grow old, quit thinking and acting as if you were aging. Instead of walking with drooped shoulders and with a slow, dragging gait, straighten up and put elasticity into your steps. Do not walk like an old man or woman whose energies are waning, whose youthful fires are spent. Step with the springiness of a young person full of life, spirit and vigor. The body is not old until the mind gives its consent. Stop thinking of yourself as an old man or an old woman. Cease manifesting symptoms of decrepitude. Remember that the impression you make upon others will react on yourself. If other people get the idea that you are going down hill physically and mentally, you will have all the more to overcome in your effort to change their convictions.

The habit of growing old must be combated as we combat, any other vicious habit, by reversing the processes by which it is formed. Instead of surrendering and giving up to old age convictions and fears, stoutly deny them and affirm the opposite. When the suggestion comes to you that your powers are waning, that you cannot do what you once did, prove its falsity by exercising the faculties which you think are weakening. Giving up is only to surrender to age.

We tend to find what we look for in this world, and if, as we advance in years, we are always looking for signs of old age we will find them. If you are constantly on the alert for symptoms of failing faculties, you will discover plenty of them; and the great danger of this is that we are apt to take our unfortunate, temporary moods for permanent symptoms. Some days, for example, perhaps you cannot think as clearly, you cannot concentrate your mind as well, you do not remember as readily as you did the day before. You then immediately jump to the conclusion that a person of your age must be beginning to fail—that you cannot expect as much of yourself as when you were younger.

In other words, when we are ambitious to obtain a certain thing, and our hearts are set on it, we strive for it, we contact with it mentally and through our thoughts we become vitally related to it. We establish a connection with the coveted object. We do everything in our power to obtain it; and the mental effort is a real force which tends to match our dream with its realization.

And so instead of fighting off age by holding the eternal youth thought and the vigor thought, many hold thoughts of weakness and declining powers. When they happen to forget something, they say their memory is beginning to go bad on them—and soon their sight will soon begin to fail. They go on anticipating signs of decline and decrepitude, until the old age visualization is built into the very structure of their bodies.

Instead of forming the habit of looking for signs of age, form the habit of looking for signs of youth. Form the habit of thinking of your body as robust and supple and your brain as strong and active. Never allow yourself to think that you are on the decline, that your faculties are on the wane, that they are not as sharp as they used to be and that you cannot think as well because your cells are becoming old and hard.

They age who think they are aging. They keep young who believe they are young.

Many of us do not realize the biological fact that Nature herself bestows upon us the power of perpetual renewal. There is not a cell in our bodies that can possibly become very old, because all of them are frequently renewed. Physiologists tell us that the tissue cells of some muscles are renewed every few months. Some authorities estimate that eighty or ninety per cent of all the cells in the body of a person of ordinary activity are entirely renewed within a couple of years.

One's mental attitude, however, is the most important of all. There is no possible way of keeping young while convinced that one must inevitably manifest the characteristics of old age. The old age thoughts stamp themselves upon the new body cells, so that they very soon look forty, fifty, sixty, or seventy years old. We should hold tenaciously the conviction that none of the cells of the body can be old because they are constantly being renewed, a large part of them every few months.

Age is not so much a matter of years as of the limpidity, the suppleness of the protoplasm of the cells of the body, and there is nothing which will age the protoplasm like such aging as worry, anxiety, fear, anger, hatred, revenge, or any discordant emotion.

Some people try to cure the physical ravages made by wrong living and wrong thinking by patching their bodies from the outside. The "beauty parlors" in our great cities are besieged by those who are desperately trying to maintain their youthful appearance, not realizing that the elixir of youth is in one's own mind, not in bottles or boxes.

You cannot repair the ravages of age on the outside. You must remove the cause, which is in the mind, in the heart. When the affections are marbleized, when one ceases to be sympathetic and helpful and interested in life, the ravages of old age will appear in spite of all the beauty doctors in the world.

Work, love, kindness, sympathy, helpfulness, unselfish interest—these are the eternal youth essences. These never age, and if you make friends with them they will act like a leaven in your life, enriching your nature, sweetening and ennobling your character, and prolonging your youth even to the century mark.

We are learning that the fabled fountain of youth lies in ourselves—in our own mentality. Perpetual rejuvenation and renewal are possible through right thinking. We look as old as we think and feel, because thought and feeling maintain or change our appearance in exact accordance with their persistence or their variations.

It is impossible to appear youthful and remain young unless we feel young.

Youthful thinking should be your life habit.

CHAPTER 43
Why Grow Old?

m any years ago, the former secretary to a justice of the New York Supreme Court committed suicide on his seventieth birthday. "The Statute of Limitations: A Brief Essay on the Osler Theory of Life," was found beside the dead body. It, and the note the man left, read in part:

"Threescore and ten—this is the scriptural statute of limitations. After that, active work for man ceases, his time on earth has expired. . . .

"I am seventy—threescore and ten—and I fit only for the chimney-corner. . . ."

This man had dwelt so long on the so-called Osler theory and the biblical limitation of life to threescore years and ten, that he made up his mind he would end it all on his seventieth birthday.

We are powerfully influenced by our self-imposed limitations and convictions; it is well known that many people die very near the limit they set for themselves—or they have been told or led to believe has been set for them—even though they are in good health when this conviction settles upon them.

There is no probability that the Psalmist had any idea of setting any limit to the life period or that he had any authority whatever for so doing. Many of the sayings in the Bible which people take so literally and accept blindly as standards of living are merely figures of speech used to illustrate an idea. So far as the Bible is concerned, there is just as much reason far setting the life limit at one hundred and twenty or even at Methuselah's age (nine hundred and sixty-nine) as at seventy or eighty. There is no evidence in the Scriptures that even suggests the existence of an age limit beyond which humans were not supposed or allowed to pass!

In fact the whole spirit of the Bible is to encourage long life through sane and healthful living. It points to the duty of living a useful and noble life, of making as much of ourselves as possible, all of which tends to prolong our years an earth.

It would be a reflection upon the Creator to suggest that He would limit human life to less than three times the age at which it reaches maturity (about thirty) where by analogy, the rest of nature, especially in the animal kingdom, lives a life at least five times the length of the maturing period. Should not the highest manifestation of God's creation have a length of life at least equal to that of the animal? Infinite wisdom does not shake the fruit off the tree before it is ripe.

We do not half realize what slaves we are to our mental attitudes, what power our convictions have to influence our lives. Multitudes of people undoubtedly shorten their lives by many years because of their deep-seated convictions that they will not live beyond a certain age—the age, perhaps, at which their parents died. How often we hear this said: "I do not expect to live to be very old; my father and mother died young."

I know of a New York man, who, in perfect health, told his family that he was certain he should die on his next birthday. On the morning of his birthday his family, alarmed because he refused to go to work, saying that he should certainly die before midnight, insisted upon calling in the family physician, who examined him and said there was nothing the matter with him. But the man refused to eat, grew weaker and weaker during the day, and actually died before midnight. The conviction that he was going to die had become so entrenched in his mind that the whole force of his mentality acted to cut off the life force—ultimately to strangle completely the life processes.

If you have convinced yourself, or if the idea has been ingrained into the very structure of your being by your training or the multitudes of examples about you, that you will begin to show the marks of age at about fifty, that at sixty you will lose the power of your faculties and your interest in the things of life; that you will become practically useless and have to retire from your business; and that thereafter you will continue to decline until you are cut off entirely, there is no power in the world that can keep the old-age processes and signs from developing in you.

Thought leads. If it is an old-age thought, old age must follow. If it is a youthful thought, a perennial young-life thought, a thought of usefulness and helpfulness, the body must correspond. Old age begins in the mind. The expression of age in the body is the harvest of old-age ideas which have been planted in the mind. We see others about our age beginning to decline, showing marks of decrepitude, and we imagine it is about time for us to show the same signs. Ultimately we do show them, because we think they are inevitable. But they are only inevitable because of our old-age mental attitude and race-habit beliefs.

If we actually refuse to grow old; if we insist on holding the youthful ideal and the young, hopeful, buoyant thought, the old-age ear-marks will not show themselves.

Be sure of this: that whatever you feel regarding your age will be expressed in your body. If you can only establish the perpetual-youth mental attitude, so that you feel young, you have won half the battle against old age.

The elixir of youth lies in the mind or nowhere. You cannot be young by trying to appear so by dressing youthfully. You must first get rid of the last vestige of thought that you are aging. As long as that is in the mind, cosmetics and youthful dress will amount to very little in changing your appearance. The conviction must first be changed; the thought which has produced the aging condition must be reversed.

It is a great aid to the perpetuation of youth to learn to feel young, however long you live, because the body expresses the habitual feeling, habitual thought. Nothing in the world will make us look young as long as we are convinced that we are aging. Correspondingly, nothing else more effectually retards age than the keeping in mind the bright, cheerful, optimistic, hopeful, buoyant picture of youth, in all its splendor, magnificence; the picture of the glories which belong to youth—youthful dreams, ideals, hopes, and all the qualities which belong to young life.

One great trouble with us is that our imaginations age prematurely. The hard, exacting conditions of our modern, strenuous life tend to harden and dry up the brain and nerve cells, and thus seriously injure the power of the imagination, which should be kept fresh, buoyant, elastic. The average routine habit of modern business life tends to destroy the flexibility, the delicacy, the sensitiveness, the exquisite fineness of the perceptive faculties.

People who take life too seriously, who seem to think everything depends upon their own individual efforts, whose lives are one continuous grind in living-getting, have a hard expression, their thought outpictures itself in their faces. These people dry up early in life, become wrinkled—their tissues become as hard as their thought.

The arbitrary, domineering, overbearing mind also tends to age the body prematurely, because the thinking is hard, strained, abnormal.

People who live on the sunny and beautiful side of life, who cultivate serenity, do not age nearly so rapidly as do those who live on the shady, the dark side.

Another reason why so many people age prematurely is that they cease to grow. It is a lamentable fact that multitudes of men and women seem incapable of receiving or accepting new ideas after they have reached middle age. Many of them, after they have reached the age of forty or fifty, come to a standstill in their mental reaching out.

Never allow yourself to get out of the habit of being young. Don't think that you must "begin to take in sail." Do not say that you cannot do this or that as you once did. Live the life that belongs to youth. Do not be afraid of being a boy or girl again in spirit, no matter how many years you have lived. Carry yourself so that you will not suggest old age in any of its phases. Remember it is the stale mind, the stale mentality, that ages the body. Keep growing, keep interested in everything about you.

If you wish to retain your youth, forget unpleasant experiences, disagreeable incidents. A lady eighty ears old was recently asked how she managed to keep herself so youthful. She replied: "I know how to forget disagreeable things."

No one can remain youthful who does not continue to grow, and no one can keep growing who does not keep alive his interest in the world. We are so constituted that we draw a large part of our nourishment from others. We cannot isolate ourselves, cannot cut ourselves off from others, without shrinking in our mental stature. The mind that is not constantly reaching out for the new, as well as keeping in touch with the old, soon reaches its limit of growth.

Nothing else is easier than for a person to age. All one has to do is to think one is growing old; to expect it, to fear it, and prepare for it;

to compare oneself with others of the same age who are prematurely old and to assume that one is like them.

To think constantly of the "end," to plan for death, to prepare and provide for declining years, is simply to acknowledge that your powers are waning, that you are losing your grip upon life. Such thinking tends to weaken your hold upon the life principle, and your body gradually corresponds with your conviction.

The very belief that our powers are waning; the consciousness that we are losing strength, that our vitality is lessening; the conviction that old age is settling upon us and that our life forces are gradually ebbing away, has a blighting, shrivelling influence upon the mental faculties and functions; the whole character deteriorates under this old-age belief. The result is that we do not use or develop the age-resisting forces within us. The refreshening, renewing, resisting powers of the body are so reduced and impaired by the conviction that we are getting on in years and cannot cope with what we once could, that we become an easy prey to disease and all sorts of physical infirmities.

The British *Lancet*, one of the highest medical authorities in the world, gave a splendid illustration of the power of the mind to keep the body young. A young woman, deserted by her lover, became insane. She lost all consciousness of the passing of time. She believed her lover would return, and for years she stood daily before her, window watching for him. While over seventy ears of age, some Americans, including physicians, who saw her, thought she was not over twenty. She did not have a single gray hair, and no wrinkles or other signs of age were visible. Her skin was as fair and smooth as a young girl's She did not age, because she believed she was still a girl. She did not count her birthdays or worry because she was getting along in years. She was thoroughly convinced that she was still living in the very time that her lover left her. This mental belief controlled her physical condition. *She was just as old as she thought she was.* Her conviction outpictured itself in her body and kept it youthful.

What has the appearance of old age to do with youth? What have gray hair, wrinkles, and other evidences of age to do with youth? Mental power should constantly increase. There should be no decline in years. Increasing wisdom and power should be the only signs that you have lived long, that you have been many years on this planet. Strength, beauty, magnificence, superiority, not weakness, uselessness, decrepitude, should characterize a person who has lived long.

As long as you hold the conviction that you are sixty, you will look it. Your thought will outpicture itself in your face, in your whole appearance. If you hold the old-age ideal, the old-age conviction, your expression must correspond. The body is the bulletin board of the mind.

On the other hand, if you think of yourself as perpetually young, vigorous, robust, and buoyant, because every cell in the body is constantly being renewed, decrepitude will not get hold of you.

If you would retain your youth, you must avoid the enemies of youth, and there are no greater enemies than the convictions of age and the gradual loss of interest in things, especially in youthful amusements and in the young life about you. When you are no longer interested in the hopes and ambitions of young people, when you decline to enter into their sports, to romp and play with children, you confess, then in effect, that you are growing old—that you are beginning to harden, your youthful spirits are drying up, and that the juices of your younger days are evaporating.

Nothing helps more to the perpetuation of youth than much association with the young.

A man quite advanced in years was asked not long ago how he retained such a youthful appearance in spite of his age. He said that he had been the principal of a high school for over thirty years, and that he loved to enter into the life and sports of the young people and to be one of them in their ambitions and interests. This, he said, had kept his mind centered on youth, progress, and abounding life, and old-age thoughts had had no room for entrance. There is not even a suggestion of age in, this man's conversation or ideas, and there is a life, a buoyancy about him which is wonderfully refreshing.

There must be a constant activity in the mind that would not age. "Keep growing or die" is nature's motto, a motto written all over everything in the universe.

Hold stoutly to, the conviction that it is natural and right for you to remain young. Constantly repeat to yourself that it is wrong for you to grow old in appearance; that weakness and decrepitude could not have been in the Creator's plan for the being made in His image of perfection; that it must have been acquired—the result of wrong race and individual training and thinking.

Constantly affirm: "I am always well, always young, I cannot grow old except by producing the old-age conditions through my thought. The Creator intended me for continual growth, perpetual advancement and betterment, and I am not going to allow myself to be cheated out of my birthright of perennial youth."

No matter if people do say to you: "You are getting along in years," "You are beginning to show signs of age." Just deny these appearances. Say to yourself: "Principle does not age, Truth, does not grow old. I am Principle. I am Truth."

Never go to sleep with the old-age picture or thought in your mind. It is of the utmost importance to make yourself feel young at night; to erase all signs, convictions, and feelings of age; to throw aside every care and worry that would carve its image on your brain and express itself in your face. The worrying mind actually generates calcareous matter in the brain and hardens the cells.

You should fall asleep holding those desires and ideals uppermost in the mind which are dearest to you, which you are the most anxious to realize. As the mind continues to work during sleep, these desires and ideals are thus intensified and increased. Purity of thought, loftiness of purpose, the highest possible aims, should dominate the mind when you fall asleep.

The great thing is to make the mind create the youth pattern instead of the old-age pattern. As the sculptor follows the model which is held in the mind, so the life processes reproduce in the body the pattern which is in our thought, our conviction.

We must get rid of the idea embedded in our very nature that the longer we live, the more experiences we have, the more work we do—the more inevitably we wear out and become old, decrepit, and useless. We must learn that living, acting, experiencing, should not exhaust life but create more life. It is a law that action increases force. Where, then, did the idea come from that one should wear out through action?

As a matter of fact, Nature has bestowed upon us perpetual youth, the power of perpetual renewal. There is not a single cell in our bodies that can possibly become old; the body is constantly being made new through cell-renewal, the cells of those parts of it that are most active being renewed most often. It must follow that the age-producing process is largely artificial and unnatural.

Physiologists tell us that the tissue cells of some muscles are renewed every few days, others every few weeks or months. The cells of the bone tissues are slower of renewal, but some authorities estimate that eighty or ninety per cent of all the cells in the body of a person of ordinary activity are entirely renewed in from six to twenty-four months.

Scientists have proved beyond question that the chemistry of the body has everything to do with the perpetuation of youthful conditions. Every discordant thought produces a chemical change in the cells, introducing foreign substances and causing reaction which is injurious to the integrity of the cells.

Whatever thought dominates the mind at any time is constantly modifying, changing the life ideal, so that every suggestion that comes into the mind from any source is registered in the cell life, etched in the character, and outpictured in the expression and appearance. The thought, the impression, the expectancy of age is thus made upon new cells. This impression is the thought. If the thought is old, the age impress appears upon the cells; If the spirit of youth dominates the thought, the impression upon the cells is youthful. In other words, the processes which result in age cannot possibly operate except through the mind, and the billions of cells composing the body are instantly affected by every thought that passes through the brain.

Putting old thoughts into a new set of cells is like putting new wine into old bottles. The result is that two-year-old cells are made to look fifty, sixty, or more years old, according to the thought. *It is marvelous how quickly old thoughts can make new cells appear old.*

All discordant and antagonistic thought materially interferes with the laws of reconstruction and self-renewal going on in the body. The great thing is, therefore, to form thought habits which will harmonize with this law of rejuvenation—perpetual renewal.

Hard, selfish, worry, and fear thoughts, and vicious habits of all kinds, produce the appearance of age and hasten its coming.

Pessimism is one of the worst enemies of youth. The pessimist ages prematurely because his or her mind dwells upon the negative, discordant, and diseased side of things. The pessimist does not progress, does not face toward youth, but goes backward—and this retrogression is fatal to youthful conditions. Brightness, cheerfulness, hopefulness characterize youth.

Selfishness is an enemy of health because it violates the very fundamental principle of our being—justice, fairness. It does not tend to produce health, harmony, or a sense of well-being, because it does not harmonize with the fundamental principle of our being.

Even prosperity can adversely affect our health. Many wealthy people do not really enjoy their possessions because of that awful consciousness that they may at any moment be forced to leave everything.

Discordant thought of every kind tends to shorten life.

As long as you think old, hard, grasping, envious thoughts, nothing in the world car keep you from growing old. As long as you harbor these enemies of youth, you cannot remain in a youthful condition. New thoughts create new life; old thoughts—canned, stereotyped thoughts—are injurious to growth, and anything which stops growth helps the aging processes.

There is a power of health latent in every cell of the body which would always keep the cell in harmony and preserve its integrity if the thought were right. This latent power of health in the cell can be so developed by right thinking and living as to retard very materially the aging processes.

Hold ever before you, like a beacon light, the youth ideal—strength, buoyancy, hopefulness, expectancy. Hold persistently to the thought that your body is the last two years product; that there may not be in it a single cell more than a year and a half old; that it is constantly young because it is perpetually being renewed and that, therefore, it ought to look fresh and youthful.

Constantly say to yourself: "If Nature makes me a new body every few months, comparatively, if the billions of tissue cells are being perpetually renewed, if the oldest of these cells is, perhaps, rarely, if ever, more than two years old, why should they appear to be sixty or seventy-five?" A two-year-old cell could not look like a seventy-year-old cell of its own accord, but we know from experience that the old-age conviction can make these youthful cells look very old.

The body would always look young if we did not make it look old by stamping old age upon it. Without realizing it, most people are using the old-age thought as a chisel to cut a little deeper the wrinkles.

Their old-age thought is stamping itself upon the new cells only a few months old, so that they very soon look to be forty, fifty, sixty, or seventy years old. We seem very adept in putting the old-age stamp upon new tissue cells. Yet it is just as easy to form the youthful-thought habit as the old-age-thought habit.

Never allow yourself to think of yourself as growing old. Under no circumstances allow the old-age thought and suggestion to remain in the mind. Remember that it is what you feel, what you are convinced of, that will be outpictured in your body. If you think you are aging, if you walk, talk, dress, and act like an old person, these conditions will be outpictured in your expression, face, manner, and body generally.

Hold the *perpetual-renewal picture* in your mind.

Youthful thought should be a life habit. It will drive out the old-age-thought habit. Every time you think of yourself make a vivid mental picture of your ideal self as the very picture of youth, of health and vigor. *Think health.* Feel the spirit of youth and hope surging through your body. Form the most perfect picture of physical manhood or womanhood that is possible to the human mind. The elixir of youth which alchemists sought so long in chemicals, we find lies in ourselves. The secret is in our own mentality. Perpetual rejuvenation is possible only by right thinking. We look as old as we think and feel because it is thought and feeling that, change our appearance.

There is a tremendous youth-retaining power in holding high ideals and lofty sentiments. The spirit cannot grow old while one is constantly aspiring to something better, higher, nobler. Employment which develops the higher self the frequent dwelling upon lofty themes and high purposes—all are powerful preservatives of youth. It is senility of the soul that makes people old

Live always in a happy mental attitude. Live in the ideal, and the aging processes cannot get hold of you. It is the ideal that keeps one young. When we think of age, we think of weakness, decrepitude, imperfection we do not think of wholeness, vigor.

I know of no remedy for old-age conditions so powerful as love—love for our work, love for our fellow men and women; love for everything.

It is the most powerful life-renewer, refreshener, re-creator, known. Love awakens the noblest sentiments, the finest sensibilities, the most exquisite qualities in man.

Harmony, peace, and serenity are absolutely necessary to perpetuate youthful conditions. All discord, all unbalanced mental operations, tend to produce aging conditions, The contemplation of the eternal verities enriches the ideals and freshens life because it destroys fear, uncertainty, and worry by adding assurance and certainty to life.

If we are convinced that the life processes can perpetuate youth instead of age, they will obey the command. *The coming man and woman will not grow old in appearance as we now do. The tendency of the race will be more and more toward perpetual youth.*

Look upon old age as an unreality, a negative, a mere phantom of your real being—for it is.

The rose that fades is not the real rose. The real rose is the ideal—the idea which pushes out a new one every time we pluck the one that fades.

9 781722 502850